UNEQUAL CITY

UNEQUAL CITY

Race, Schools, and
Perceptions of Injustice

Carla Shedd

Russell Sage Foundation • New York

The Russell Sage Foundation

The Russell Sage Foundation, one of the oldest of America's general purpose foundations, was established in 1907 by Mrs. Margaret Olivia Sage for "the improvement of social and living conditions in the United States." The foundation seeks to fulfill this mandate by fostering the development and dissemination of knowledge about the country's political, social, and economic problems. While the foundation endeavors to assure the accuracy and objectivity of each book it publishes, the conclusions and interpretations in Russell Sage Foundation publications are those of the authors and not of the foundation, its trustees, or its staff. Publication by Russell Sage, therefore, does not imply foundation endorsement.

Library of Congress Cataloging-in-Publication Data

Shedd, Carla.
  Unequal city : race, schools, and perceptions of injustice / Carla Shedd.
    pages cm
  Includes bibliographical references and index.
  ISBN 978-0-87154-796-5 (pbk. : alk. paper) — ISBN 978-1-61044-852-9 (ebook) 1. Minority students—Illinois—Chicago. 2. Segregation in education—Illinois—Chicago. 3. Discrimination in education—Illinois—Chicago. 4. Social stratification—Illinois—Chicago. 5. Equality—Illinois—Chicago. 6. Racism—Illinois—Chicago. I. Title.
  LC3733.C4S54 2015
  371.8290773'11—dc23   2015008748

The paper used in this publication meets the minimum requirements of American National Standard for Information Sciences—Permanence of Paper for Printed Library Materials. ANSI Z39.48-1992.

Text design by Suzanne Nichols

RUSSELL SAGE FOUNDATION
112 East 64th Street, New York, New York 10065
10 9 8 7 6 5 4 3 2 1

CONTENTS

LIST OF ILLUSTRATIONS

ABOUT THE AUTHOR

CARLA SHEDD is assistant professor of sociology and African American studies at Columbia University.

One day in late May 2000, I left Massachusetts just as dawn was breaking and headed halfway across the country to Chicago. The week before I had graduated from Smith College, an all-women's college in western Massachusetts, and now I was beginning the next phase of my academic journey in the doctoral sociology program at Northwestern University. Later that evening I arrived at my aunt's home on Drexel Boulevard, located on the South Side, on the border between the neighborhoods of Kenwood and Hyde Park. Drexel was a grand boulevard indeed. It had a rich past as a major promenade for the upper-class residents who lived in Kenwood, but it also served to separate the racially diverse Kenwood and Hyde Park neighborhoods from the Black,[1] lower-class neighborhood to its west, Washington Park. My Aunt Patricia, who is African American, owned an apartment building on the east side of Drexel where I would live for the next few years as a graduate student. It was a familiar place since, as a Black child of the Deep South, I would often fly from Jackson, Mississippi, to Chicago during summers and holidays to get my taste of the big city. Now I was here pursuing my own agenda, and it felt liberating. However, that sense of freedom was soon constrained.

My first lesson about Chicago came with the detailed directions I received on how to drive from Drexel Boulevard to my aunt's child care center. My plan was to work for her that summer as a preschool teaching assistant, starting the day after I arrived, until my graduate classes began that fall. The school was located in the predominantly Black, majority-low-income Auburn-Gresham neighborhood just over six miles southwest of my new home. Aunt Patricia told me that the southwest shortcut through Washington Park to Fifty-Fifth Street was the best way to get to the Dan Ryan Expressway, which bisected the traditional Black Belt from what were, until recently, fiercely defended Irish American neighborhoods. I could then take the highway south, exit at Seventy-Ninth Street, and drive west until I arrived at the center.

My male cousins saw this commute differently, however, and were quick to revise Aunt Patricia's straightforward instructions. Shortcuts were less important than safety. I was a newcomer, after all. So they told me ways to avoid major street traffic, gang territories that were in dispute, and streets riddled with potholes. I eventually found my way.

In the coming weeks—and indeed, for as long as I lived in the city—I would receive many more directives for how I should navigate the city during my free time. According to one cousin, I should never venture to Chicago's West Side. Another told me to avoid driving too far south. A third told me that I should stick to the major highways, avoid going through White neighborhoods, and try not to visit Black neighborhoods aside from Kenwood/Hyde Park and Chatham. They all agreed that I should always keep my car windows up and never linger at red lights once they turned green. My relatives meant well, but their orders were infuriating. How much danger could my choice of route really present? Before long, however, I started to realize that the paths you take each day in Chicago matter a great deal.

My second lesson on how much your place of residence matters in Chicago came as I talked to a twenty-year-old from my neighborhood. He asked me exactly where I lived. I told him my block on Drexel, and he immediately exclaimed, "Oh, you're a Black P. Stone." I was obviously confused, so he explained: the Black P. Stones was my neighborhood's gang, so that meant I too was a Black P. Stone. He even demonstrated the gang sign. I gently reminded him that we were no longer in the 1980s. I was getting my doctorate, after all, and he was a middle-class college student himself. Gangs couldn't possibly be that important to our lives. He was as baffled by my response as I was by his insistence. As it turned out, I had a lot to learn about how your address might shape your future and about an America defined—far more than we care to admit—by the sometimes brutal intersection of race and place.

My third, and most important, lesson on how much our expectations and experiences depend on racial and spatial characteristics and attributes came after my first year in graduate school, during the summer of 2001. I was involved in a study commissioned by the National Research Council (NRC) to examine the antecedents of lethal school violence in the late 1990s, a direct response to several highly publicized "rampage shootings" in rural and suburban America—most notably, the "Columbine Massacre" in Littleton, Colorado, in April 1999. After much deliberation on whether urban school shootings should be included in the study, as there had been no incidents of multiple victims of lethal violence in urban schools from 1997 to 1999, our small research team at Northwestern was given the task of studying a "negative" case—that is, an incident that did not fit the parameters—in order to learn more about what might be happening differently in urban school contexts.[2] Our investigation of the social causes and consequences of a lethal, in-school incident with multiple victims at Chicago's Edward J. Tilden High

School on November 20, 1992, would profoundly shape my perspective and my research trajectory.

This was my first encounter with Tilden High, located in the historically Irish American Canaryville neighborhood and bordered by Back of the Yards—an area made famous by Upton Sinclair's book *The Jungle,* which detailed the pollution and poverty surrounding the Union Stockyards meat-packing plants in the early twentieth century. In 1992, fifteen-year-old Joseph White, a Black ninth-grader at Tilden, brought a gun to school anticipating that he might need extra protection while walking home. He had received a few threats about some money missing from a dice game in the school bathroom, for which he and another boy had been suspended just a few days earlier. On that fateful day, Joseph got into a shoving match in the school hallway. He fired several shots, which he said were in self-defense, killing one of his schoolmates and injuring two others.

As part of our research team's retrospective ethnography of the shooting, we combed through newspaper articles, court transcripts, and other documents related to the case; we also conducted interviews with lawyers, teachers, community leaders, and students who went to Tilden during that time, as well as many of the main actors involved, including Joseph. As the budding ethnographer on our three-person team, I was selected to do much of the field research in the neighborhood surrounding Tilden and in Joseph's home neighborhood, several blocks southeast of the school. I would discover that they were two very different worlds.

I experienced a range of emotions as I navigated between those two places, from anguish at the nonchalant answer when I asked how a fifteen-year-old could get a gun so easily in Englewood ("It's easy to get a gun, we can get you one right now") to trepidation after I saw the quizzical looks on a couple of White people's faces from their porch, followed by a watchful "wassup" from one young White male as I was en route to an interview with a Canaryville community leader. This fear was magnified by my interviewee's insistence that he escort me to my car afterward. After learning more about the Canaryville neighborhood, I decided that my fears were not unfounded. I knew that Blacks didn't "belong" there, but I was unclear on the consequences of being there without an apparent purpose. More research clued me into the neighborhood's racial dynamics.

In 1985 two African American men stopped in front of Tilden High to help a stalled car ahead of them. Suddenly, a group of White youths surrounded their car, smashed all the windows, and struck one of the men in the neck and head before chasing them out of the area. In 1991 two African American fourteen-year-olds were waiting on a bus in Bridgeport that would take them to their homes in Englewood. They had just left a White Sox game in the seventh inning. According to the boys, two White police officers pulled up, told them that they did not belong in the community and were violating curfew, and ordered them inside the police car, while cursing at them. The police allegedly drove them to another White neighborhood just two blocks from Tilden High, near Forty-Fifth and Union Avenue, whereupon, the boys alleged, the female officer slapped them with a half-closed fist and kicked them out of the car. As they started walking, according to testimony, they were set upon by a group of White boys; one of the victims said that the White boys were shouting racial epithets and throwing bottles.[3] One boy was able to elude capture, but the group caught the other, beating him until he was unconscious. He was later hospitalized. Almost two years later, three juveniles were convicted of aggravated battery and ethnic intimidation.[4] The officers were cleared of criminal misconduct charges for dropping the kids in the Canaryville neighborhood in 1991, but in 1992 both were fired for violating several police department rules, including "engaging in any unjustified verbal or physical altercation with any person on or off duty."[5]

Later that same year, Joseph White was in trouble in the same neighborhood, but he was not running from a gang of White youths. Instead, he had acquired a gun to protect himself from rival African American gang members as he walked to and from school. I was intrigued by the idea that teens have to make alliances throughout the day; more importantly, do their friends, enemies, and expectations change depending on who they are and where they are? For instance, around Joseph's home the Mickey Cobras were the dominant gang, but the Black P. Stones ruled the hallways of Tilden. These two gangs were often friendly to one another because they created a racially united front against the Latin Kings, who also attended the school. But if a Black or Hispanic student of any gang left school too late, without the safety of numbers, he might have to deal with the White members of that community for being in the wrong place at the wrong time.

Joseph might have considered calling the police if his mother was robbed, but he felt compelled by the unspoken, life-altering adolescent male code of behavior to protect himself by himself, with no help from school officials or the law. In the years since, Joseph's plight—he was sentenced to forty-five years in prison—and the look of sadness and resignation on his mother's face when I interviewed her in that summer of 2001 have never left me.

This book takes readers on a sociological journey into the minds and lives of young people in Chicago to understand how often they face conflicts like Joseph's, with potentially deadly consequences, as they travel to and from school, or even while they sit in classrooms. Both the sociological literature and our national discussions of opportunity and discrimination have given the perceptions and experiences of young people short shrift. Although as educators and researchers, as politicians and cultural critics, we routinely lament the problems of youth today, we spend precious little time seriously trying to understand their motivations and their experiences. Teenagers have remarkable vantage points on the cities they live in—not only on how their city functions but also on how it does not. They are a walking experiment in the effects that city agencies—in this case, the board of education and the city policing apparatus—can have on a generation of people who are especially vulnerable and may even be harmed by the policies and procedures that seek to ensure their safety. It is long past time to let their voices be heard.

CHAPTER 1

Introduction: Crossing Boundaries of Race, Class, and Neighborhood

> I need to go check out the suburbs and see how they treat them out there, and then maybe I can put two and two together to see what's going on.
>
> —Keisha, African American tenth-grader, Harper High

Imagine the scene: Students from a public school located on the South Side of Chicago disembark from their bus in front of a stunning $65 million educational facility located in the suburbs. One African American student exclaims, "This school is way better than I thought it would be!"[1] She says this before even entering the school to tour the Olympic-sized pool and other world-class athletic facilities, walk the well-lit hallways, and attend several classes. Until this day, having no concrete comparison with which to measure the education she is receiving in her school on Chicago's South Side, this young lady has not been able to really fathom or comprehend the short shrift she receives in her education. Her statement succinctly reveals the importance of the concept of "relative deprivation"—that is, the way people compare their plight with similarly situated others.

These students were highlighted in a 2006 episode of *The Oprah Winfrey Show* that I viewed nearly a year after conducting my field research in four Chicago public high schools, including Harper High. Inspired by Rev. Jesse Jackson to expose "America's School Crisis," Oprah had decided to use these vastly different settings to reveal the disparities in educational opportunities and achievements. The episode begins with Microsoft founder and philanthropist Bill Gates and his wife Melinda lamenting that lagging behind other industrialized countries in educational achievement has greatly harmed America's stature as the most powerful country in the world. The Gateses outline their efforts to fund schools and scholarships for students to overhaul all that is not working in our system of public schooling.

Oprah's cameras track students who have left Harper, their all-Black school in the South Side Chicago neighborhood of Englewood, to attend Neuqua

Valley High School located in Naperville, Illinois, less than one hour west of the Windy City. The experience of the students from Naperville who venture into Harper from their suburban enclave is also filmed. The contrast between the two schools is vividly shown: the inner-city school's surrounding "low-income community" is portrayed as devastated and disorganized; the suburban public school located only thirty-five miles away, in contrast, is depicted as neat and clean.[2] The physical condition of the school buildings foretells the accomplishments of the students therein: whereas 99 percent of the suburban school students graduate in four years, only 40 percent of the Harper students do so.

The suburban students' first shock upon their arrival at the South Side school is having to go through metal detectors to enter—and that is just the beginning of the stark differences they notice between the two schools. Not surprisingly, the suburban students are used to facilities that are infinitely superior to those at the city school. For instance, they have actual instruments for music class; only a few working instruments are available in the South Side school, and most of the students improvise by pounding out notes with their hands on their desks. The suburban students seem not to grasp how privileged they are to have a working Olympic-sized pool and state-of-the-art fitness equipment, while the inner-city students have only a dilapidated gym with peeling walls, an empty pool, and broken and tattered fitness equipment. Their academic experiences are worlds apart as well: students at Neuqua Valley High have a couple of dozen advanced placement (AP) courses to choose from, while the city school offers only two. One suburban student sums up the experience for all who are participating from her school: "We really take our resources for granted."

The chasm between the two schools' test scores is as wide as their physical differences. While 77 percent of students at the suburban school meet the Illinois math standards, fewer than 1 percent meet the standards at the city school. One girl somberly remarks that, even though she is an A student in math at Harper, she is totally dumbfounded by the trigonometry class she has attended that day in the suburbs: "I was looking at the math problems that they're doing [at Neuqua Valley], and I'm like, 'What language is that?'. . . As soon as I get to college, I'm going to be lost."

The cameras then show the great disappointment registering on the face of an inner-city female student as she realizes that nothing comparable to this suburban educational experience is available in the city. Accompanied by her classmates' vigorous nods of agreement, she states, "The best school in Chicago can't even compare to this." Viewing this episode, I found it distressing to see the disappointment on each of the Harper students' brown faces as they confront the truth about their substandard educational experience back in Chicago. One student speaks for them all in commenting bitterly, "I feel like I've been cheated."

In this case, ignorance can truly be bliss. Whereas visiting the inner-city school confirms for suburban students their relative advantage as a group, visiting the suburban school only substantiates for the city students their relative subordination. A South Side female student generously states, "I'm glad that y'all have it, 'cuz if we don't have it, I'm glad somebody have it. But it's the simple fact that we see y'all doing well and we want to do well too."

This story is about *place* as much as it is about *race*. In this episode of *Oprah*, only one student in the suburban school looks like she could be identified as a person of color (White-Hispanic); her classmates are all White. The entire group of city students are African American, but that is not the crucial issue. Students in the city of Chicago (and many other urban and rural communities) have been consigned to a separate and *unequal* education simply because of where they live. If the cameras had still been rolling the next day when the inner-city students returned to school, we most likely would have seen profound disillusionment with their school experience and disappointment in the opportunities they were given simply because of where they attended school—a public school in the city instead of the suburbs.

Unequal City provides an in-depth discussion of exactly this issue: how adolescents' perceptions of themselves and the larger social world are shaped by their daily interactions with others, particularly as they travel back and forth from school. This book examines Chicago adolescents' experiences within and navigation through ostensibly free yet potentially penalizing places like urban schools and neighborhoods to reveal that their perceptions of social and criminal injustice are both stratified by race and rooted in place.

Chicago's streets and neighborhoods are defined by a long legacy of racial and class stratification, discrimination, and poverty. The inequalities in resources and opportunities resulting from racial stratification dominate its central social institutions—and most dramatically, its public schools. Adolescents in particular have to traverse social and physical terrain that can powerfully shape both their immediate experiences and their long-term perceptions. Like every urban school system, the Chicago public school system requires that adolescents navigate its "geography of opportunity."[3] Urban high schools play a major role in either ameliorating or further reinforcing adolescents' racially divergent social worlds, particularly their perceptions of and experiences with authoritative figures across many different social contexts.

Much of the story told in this book is shaped by the journeys that tens of millions of adolescents take each day as they go from home to school and back. This daily routine may be familiar, but it is anything but banal, especially for urban teenagers, who typically go to school by themselves and often travel greater distances than elementary school students. Their trek may involve crossing multiple boundaries of race, class, and neighborhood. It is a central finding of this book that how adolescents traverse this geography has a significant influence on their worldviews, particularly their perceptions of social and criminal injustice.

This is a timely story of race, place, education, and the expansion of the carceral state. The findings are critical because adolescents' perceptions shape their decisionmaking, behaviors, and outcomes; thus, the social-psychological, educational policy, and urban policy dimensions of this work are clear. The rich description and analysis of students' socialization to the justice system and the activation of their various identities (race, ethnicity, gender, age, class) reveal the differences in how adolescents navigate urban geographies of inequality and opportunity.

I conducted the research at the heart of this study during a decade (2001–2010) of monumental transformation in Chicago's public housing and public schooling that wholly shifted urban lives and wrought vast unintended consequences. Reforms since the early 2000s, such as "Renaissance 2010," which closed or combined many public schools, coupled with the transformation and demolition of Chicago's vast stock of high-rise public housing, have drastically reshaped the city's overlapping housing and educational landscapes. One result is that schools continue to play a major role in either subverting or reinforcing young people's divergent social worlds—that is, the vastly different social conditions, economic conditions, and distinct experiences by race and place that they confront every day.[4]

Unequal City addresses these issues by focusing on three interrelated themes. First, it explores how high school students from different social, racial, and economic backgrounds experience police contact and perceive injustice along a gradient that diverges along racial and ethnic lines. Second, it uses the experiences of youth, particularly their interactions with teachers, police, and parents, to uncover how their experiences shape their perceptions of themselves and their wider social worlds. Finally, this book uncovers the driving forces behind, and consequences of, policies that have intricately linked the public school system and the criminal justice system.

This study's use of both quantitative and qualitative data is a unique contribution to urban sociology. I have used a distinctive array of data sources to document the mechanisms and processes by which high school students' decisions and behaviors profoundly shape the trajectories of their adult lives, as well as their perspectives and experiences: a 2001 survey of approximately 20,000 Chicago public school ninth- and tenth-graders; a survey and in-depth interviews conducted in 2005 with forty ninth- and tenth-graders across four different public schools; a follow-up survey and interviews in 2010 with four students; ethnographic observations in the schools and neighborhoods; and newspaper archives. The variable at the center of this work, "perceived injustice," measures young people's attitudes about social and structural disadvantage, which may include their awareness of differential opportunities to achieve economic or educational success. This study also focuses on adolescents' personal and vicarious interactions with authorit₂ institutions and their representatives, such as teachers in school and police officers on the street.

Neither Child nor Adult

We laud young people as "the future," and yet more often than not their voices remain unheard or ignored. Youth are often the focus of public policy decisions—such as policy on school curricula, policing tactics, or the deployment of neighborhood resources—but we usually do not view them as subjects with opinions that should be solicited and incorporated into policy decisions, even if they are the ones most affected by them. Scholars' understanding of children and teenagers is not much better than that of the general public. There is a dearth of sociological research that both presents the perspectives and experiences of youth in their own words and embeds these perspectives and experiences within the formative social institutions that shape their lives.[5] This is especially the case for marginalized minors who are deeply enmeshed in the state through the provision of public housing and public schooling and matters of public safety and who do not feel that they have much agency to determine the substance and impact of their encounters with state agencies.

The only way to address this fundamental gap is to penetrate the worlds of these teens, and that effort requires going to their schools and neighborhoods, observing the interactions in their daily world, and sitting down and talking with them. Teenagers have a great deal to share, and they offer many challenges to the conventional vision of how school works and what day-to-day justice and equality feel like. Society cannot afford to ignore their voices any longer.

Youth are highly attuned to the distribution of opportunity and the presence of social inequality. They are also aware that their "pathways of opportunity can be modified, arrested, or deflected by social interventions, including the actions of government and the leaders of key social institutions."[6] As we shall see, the Chicago students I followed offer a profound reminder that we must broaden our concept of "justice" from an exclusive focus on courts, jails, and police to the broader context formed by the social institutions, such as schools, that influence how youth learn about and experience equality and inequality.

I document the gradient—along lines of race and ethnicity—of adolescents' actual contact with police. Just as important, I analyze their perceptions of social and criminal injustice, paying particular attention to how their race and ethnic identity, class, and gender shape their beliefs and experiences. For instance, one African American male student I spoke with, Dewayne, told me that the police "don't represent the law. . . . They figure since they got that badge they want to play God. . . . All the government is doing is letting them play God." And what could send a stronger message to students about their relationship with legal authorities than to have the police—those who provide the jailhouse with its inhabitants—standing guard inside and outside the schoolhouse?[7] These perceptions offer a great deal of insight into young people's perspectives at the formative stage when their decisions and resultant behaviors can dramatically shape the trajectories of their lives.

Adolescence is a life stage that is full of meaning making. Young people are making sense of both internal and external forces, from their inexplicable, inextinguishable feelings about the girl or boy next door to their concerns about violence in their neighborhoods. The high school students in this study are dealing with very important transitional life events, including moves to new high schools, searches for after-school jobs, and navigation of the world as a young adult with greater independence. These transitions are fraught with major social adjustments that involve changes in status, peers, and, most importantly, the social circumstances they are likely to confront each day.[8] Understanding that adolescence is also a critical and formative period of politically sensitive beliefs underscores the importance of exploring the development and evolution of adolescent perceptions of inequality.[9] What young people believe and the stories they tell about their position in the larger social and economic strata must be given serious scholarly attention. Youth are rather accurate about—and sometimes frighteningly aware of—their chances in the world in which we live.

The uses and definitions of the terms "adolescence" and "youth," which I use interchangeably, have changed over time.[10] The extension of the time between childhood and adulthood in the twentieth century led to the revival of the term "adolescence" to denote a period when youth are in flux with regard to their responsibilities and society's expectations for them. For instance, adolescents have much more agency than children when it comes to traveling farther from home or taking on low-wage or low-skill work, but they remain subject to the authority of parents, teachers, and even police. The restricted ability of people under eighteen to determine the course of their own lives—where to live or who to vote for when they are old enough or what to do with their days—may actually make their thoughts about the world that much more important.

Race, Place, and Perceived Inequality

I use the notion of "perceived injustice" as a means of capturing public high school students' attitudes about social and structural disadvantage in general and, more specifically, their awareness of how opportunities for economic or educational success may differ by race, ethnicity, gender, or class. The concept of perceived injustice can also spotlight students' personal and vicarious interactions with authoritative institutions and their representatives, whether teachers in the schools or police officers on the street. This study offers a revealing look at a generation of teens whose experiences are relegated to society's margins but whose life outcomes continually demonstrate the inequality of educational and economic chances in a purportedly democratic society.

The focus here on youth's perceptions of injustice draws on foundational research conducted by Herbert Jacob in Milwaukee in 1969 during a "period of relative calm" after the urban riots that had rocked the United States the previous year.[11] Jacob defined and measured justice as the congruence between actors' expectations about key agents in the justice system (police, courts, and other legal offices) and their perceptions of the actual behavior of these agents, with injustice denoted as the gap between those expectations and perceptions. Too often scholarship simply reports that African Americans and Whites have different attitudes about the criminal justice system, but Jacob made place central to his analyses of racialized perceptions of justice. He focused his study on three neighborhoods with varying race-class compositions—a "Black ghetto neighborhood," a "White working-class neighborhood," and a "White middle-class neighborhood"—and found that his subjects' evaluations of the police were rooted, to some extent, in neighborhood cultures. As he put it, "Although individual Blacks may report satisfactory experiences, they are much more likely to know persons who have had worse experiences [with police]."[12] Jacob's article was also groundbreaking in its examination of the distribution of perceptions of injustice as an outcome instead of as an explanatory variable.

An individual must have a conception of justice to have a conception of injustice. The same can be said for a person's ability to understand his or her personal plight as deficient or advantageous. The theory of "relative deprivation," or "relative subordination," is useful here. This theory, as articulated in the foundational works of James Davis and extended by William Runciman, stems from "a familiar truism: that people's attitudes, aspirations and grievances largely depend on the frame of reference within which they are conceived."[13] Relative deprivation applies when people compare their individual plight with that of others, whereas relative subordination is a group-based comparison of status or outcomes. The theory is applicable to both racial and class hierarchies.

According to Runciman, "Steady poverty is the best guarantee of [aspirational] conservatism: if people have no reason to expect or hope for more than they can achieve, they will be less discontented with what they have, or even grateful to simply be able to hold on to it."[14] In Runciman's theory, the poor wish for less than the rich do; they do not seem conscious of another possibility. But there is also reason to argue that something more complex is often at work. Those who face the most daunting challenges—young, poor African Americans in particular—may be willing to limit their hopes and expectations because that is less painful than confronting their disappointment.

As we would suspect from endless anecdotal evidence (including Oprah Winfrey's school swap), and as is confirmed by numerous social indicators (such as poverty, unemployment, education, and homeownership), life in America is shaped by a well-established racial hierarchy. However we attempt to explain it, the presence of a racial gradient, with stagnant extremes, is undeniable in this country. Typically Whites and Blacks are at the poles of the spectrum, with Latinos, Asians, and Native Americans (when counted) falling somewhere in between.[15]

African Americans also have the highest perceptions of injustice along a racial gradient, with Whites (and Asian Americans) at the opposite end of the spectrum.[16] A strong perception of inequality does not mean that those who rank high on perceptions of injustice—those, as discussed earlier, who believe the world is fundamentally unjust—are defeatists. In fact, much of the sociological research on perceptions of justice reveals minimal differences between the races in their endorsement of basic principles of justice. Indeed, although as a group African Americans have historically experienced some of the country's highest levels of discrimination, they report some of the highest commitments to education, equity, and opportunity.[17] They have not "given up." Instead, the stark differences come into play when we look at experiential justice—that is, perceptions of the way justice is distributed *in fact*.[18]

The next iteration of perceptions research by sociologists, criminologists, and economists provided even more nuance in this area of study by incorporating class into the analyses and pushing us to think more about the processes and mechanisms that shape individuals' perceptions of injustice; such analyses are also well served by social-psychological research methods.[19] The psychologist Tom Tyler and his colleagues have done much to advance the study of perceptions via their rich line of research on the topic.[20] Tyler's work reveals that people comply with the law because they believe it is proper to do so, that they react to their experiences by evaluating their sense of justice or injustice, and that they evaluate the process independently of the outcome. These findings have spurred many new studies and extensively shaped police policy and practices.[21]

Unequal City extends these research traditions in that it "maps the terrain" of perceived injustice across school and residential contexts as informed by race, gender, and class.[22] A "place-sensitive" sociology that understands place not just as a backdrop to our social lives but also as an agentic player in our social lives, with measurable and independent effects, is necessary to answer these sorts of questions.[23] The formation and transformation of the Chicago public schools has enormously shaped the social and cultural lives of its students. This relationship is manifest in the various ways in which the Chicago schools reflect and sustain difference while also facilitating either social engagement or social estrangement.[24]

Of Journeys and Destinations

"Adolescent geographies" determine both the paths that young people take and their social and physical destinations. Another useful conceptual tool for understanding how schools provide experiences and shape perceptions in a discernibly stratified way is the social geographer and theorist David Sibley's notion of "geographies of exclusion." Geographies of exclusion are the literal mappings of power relations onto geographic places and their commensurate social spaces, such as schools and neighborhoods. Through this frame we can begin to understand social boundaries and exclusionary landscapes, particularly how physical terrain becomes imbued with social meaning and markers, which together shape what Sibley terms the "ecological self."[25]

People both shape and are shaped by places. This is certainly true for the physical boundaries circumscribed by the paths we travel (such as arterial streets, highways, railroad tracks, and viaducts), and it is just as true for the social boundaries of race-ethnicity, class, and gender that we draw around ourselves and others—through the friends we hang out with, the organizations or gangs we belong to, and the many other components of identity.

We all feel varying degrees of possessiveness about the different spaces we inhabit, whether home, neighborhood, school, or nation. The social composition of these spaces is a key factor in our feelings about them. Possessiveness—that is, the desire to control space—governs social interactions at all of these levels, but particularly at the neighborhood and school levels, where homogeneity paints differences as a threat.[26] In our very human desire to feel safe in our surroundings and confident that we can protect our loved ones, we can all too easily become suspicious of anyone who does not look or talk or walk like us. From this perspective, we all become defined by place—both by the places where we do not belong and by those where we do.

Crossing boundaries from the familiar to the alien can produce a gamut of emotions in young people, from anxiety to exhilaration. Border crossing, Sibley notes, can produce the "thrill of transgression," but it can also result in harassment, physical danger, or even arrest.[27] Because they are moving from childhood to adulthood, teenagers are inherently border-crossers: they do not fit comfortably in either category. Adults are not comfortable continuing to give them the benefits of childhood, which they seem to have outgrown, but they are equally uncomfortable extending to teenagers the privileges of adulthood, which they may not yet deserve. At the same time, social behavioral expectations for teenagers—what they are expected to do and how they are expected to act—are invariably bound up with the places they either inhabit or are excluded from. Physical place is thus inextricable from our moral judgments about teenagers as well as our tolerance (or lack thereof) for their deviant practices.[28]

The connection between our ecological and imagined realities has become clearer in a recent line of scholarship that centers on "cognitive landscapes." Building on Gerald Suttles's idea of "cognitive maps," Robert Sampson and Dawn Bartusch suggest the metaphor of "cognitive landscapes" to describe the demographic and ecological structures of those troubled American settings in which the presence of crime and disorder may be seen as the norm.[29] The idea of cognitive landscapes complements other scholars' theoretical contributions to our understanding of how place and physical mobility shape individuals' perceptions of social success and mobility.[30]

This book adopts these ideas to make sense of how adolescents reconcile their particular position in the reigning social hierarchy with their personal aspirations and life experiences. For the young people in this study, as for all of us, specific social locations—that is, their peer networks, neighborhoods, and schools—act as frames of reference. What they perceive and experience as normal is affected by their individual place in the larger social structure and cultural milieu.[31] Youth's socioecologically structured "cognitive landscapes" involve interactions with authority figures, which may have an impact on their feelings of injustice. This book combines awareness of the multiplicative influences of place, race, age, gender, class, and other components of identity to present a richer, fuller account of the variation in youth perceptions of inequality and opportunity.

An Urban Laboratory Like No Other

Just as there is great racial stratification in urban school systems, there is a concomitant geography of opportunity in America's urban centers. The city of Chicago, the site of so many great sociological studies, provides an especially interesting locale to use in evaluating the confluence of racial inequality, economic instability, spatial segregation, and crime with the research focus of this book—youth perceptions of injustice.[32]

The defining experience for Chicago's young people of attending the city's public schools is being forced to navigate its "geography of opportunity," or more accurately, the city's "geography of inequality."[33] Chicago's racial stratifications are well known and long-standing—and, for many of us, so taken for granted that it is easy to forget that these racial divides permeate the city's social institutions. These institutions, especially urban neighborhoods and schools, are the central sites that create, maintain, and perpetuate inequality.

Because public schools are typically organized around geographical catchment areas, they reinforce and exacerbate the effects of residential segregation and social isolation.[34] The majority of African American and Hispanic students living on the South and West Sides of Chicago and attending schools there have a radically different educational experience than their counterparts in the Loop, Chicago's downtown, and the communities farther north, who are typically Whiter and wealthier. Those on the South Side are literally "out of the loop" in comparison to their peers just a few miles north, where schools have tremendously different resources. This geographical variance in school quality has been the cause and consequence of students leaving their neighborhoods to take advantage of an expanded portfolio of "educational options" within the Chicago public schools system.

After the Illinois Charter Schools Law was passed in April 1996, the state and city leadership began allowing—and even encouraging—parents to apply to send their children to schools outside their neighborhood's borders. The lawmakers' intent "in authorizing charter schools," they said, was "to create a legitimate avenue for parents, teacher, and community members to take responsible risks and create new, innovative, and more flexible ways of educating children within the public school system."[35] Former mayor Richard M. Daley and U.S. education secretary Arne Duncan began the push that increased the number of privately run public charter schools from zero in the mid-1990s to 133 in 2014, serving approximately 57,000 students in the city of Chicago.[36] The rapid growth of the charter school movement has only accelerated the decline in neighborhood high school enrollments.[37] Dozens of neighborhood public schools have closed since 2011 under the mayoralty of Rahm Emmanuel, fifty of them in predominantly African American South and West Side neighborhoods.[38] As a result, "some 10,000 high school students and 6,000 elementary school students of CPS students, travel as far as six miles" to get to school each day, crossing boundaries of race, class, and opportunity.[39]

It is not always a bad thing for adolescents to cross boundaries, whether those borders are defined by geography or by social convention. For instance, the teens who attend the magnet school downtown or commute from across the city to Lincoln Park High for its International Baccalaureate (IB) program have an opportunity to see and experience more than their peers who attend school in their home neighborhoods. Their "temporary exile" for the purpose of achieving an education superior to what is available closer to home undoubtedly increases their chances for success and upward mobility relative to their peers who stay in the neighborhood. However, they may also have to grapple with feelings of being seen as out of place in those same neighborhoods, hallways, and classrooms where other students have different skin colors, class status, and experiences. That is why it is important to understand the development and evolution of youth's perceptions of social and criminal injustice from an ecological perspective, not just as these perceptions originate from their race, class, gender, and other foundational aspects of identity.

Moreover, this is not merely a theoretical exercise: the perception of injus-

tice has real and important effects on people's lives. A burgeoning area of research has concluded that perceptions of social injustice are positively related
to crime and delinquency, showing that perceptions of injustice have an impact not only on individual lives but also on all aspects of our society.[40] The
stakes are high. We should all be interested in discovering how young people
form perceptions of injustice through contact with authorities such as school
officials and police officers.

Four Chicago Public High Schools

The four Chicago schools highlighted in this book—Lincoln Park High, Payton College Prep, Tilden Career Community Academy, and Harper High—
were selected primarily on the basis of their racial composition and neighborhood settings so as to represent four unique contexts (see table 1.1).

Lincoln Park High School has programs that attract students from across
the district, including the International Baccalaureate program, an accelerated curriculum with "an emphasis on problem solving and integration of
knowledge." The other two programs into which students are sorted at the
application stage are a double honors/Advanced Placement (AP) program and
the performing arts curriculum. Approximately three-fourths of the school's
2,200 students enter Lincoln Park through one of these special programs.
The remaining pupils are admitted from within the school's attendance
boundaries. These admittance criteria bring together a diverse group that includes upper-middle-class students who live in condo buildings on Armitage
Avenue as well as lower-income students from the Cabrini-Green high-rise
housing projects (all completely razed by early 2011) to the south of the
school.[41] The average household income in the neighborhood is nearly
$87,000, and the poverty rate is 12 percent.[42]

The Lincoln Park High School campus consists of two buildings. The
main structure, a Greek Revival–style building with beautiful columns that
frame the grand entry, is paired with a more modern, two-story building that
serves the freshman class. In this separate building, the younger teens have a
space all their own in which to bond with each other and transition to high
school in a relatively structured setting. Orchard Street was closed in 1979 to
make way for a tree-lined mall between the two school buildings. This public
space exclusively reserved for the school community gives Lincoln Park the
feeling of a small college campus.

Walter Payton College Preparatory High School sits less than two miles
southeast of Lincoln Park. Payton, established in 2000, is the newest school
of the four studied in this book. It is a selective enrollment school: every
student has to pass an entrance exam to be admitted and the school has no
enrollment boundaries.[43] Payton's administration prides itself on maintain-

Table 1.1   Characteristics of Four Chicago Schools, 2006

	Lincoln Park High School	Walter Payton College Preparatory High School	Tilden Career Community Academy High School	Harper High School
Official school classification	Mixed-race	Integrated	Predominantly minority	Predominantly Black
White	29.4%	40.4%	5.1%	0.1%
Black	35.1	27.5	60.0	99.3
Latino	19.9	22.8	32.3	0.6
Asian	15.3	8.8	1.6	—
Native American	0.3	0.6	0.1	—
ACT composite	21	26	15	14
Percentage low-income	51%	34%	95%	84%
Graduation rate	81	89	56	66

Source: 2006 official school reports.

ing "a student body that is economically, geographically, and racially diverse."[44] In fact, this seems be the case: in 2005, when I conducted my interviews with students, the school's racial composition was 40 percent White, 28 percent African American, 23 percent Hispanic, and 9 percent Asian/Asian American.

Payton is situated one mile east of (what was) the heart of the Cabrini-Green projects and one mile west of Chicago's famous "Magnificent Mile," which consists of high-end retail stores, smaller boutiques, and restaurants. The average household income of residents in the school's neighborhood, according to the 2008–2012 American Community Survey, is approaching $72,000, and the poverty level in the neighborhood is slightly under 20 percent.[45]

Payton's physical appearance is breathtaking. In the entryway behind its grand modernist glass facade, flags representing countries around the world hang from the ceiling. Looking deeper, a visitor notices the school's generously wide corridors and high ceilings. The structure in which learning takes place is commensurate with the substance. Payton's curriculum focuses on math, science, and world languages and consists solely of honors and AP courses. It is difficult to get into Payton, and upon being accepted, students usually rise to the challenge. The graduation rate for the school since 2005 has consistently been around 90 percent.[46]

Tilden Career Community Academy High School, the third school in the study, provides a stark contrast to Payton. The median household income of the surrounding neighborhood is approximately $37,000, with a corresponding 29 percent living below the poverty rate.[47] The racial composition of Tilden in 2005, when the first interviews were conducted, was fewer than 2 percent Asian and Native American, 5 percent White, 32 percent Hispanic, and 60 percent African American. Since the 2004–2005 academic year, the number of students residing in Tilden's attendance area who choose to attend Tilden has dramatically declined. According to recent data procured through several Freedom of Information Act (FOIA) requests, 732 area ninth-graders chose other public schools in 2005, while 425 neighborhood students enrolled at Tilden. In 2013–2014, 582 area students enrolled elsewhere, while only 46 students living in the area chose Tilden.[48]

The history of Tilden is both intriguing, as outlined in the preface, and complicated. The current building was constructed before the area's annexation to the city of Chicago. Tilden began as Lake High School in 1881, became part of Chicago Public Schools in 1889, was rebuilt in 1905, and was renamed for the banker and former Board of Education president Edward Tilden in 1915.[49] The L-shaped, three-and-a-half-story building was the all-boys Tilden Technical School from 1917 until the early 1960s. At that point, it educated over 2,000 students at any given time—a far cry from the 327 students who attended the school in 2014.

Walking through the main entrance at 4747 South Union Avenue, with its navy blue doors flanked by four Ionic columns, gives the visitor a sense of the school in its former days of glory. As Tilden Technical School in the middle of the twentieth century, the school focused on training future engineers, electricians, and machinists.[50] The school continues to take pride in its history while imagining a brighter future. The visitor walking Tilden's halls will find recently affixed messages of uplift interspersed between about fifty newly restored murals depicting famous architects, scientists, engineers, and writers who graduated from the school.[51] The visitor might also find the interior foreboding, however; everyone entering the building must pass through metal detectors and proceed down dimly lit hallways. The physical atmosphere no doubt shapes the tone and tenor of the behavior of the schools' inhabitants, who are playful and open at times, but guarded and resolute at others. To this day, Tilden is constantly fighting against the middle, with a graduation rate that has hovered around 55 percent every year since this study began in 2005. The average ACT composite score for Tilden students is 15.

Located three and a half miles southwest of Tilden, Harper High School is nestled in the middle of a residential area in West Englewood that is lined with small bungalows with porches where residents hang out and people-watch. The surrounding blocks are dotted with prominent notices of Block Club Rules, wooden placards that broadcast the residents' disapproval of ball-playing, profanity, and loud music. The average household income of residents in the neighborhood is around $30,000, with a 40 percent poverty level.[52]

The curriculum at Harper is organized into six small school programs that focus on combining academic studies with job skill training in business and entrepreneurship, communications, construction, culinary arts, language arts, and writing arts. The majority of Harper's students (85 percent) join these small schools after successfully completing their first year in the Freshman Academy; the other 15 percent continue with a general high school curriculum.[53] In 2006, Harper's graduation rate was 66 percent, and the average ACT composite score was 14.

Harper's sprawling four-story brown brick building dominates more than half of its block on South Wood Avenue. The outside of the building features gorgeous murals that complement the school's decor, which is inspired by its cardinal-red mascot. Once inside, the visitor to Harper sees wide hallways and bright corridors filled with students who are drawn from the surrounding neighborhood. These young people, and their school, have been on the local and national radar for nearly a decade since Oprah's "school swap" experiment. In 2008 Harper was designated one of the first "Turnaround Schools"; in February 2013 a two-part series on the critically acclaimed public radio show *This American Life* documented the violence that pervades the lives of Harper's students, both inside and outside school walls. First Lady Michelle Obama visited Harper in April 2013 to listen to students' firsthand accounts of confronting violence.[54] Twenty-six Harper students visited the White House in June 2013.

All four of these schools have rich histories and fascinating present-day dynamics that contextualize the numbers and narratives of the participants in my research. Lincoln Park, Payton, Tilden, and Harper are not simply educational institutions that play the enormously important role of shaping the hearts and minds of Chicago adolescents. They are also institutionalized spaces that create a climate and provide experiences that profoundly shape the perceptions and experiences of their inhabitants. The account that follows reveals both the simple and complex notions that young people have about themselves and the world in which they live that are directly informed by their race, neighborhood, and school contexts.

The Outline of the Book

Unequal City builds a crucial case for why social scientists, politicians, policy-makers, teachers, and parents should focus on the home and school contexts of youth to understand how their perceptions of inequality are shaped by their racially divergent worlds and their interactions with authority figures within and across those social spaces.

Each day Chicago residents navigate streets and neighborhoods that are still strictly demarcated by the identities of their inhabitants. Adolescents have to traverse social and physical terrain that powerfully shapes their immediate and long-term perceptions and experiences. As I will show, the passage from home to school each day embodies the curious predicament of the urban American teenager, who will learn as much, if not much more, about his or her identity, social inequality, and the workings of the larger social structure of authority during these journeys as he or she will at school. This is especially the case for the tens of thousands of students who travel more than two miles to attend high school.

Chapter 2 chronicles the perpetually changing educational landscape in Chicago, whose educational and residential policies, instead of shoring up schools as formative social institutions that can create and maintain social solidarity, have often wrought instability and conflict. When social cohesion is interrupted, danger can arise. A Chicago teenager's daily routine of traveling to school can be a theater of both sociability and violence. Day in and day out, students must work to avoid danger from peers and neighbors, as well as the police meant to protect them.

Safe passage between places, just like the broader passage from adolescence to adulthood, is not a uniform experience for all young people. This is abundantly clear in American cities. So how do urban adolescents navigate the passage between home and school? What do they think about their experiences? In chapter 2, I use four students' journeys to their schools to answer these questions through the lens of "geographies of inequality." Their perceptions of safety further restrict or expand their visions of the city and inform how they navigate within and across its various physical and social borders.

Chapter 3 takes a closer look at Chicago, a "city of neighborhoods" in which a major anchor of the community, the neighborhood school, has been displaced. The "racial-spatial divide" in the United States, according to the sociologists Ruth Peterson and Lauren Krivo, is characterized by "a social arrangement in which substantial ethno-racial inequality in social and economic circumstances and power in society is combined with segregated and unequal residential locations across racial and ethnic groups."[55] The racial-spatial divide is a significant structural mechanism that captures the array of resources, opportunities, and diversity available to young people and also shapes their ability to perceive, experience, and adapt to discriminatory treatment in education, employment, and housing. This chapter's examination of the school as a central, organizing social institution lays the foundation for the analyses that follow, demonstrating how teens who daily cross race, class, neighborhood, or gang lines to attend school have an "expanded frame" for understanding social and structural hierarchies, and how this frame affects their view of themselves and their prospects for mobility.

Chapter 4 investigates the claim that contemporary urban youth are increasingly exposed to police contact, and at earlier ages, than urban youth in the past, owing to the implementation of the surveillance practices and disciplinary policies of an overtly carceral institution and its accompanying carceral apparatus. Schools are ostensibly free but have come to resemble correctional facilities. Metal detectors, surveillance cameras, and other mechanisms designed to monitor and control inhabitants are now standard equipment. Youth who must navigate these spaces risk police contact, and their response to these penalizing "routines and rituals" within their educational institutions varies depending on their safety concerns and their relationships with the enforcers of the law.

The descriptions of four types of Chicago school environments earlier in this chapter reveal some of the prisonlike practices endorsed by our education system even when safety threats are improbable. Every day students encounter pat-downs and are monitored on live video surveillance cameras by police officers. Chapter 4 also broadly examines the criminalization of adolescence, revealing who it is students believe police are there to "serve and protect" and detailing their ambivalence about the presence and purpose of the police and security guards patrolling their hallways and classrooms.

If teens have been deemed "criminal" or "suspicious" and made subject to police searches while walking to school, have they already left adolescence and entered into some netherworld of adulthood? Through this example and countless others, young people are often introduced to the criminal justice system without setting foot in a jail or courtroom. Chapter 5 explores how these personal and vicarious encounters with justice and injustice, usually experienced as students travel from their neighborhoods to their schools and back home again, shape their attitudes toward authorities. When young people are formally stopped, searched, and sometimes arrested, or when they know someone else who has had that experience, they develop well-formed opinions about the prejudices and practices of the police with whom they interact, regardless of their visceral responses to the experience.

Many of the youth surveyed and interviewed for this work expressed feelings of powerlessness and an understanding of inequality that originated in one or more of the essential components of identity—age, race, gender, and class. Each of these categories can be a marker of power or its opposite; these young people often experienced the latter, powerlessness, in at least one (if not all) of these categories. These components of identity—and the relative power or powerlessness deriving from each—shaped these teens' beliefs about their opportunities for mobility, from finding a good job to living in a nice house to driving a fancy car. For these young people, as it is for all of us, their visions of the future were shaped to a great extent by their experiences in the present. As we shall see, the sense of the social mobility they would have as adults was influenced by their physical mobility as teenagers.

Chances are that most of the people reading this book were not stopped by a police officer when they were a teenager; nor were they frisked or brought in for questioning. Most of us think of the police—when we think of them at all—as a benign force on the periphery of our lives that serves to protect us when we call them. For many urban young people, however, especially males of color, police play a much more aggressive and proactive role in their lives. Many of these young people routinely have contact with the justice system, and I join the call of criminologists to policymakers to take note of the uneven impacts of the justice system.[56] The justice system's impact is concentrated squarely on young males of color, particularly those who are identified as African American or Hispanic. One aim of this research is to learn how their hopes and dreams have been affected by the opportunity structure made available to them in our purportedly democratic society.

What we shall see is that schools, which should be an equalizing force in American society, are instead more likely to reproduce existing social stratification by race, gender, class, and neighborhood. Schools are essentially institutionalized spaces in which structures of power re-create themselves. They are also social sites where the ultimate objective is to shape the formation of students' knowledge of self, community, nation, and world. Thus, we must confront crucial questions: What exactly are our young people learning in school—not just about math and science but also about their own importance and the relative worth of their peers? What signals are they receiving about what the future holds?

Let us begin to explore the minds of marginalized minors by delving into the realities of their worlds. As we learn a bit more about life in Chicago, and about the wide variety within and across young people's school and home environments, we will see how their sense of racial hierarchies is constructed and how their adolescent visions compare to our understandings of ourselves and our fellow adults. The perspectives of these young people and their horizon of expectations, which are so often ignored, give us a moving and at times disturbing look into our future. We will see that their beliefs and understandings are both stratified by their race and rooted in their place. The potent mix of these forces has a lot to tell us about ourselves, and about the world we create each day for our youth.

CHAPTER 2

"And We Are Not Saved": Safe Passage Through a Changing Educational Landscape

Law is more than logic: it is experience.

—Derrick Bell, *And We Are Not Saved: The Elusive Quest for Racial Justice* (1987)

The life of the law has not been logic; it has been experience.

—Justice Oliver Wendell Holmes, *The Common Law* (1881)

Every day young people are given the task of navigating the spaces between home and school (and sometimes work and play). They do so under the watchful, and sometimes not so watchful, eyes of authorities, families, and peers. These journeys, whether safe or dangerous, are a central force in the lives of America's urban adolescents. If we examine the protections historically deemed necessary to provide safe passage to school—from the integration struggles of the 1950s through the turbulent 1960s and the White flight of the 1980s, and into the present—we find that only the race and age of those making these passages unsafe have changed. During the most pitched battles for school desegregation, National Guardsmen protected Black students from segregationist mobs; now city policymakers protect Black students from one another. This transformation masks a more important change: police officers and other mechanisms of social control have become a central feature of urban schools since the early 1990s, in tandem with the peak in violent crime in large urban cities in this nation.[1] Moreover, police are simply one flavor of the variety of authority figures encountered by these students in their journeys. Besides the police, students encounter parents, teachers, counselors, and social workers each day. Once seen as a group in need of societal protection, urban students are now more commonly seen as the problem. And yet, they still are not safe and we are not saved.[2]

One of the most egregious cases of the failure of safe passage is that of Der-

Photo 2.1   Police Outside Fenger Academy High School, Chicago, in 2009

Source: Photo by Scott Olson, courtesy Getty Images. http://www.gettyimages.com/detail /news-photo/police-patrol-at-a-gathering-outside-fenger-high-school-to-news-photo/91223992.

rion Albert, a sixteen-year-old Fenger Academy student whose murder in 2009 precipitated a police presence outside that school that continues to this day (see photo 2.1). Albert's death serves as a vivid reminder of the dangers of crossing neighborhood boundaries for educational purposes. Although Albert's murder is an extreme case, it heightened the safety concerns of Chicago students and parents, even prompting the mayor at the time, Richard M. Daley, to initiate a "Safe Passage" program that positioned adults along the paths that kids took to and from school.[3] It also put the plight of Chicago youth on the national news radar.[4]

Albert was fatally beaten in September 2009 with a wooden plank from a railroad tie in the shadow of the Agape Community Center at 342 West 111th Street in the Roseland neighborhood on the South Side of Chicago (see photo 2.2).[5] Albert and his killers were all students at Christian Fenger Academy, a high school located in a section of the neighborhood known as "the Ville." Fenger had recently taken in students who lived in a rival community, Altgeld Gardens, whose neighborhood school had been converted into a military academy under the direction of Arne Duncan, then the CEO of Chicago Public Schools (CPS).[6] Albert was an Altgeld resident and, according to prosecutors, an innocent bystander: Albert unknowingly walked into the path of an escalating fight between rival factions from each neighborhood who, earlier in the day, had been shooting at one another outside Fenger.[7]

The irony of the beating next to the community center was brutal: that

Photo 2.2 "Love RIP": Agape Community Center, 342 West 111th Street, Chicago, the Site of Derrion Albert's Fatal Beating in 2009

Source: Photo taken by Carla Shedd, August 26, 2010.

day there was no sign of "agape"—an all-encompassing love—between the students who spent their days together at Fenger. In Chicago place and gang boundaries are socially organized in a reciprocal relationship, and there are many long-standing institutionalized gangs that have deep ties within the neighborhoods.[8] One prominent gang researcher describes Chicago gangs as a "neighborhood tradition" for more than 100 years.[9] The gang influence remains strong to this day, so much so that even teenagers who are not officially in a gang are perceived to have an unavoidable allegiance to the gang in their neighborhood. And high school—one of the most common mixing grounds for people from different areas—becomes a staging ground where students may be forced to defend all the components of their identity, including their residential address.[10]

Even so, young people move around all the time, and the gangs generally have informal agreements about shared spaces that are relatively safe. The fight occurred just past the railroad tracks at 111th and Stewart Avenue, which both sides considered an unofficial safe zone for Altgeld Gardens residents walking east toward Michigan Avenue on 111th Street in order to be able to take only one CTA bus home (see photo 2.3).[11]

Photo 2.3   Looking from the East Toward Agape Community Center, Across
             the Unofficial "Safe" Zone for Students Traveling Home to Altgeld
             Gardens from Fenger Academy High School

Source: Photo taken by Carla Shedd, August 26, 2010.

In Chicago—and indeed, throughout urban America—young people's affiliation and identification with a place can wholly change the trajectory of
their lives. This fight just beyond the schoolhouse grounds not only extin-
guished Albert's life but also diminished the life chances of the five young
men convicted of his murder.[12] And it is likely that these young men would
have never crossed paths had they not been assigned to the same school across
fractious neighborhood borders. The policing of boundaries, both formal and
informal, internal and external, has shifted since the modern civil rights era;
today intraracial boundaries can be just as fraught as the long-standing interracial boundaries seen prior to the 1960s. These boundaries both create and
sustain attachment to group membership.[13]

Crossing Boundaries: Race, Place, and History

Chicago's already stratified residential geography becomes even more complicated when overlaid with its educational landscape. The intersection of race
and place in Chicago schools has profoundly disadvantaged African American students in recent history.[14] Before court-mandated desegregation in the
1950s, Chicago schools were intensely segregated, and the Chicago public

school system's policies during the first half of the twentieth century reinforced racial and ethnic inequality in myriad ways. African American public school students confronted educational institutions vastly different from those of their White immigrant counterparts.

The racial and ethnic composition of schools had a significant impact on school policies and resource allocation. Compared to schools that educated White students, even immigrant White students, schools with a majority of students of color had less-experienced teachers, the facilities were poorer, and they lacked textbooks and libraries—let alone laboratories and specialized curricula.[15] From 1900 to at least 1960, African Americans and White immigrants living in Chicago faced distinct educational trajectories fueled by racial discrimination and entrenched poverty—a group plight only worsened by the demographic pressures of Black migration to the city known as the "promised land."[16]

The boundary crossing at the heart of this book is a product of several recent attempts to desegregate Chicago's public schools. The costs of transgressing borders are borne by all members of our society, but they especially weigh on the children who are tasked with crossing racial, class, and geographical boundaries. Moving to a different school, outside of the familiar neighborhood and social group, requires substantial adjustments. Young people making these longer journeys to school may become more aware of their disadvantage; in addition, sending students from "bad" neighborhood schools to "good" schools elsewhere inadvertently exposes them to new kinds of dangers besides threats to their physical safety, including the danger of possibly negative encounters with the police.

School desegregation has been a crucial battle in the ongoing quest for racial equality. Although rife with problems in both concept and execution, desegregation in our schools has moved faster in important geographic ways than in the rest of our society. Neighborhoods, in other words, are often still more segregated than the schools located in them. Whether we are talking about African American students who were bused to predominantly White schools after the landmark 1954 school desegregation case Brown v. Board of Education or students of all racial and ethnic minority backgrounds whose parents today enroll them in the "best" schools possible (schools that are often in White or wealthy neighborhoods), all of these students might be crossing more boundaries to get an education than the rest of us do in any other pursuit. The tensions around this adjustment from Jim Crow–era residential and educational segregation to the more muddled situation of post–civil rights era stratification remain palpable.

Supreme Court chief justice Earl Warren, in his majority opinion for Brown v. Board of Education, proclaimed that education is "perhaps the most important function of state and local governments. . . . It is a principal instrument in awakening the child to cultural values, in preparing him for later professional training, and in helping him to adjust normally to his environment." The phrase "adjust normally to his environment" is crucial, because there is much about many urban public school environments that is not normal—and should not be perceived as normal. For many young people, navigating through danger and social deprivation in their school setting is their typical experience; they have no choice but to figure out how to adapt to their environment.

The road to Brown v. Board of Education was long and hard-fought, and it was so challenging that the decision was broken down into two phases. The first Brown decision, a compendium of cases from four states and the District of Columbia, overturned the "separate but equal" doctrine adopted in the Court's 1896 Plessy v. Ferguson decision. The Brown decision was a bold declaration that segregation has no place in the field of public education.[17] This effectively shut down states' right to prohibit Blacks from using the same public services and facilities as Whites because legally mandated segregation deprived Blacks of the "equal protection of the laws" guaranteed by the Fourteenth Amendment. The second phase of Brown, decided one year later on May 31, 1955, dealt with the implementation of the Court's mandate to desegregate public schools, but it lacked enforcement provisions. A decade would pass before passage of the Civil Rights Act of 1964 gave the executive branch the power to enforce school desegregation. The Department of Justice was given the authority to file lawsuits seeking school desegregation, and the federal government also used the tactic of cutting funding to schools that continued to segregate their students.[18]

Widespread school integration did not begin until a 1971 Supreme Court case brought from North Carolina, Swann v. Charlotte-Mecklenburg Board of Education, allowed busing as a means of integrating schools in racially segregated neighborhoods.[19] After Swann, some areas of both the South and North achieved the highest levels of school integration ever seen in the 1970s and 1980s. Chicago schools, however, would not integrate as successfully.

Because of "White flight" from the city to the suburbs, and from public to private schools, Chicago's Black and Hispanic students were left behind in the city's public school system. Unlike districts elsewhere that experienced "successful" integration, Chicago public schools, the largest school district in Illinois, seemed to give up. In 1980 the student population of Chicago public schools was approximately 18 percent White, 60 percent African American, and 14 percent Hispanic.[20] These changes in Chicago were typical of what happened in large urban school districts across the United States (see table 2.1) and would have a major impact on the life chances and life trajectories of the Black and Hispanic youth left behind.

On September 24, 1980, the U.S. Justice Department filed a lawsuit against the Board of Education of the City of Chicago in which it alleged that the Board "operated a dual school system that segregated students on the basis of race and ethnic origin in violation of the Equal Protection Clause of the Fourteenth Amendment to the United States Constitution and Titles IV

Table 2.1   Racial Demographic Data on Pre-K Through Twelfth-Grade Students in the Largest U.S. Public School Districts, 1987–2009

	New York[a]		Los Angeles		Houston		Philadelphia	
	1990–1991	2008–2009	1987–1988	2008–2009	1987–1988	2008–2009	1987–1988	2008–2009
White	19%	n.a.	17%	9%	16%	8%	24%	13%
Black	38	n.a.	18	11	42	28	63	61
Hispanic	35	n.a.	57	73	39	61	9	17
Asian	8	n.a.	8	6	3	3	3	6
Total	943,969		589,311	625,073	191,708	200,225	194,698	159,867

Source: National Center for Education Statistics (NCES), Common Core of Data (CCD), "Public Elementary/Secondary School Universe Survey," 1987–1988, 1990–91 (version 1a), and 2008–2009 (version 1b) for New York, Los Angeles, Houston, and Philadelphia.
[a]New York data was unavailable for 1987–1988 and 2009–2009. Data for 1990–1991 was available as an early comparison to the other largest U.S. public school districts.

and VI of the Civil Rights Act of 1964."[21] The investigation found that school attendance zones had been gerrymandered to perpetuate segregation. They also charged the Chicago school board with underutilizing White schools while using mobile classrooms to ease overcrowding in Black schools. According to a *Washington Post* report, "Federal officials found that the school board had bused 300 children out of a severely overcrowded Black South Side school to another all-Black school four miles away. A largely White school sat less than two miles away with six empty classrooms."[22]

In addition, the lawsuit accused the Board of tracking students to create or maintain segregation; maintaining racially segregated branches of schools; race-matching teachers and staff to students; allowing White students to avoid assigned schools when their race was in the minority in favor of attendance at other schools where Whites were the majority; and lastly, associating segregated schools with segregated housing projects.[23] This was said to have happened over a "substantial period of time and in a substantial portion of Chicago public schools"; continuance of these policies would result in the Board operating in violation of the U.S. Constitution, thereby causing "immediate, severe and irreparable harm."[24]

After extensive negotiations, a consent decree was entered requiring the Board to desegregate as many schools as possible, "considering all the circumstances in Chicago," and to provide supplemental resources for any majority-Black or -Hispanic schools that remained segregated.[25] Like the Brown v. Board of Education II decision, this legal remedy provided no specific goalposts or enforcement provisions. The predictable result was lackluster and halfhearted actions.[26] The Board's minimal efforts in the 1960s, the 1980s, and the early 2000s did little to redress the unequal racial and spatial order of Chicagoans' residential and educational lives. As detailed in table 2.2, segregation has exponentially increased in Chicago in the last thirty years.

Since 2009, when a federal judge lifted the thirty-year-old consent decree ordering desegregation in Chicago public schools, the Board has not faced any legal requirement to improve the situation. This means that the school system is no longer required to try to achieve greater racial balance in the schools by busing or allocating school slots by racial demographics. The decision to lift the consent decree has exacerbated segregation by further restricting equal access to the city's selective enrollment and magnet schools. Currently, fewer than 10 percent of school-age White students in Chicago attend public high schools, and the majority of those attending public schools are enrolled in the city's better-resourced magnet schools.[27] The remaining population of White students attend private and parochial schools inside and outside the city limits.

This is the context in which then-CEO of Chicago Public Schools Arne Duncan (now the U.S. secretary of education) proposed a plan to restructure the spatial organization of public schooling in Chicago. The stated goal of this plan, launched in 2004, was to replace "underperforming" schools with 100 new high-quality elementary and high schools with innovative learning approaches by the year 2010.[28] Chicago's "Renaissance 2010" program—which was designed to increase the "portfolio" of options (curricular, locational, and so on) that parents and students could choose to enhance their educational experience and further their educational trajectory—has drastically reshaped the city's educational landscape.[29] But the new availability of "school choice" also shut students and parents *out* of options; familiar neighborhood schools were closed, combined, and put on notice. The Renaissance 2010 plan, like court-ordered desegregation before it, led to some children having to journey farther from their home neighborhoods to attend school.

The impact of this overhaul in education on young people's school lives was intensified by a simultaneous change in their residential lives, especially those youth who resided in public housing. In 1999 the U.S. Department of Housing and Urban Development approved the "Plan for Transformation" developed by the Chicago Housing Authority (CHA). This effort, costing over $1 billion, called for the demolition and replacement of eleven high-rise housing developments and the rehabilitation of 10,000 units in low-rise and senior housing facilities. In addition, nearly 38,000 families were given Housing Choice Vouchers to seek residences in the private rental market with the assistance of a government subsidy.[30] The youth who were directly affected by the CHA Plan for Transformation were tasked with moving from extremely distressed environments to settle in neighborhoods that were still impoverished, still hypersegregated, and still perceived to be unsafe.[31] In fact, families

Table 2.2 Racial Demographic Data for Chicago Schools, Pre-K Through Twelfth Grade, While Under the Desegregation Consent Decree, 1987–2009

	1987–1988	1990–1991	1993–1994	1996–1997	1999–2000	2002–2003	2005–2006	2008–2009
White	54,276	48,367	46,834	44,108	42,970	40,515	33,945	37,488
	13%	12%	11%	9%	10%	9%	8%	9%
Black	251,705	236,914	227,604	227,852	226,611	221,221	204,664	196,200
	60%	58%	56%	49%	52%	51%	49%	47%
Hispanic	100,741	110,707	121,343	135,206	147,705	159,284	158,270	172,106
	24%	27%	30%	29%	34%	37%	38%	41%
Asian	12,126	11,994	12,848	13,370	13,731	14,236	13,361	14,862
	3%	3%	3%	3%	3%	3%	3%	4%
Total	419,537	408,830	409,499	469,098	431,750	436,048	420,982	421,430

Source: National Center for Education Statistics (NCES), City of Chicago, School District 299, Common Core of Data (CCD), "Public Elementary/ Secondary School Universe Survey," 1987–1988, 1990–1991, 1993–1994, 1996–1997, 2002–2003, and 2005–2006 (version 1a) and 1999–2000 and 2008–2009 (version 1b).

who moved from housing developments to Black communities like Engle-wood, where Harper High is located, reported greater fear and greater vio-lence in comparison to those families who lived in traditional CHA develop-ments. For most families required to move, the relocations were rushed, proceeded without any substantive mobility counseling, and were often out of sync with public school schedules.[32]

Not surprisingly, this housing instability led to greater school instability. The young people who had to move were sometimes able to continue in the same school, but many were forced to move far from both their residential and educational communities. Also perhaps unsurprisingly, these moves cor-related with school disengagement. One study of CHA youth conducted at the same time as this research found that one in three teens were academically off-track—that is, not in the appropriate grade for their age.[33] Although these extensive changes in school and housing policies were instituted to increase educational opportunity and enhance quality of life, they often dramatically upended the lives of youth in ways that policymakers did not anticipate.

These transformations have changed both the physical and mental land-scapes for hundreds of thousands of youth in Chicago. Attending high school is one of the primary reasons—sometimes the only reason—that young peo-ple leave their racially and socioeconomically cloistered home environments; paradoxically, for other students who attend the school as local residents it is the reason they remain ensconced in their environment. So school, as an in-stitution that structures life experiences and interactions, becomes even more important than the neighborhood.[34] Many of the students whose stories are told in this book leave the land of the "have-nots" to be educated with the "haves." Some "haves" and "have-nots," meanwhile, get their education in their respective advantaged or disadvantaged quarters. Finally, there are oth-ers who leave nice neighborhoods where they attended private or parochial schools to join the "haves" and the "have-nots," who hail from their respec-tive residential neighborhoods, to learn in selective public schools with no attendance boundaries, like Payton Prep, or neighborhood schools with a rigorous curriculum accessible via application, like Lincoln Park. Thus, these young people daily navigate a racially ordered "geography of opportunity" wherein the resources for improving school and life chances are meted out by race, class, and zip code.[35] Understanding the danger and conflicts they in-evitably encounter along the way requires a closer look at the spatial politics of the city they call home.

The Segregated City

Chicago is a racially stratified city, a place where employment trends, housing policies, and school conditions have long revealed and perpetuated the divide between Whites and African Americans. The stark chasm between what used to be the towering Cabrini-Green housing projects and the glittering wealth of the "Gold Coast" on Michigan Avenue, just one mile east, is one of the better-publicized examples of the separate and unequal worlds that African Americans and Whites generally inhabit in "the Second City."[36] According to recent evidence, this ethnic divide is only becoming more pronounced as the city's diversity increases, with growing populations of Hispanics and Asians and increasing gentrification of the city center.

Class also divides the city of Chicago. Well-marked physical and social boundaries shape the perceptions and experiences of the people who live within them. From the early work of Robert E. Park, St. Clair Drake, Horace Cayton, and Gerald Suttles, through the groundbreaking efforts of William Julius Wilson, researchers studying Chicago's social ecology have shown that concentrated poverty marks many neighborhoods, sealing their status and determining their access to resources. The maps reproduced here and the large-scale survey results I discuss are all drawn from Chicago neighborhood and public high school data collected by the Consortium on Chicago School Research (CCSR).[37] The CCSR data, which are mapped to depict the levels of concentrated poverty as measured by the percentage of adult male unemployment and the percentage of families living below the poverty line across the city, underlie a later discussion of the distribution of perceptions of injustice.

Even without intimate knowledge of Chicago neighborhoods, anyone looking at map 2.1 can clearly see the stratification of poverty by neighborhood and the great overlap between ethnicity, poverty, and place. Neighborhoods that are predominantly African American, such as Englewood and Greater Grand Crossing on the South Side (community areas 68 and 69, respectively) and West Garfield Park and East Garfield Park on the West Side (community areas 26 and 27, respectively), have many more inhabitants who are unemployed and living below the poverty line, as denoted by the darker shades of those areas on the map. The inhabitants of the neighborhoods on the North Side and Southwest Side, which have the lightest shading, have lower levels of poverty and unemployment. The flags on the concentrated poverty map depict the four public high schools in this study—Lincoln Park (7), Payton (8), Tilden (61), and Harper (67).

Several outlier communities make the larger neighborhood patterns even more striking. On the North Side of Chicago, the Uptown and Logan Square community areas have moderate to high levels of poverty, but their populations differ from their surrounding communities by ethnicity (more African American and Hispanic), by housing stock, and by resources for the mentally ill and the formerly incarcerated.[38] Neighborhood isolation or contiguity also matters. Logan Square (community area 22) is adjacent on the north to the

Map 2.1   The Concentration of Poverty in Chicago by Community Area

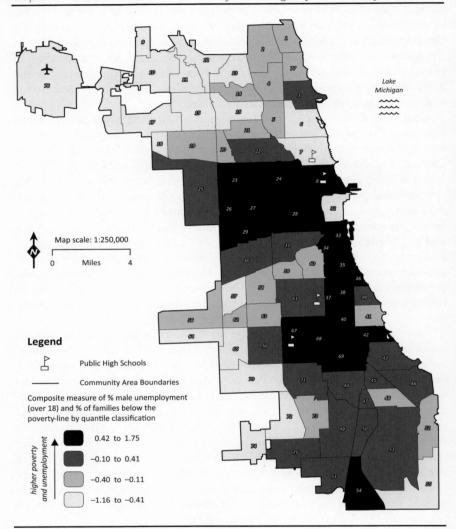

Source: CCSR data, 2001.

more impoverished West Side neighborhoods, while Uptown (community area 3) is an island of concentrated poverty in comparison to neighboring areas that are less impoverished and have higher employment rates.[39] According to a recent report on Chicago's long-standing segregation by race and class, "Ten of the city's seventy-seven community areas have poverty rates above 40 percent"; conversely, "ten others have poverty rates below 10 percent."[40]

The racial stratification across neighborhoods is inextricably linked with the geographical class divisions in the city. The same report notes that in thirty-two community areas fewer than 10 percent of residents are African American (and twenty-seven of those are fewer than 5 percent African American). Moreover, 52 percent of the city's Black population "lives in only 20 of Chicago's 77 community areas—neighborhoods that are each more than 90 percent Black."[41] A stark geography of inequality operates as a social force and a social product—that is, as both cause and consequence. This visual representation of social inequality reveals the bounded nature of residents' lives and hints at the degree of socialization involved in navigating Chicago's spatial divide.[42]

The city's geography also includes sharp social-psychological divisions. Map 2.2 shows the CCSR school survey respondents' perceptions of safety across these same areas of Chicago. The neighborhoods with the lightest shading are those considered the safest; the majority of the neighborhood areas that are considered the least safe (darkest shading) overlap with the communities that have higher levels of concentrated poverty. The flags denote public high schools (excluding charter, contract, and special education schools) to demonstrate the various locations and densities of educational institutions across the various neighborhoods.

Two of the four items in the perception of safety scale concern students' assessments of their safety while in their school's classrooms and hallways. The other two ask about their perceptions of insecurity outside of school and while traveling to and from school. The data can be interpreted in several different ways. On the one hand, crime levels are in fact higher in many of the neighborhoods that students perceive as very unsafe.[43] On the other hand, these same neighborhoods also usually include a high police presence that does not always translate into its residents feeling safer.[44] In fact, greater numbers of police in a neighborhood can lead to a stronger feeling of insecurity. Safety means different things to different people, particularly to young people of color who disproportionately feel harassed by the police.

In Chicago, neighborhoods that are mere miles away can be worlds apart with regard to their residents' perceptions and experiences. Chicago residents' "divergent social worlds" rest heavily on their starkly contrasting resources and opportunities, which particularly shape their experiences with crime and policing.[45] Thus, the time and energy accorded to achieving safe passage is also stratified by race, place, and circumstance.

Students' perceptions of safety and their actual exposure to violence and crime are heightened when they cross social and symbolic boundaries. Those who live in a city learn certain things about how to "stay safe" in their neighborhood. There, they may know the problem areas and even the problem

Map 2.2   Perceptions of Safety Among Surveyed Chicago Youth

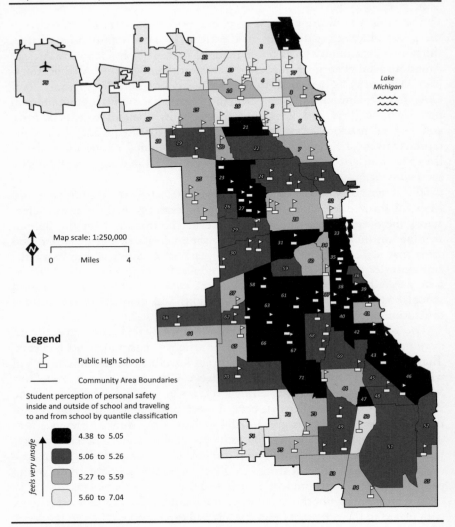

Source: CCSR data, 2001.

people, but that knowledge is missing when they pass through less familiar places. Over time students on their way to and from school may acquire some knowledge about those passages, but the sheer amount of instability and mobility inevitably exposes them to places whose rules they do not know and where they may not resemble the residents.

Formation and Reformation in Chicago Schools

Although the most idealistic portrayal of schools holds them up to be institutions where students are inculcated with democratic ideals and academic knowledge, in reality schools have a variety of other functions as well. They socialize students to mainstream societal norms and promote social integration across and within groups. They also create and reinforce social hierarchies.[46] Schools require that students interact with both peers and authority figures whose identities and experiences may either be similar to theirs or be the total opposite. What students take from these encounters indelibly shapes their perceptions of both the larger social world and themselves.

Schools have long been understood as places of "formation," which provide knowledge and skills to further the social and cultural development of students, in contrast to places of "reformation," such as workhouses and prisons, which strive to correct individuals' behavioral dysfunctions and to rehabilitate them and their standing in society. We as a country trust that schools will shape our young; promote their social, intellectual, and emotional development; and (in ways not often defined) prepare them for the experience of being an adult. These tasks are considered so essential that for almost a century school has been mandatory across the country.[47] In 2004 Illinois state law mandated that children between ages seven and seventeen be enrolled in school unless they had already received a high school degree or some equivalent degree or were eligible for other exceptions.[48]

The uniqueness in American society of a requirement applicable to everyone—we must *all* attend school—makes evident the enormous trust our society has in the public school system. It should also be clear that society as a whole benefits when schools accomplish their missions of socialization and acculturation. Students are taught to respect and obey authority, to follow directions, to be on time and follow schedules, to meet deadlines, and much more. Where those lessons are not learned, certain properties of reform within educational institutions become apparent. The meaning of school misconduct has expanded in the last two decades, and the consequences of misbehavior, which may include detention, suspension, or expulsion, have become increasingly severe.[49] Schools are a central mechanism influencing the subsequent institutional paths taken by young people, whether toward the labor force, toward higher education, or toward the prison system, and young people daily experience and adapt to the universal carceral apparatus present in these institutions.[50]

After the home, school is the second-most-important place for socialization; at school we figure out who we are and how we are supposed to engage with the rest of the world. Whether or not they were explicitly conceived that way, schools thus act as structural forces. "Schools are not just places where learning comprises how to read, compute, analyze, and synthesize information," notes the sociologist Prudence Carter. "They are also key sites of social-ization and cultural reproduction."[51] The "powerful cultural dynamics" that Carter sees as permeating our schools—such as teachers' evaluations of stu-dents' language, style, and tastes in relation to the dominant culture—act in concert with the social dynamics inherent not only in the curriculum but also in students' interactions with authority figures in the school as well as with one another. Young people understand a great deal about their value, both the value they assign to themselves and the value they believe others see in them, by examining the state of their surroundings.

A school is generally assumed to be a safe haven, but depending on its lo-cation, security and quality can vary enormously. Our nation's most com-petitive high schools, though not without their problems, are models of what public education can achieve: they offer an astounding array of challenging courses, training in music and art, and guidance that shepherds students into the nation's top colleges, all the while nurturing the social, psychological, and emotional development of the future leaders of our country. The other end of the spectrum seems like an entirely different universe: failing urban schools are overused facilities stuffed with too many students, who are not stimulated by the often meager intellectual offerings but are amply punished for acting out. Nor do young people feel safe once they enter the highly securitized space of an urban school.

Schools, in other words, are ambiguous places because of their multiple meanings and purposes. Contemporary urban public high schools are simul-taneously sites of both danger and refuge, places where adolescents negotiate their identities, learn how to represent themselves to society, and manage multiple external forces of social control. In effect, the societal microcosm that schools represent can also be interpreted as a distortion of our society, rather than as a true reflection of it. Schools, with their bell schedules, class-room routines, and standard lunch and recreation times, are designed to re-move the unpredictability at the heart of young people's daily lives, to replace uncertainty with consistency. We believe that such procedures will better teach and socialize our children, but school—which should be an equalizing force in American society—may also reproduce existing social stratification by race, gender, class, and neighborhood.[52]

Perceptions of Safety Among Chicago Youth

A central premise of this book is that schools and neighborhoods—and the passages between them—are integral to shaping youth attitudes and experi-ences. In addition, race, gender, and neighborhood also affect students' views of their own safety.

When students evaluate their sense of safety in the various places they visit throughout their days, striking differences emerge among racial and ethnic

Figure 2.1   Chicago High School Students' Perceptions of Insecurity, by Race, 2001

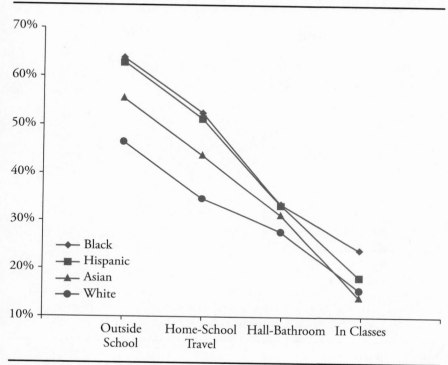

Source: CCSR data, 2001.

groups in Chicago schools, with African Americans reporting the most pervasive sense of danger (see figure 2.1). A clear majority of African American, Hispanic, and Asian American students feel the least safe outside their school environments. Nearly half of Blacks and Hispanics feel insecure while traveling between home and school. Strikingly, a sizable number of students in all racial groups, from 28 to 40 percent, feel unsafe in their schools' hallways and bathrooms. Finally, approximately 25 percent of African American youth feel unsafe in their classrooms. And school is supposed to be a safe place?

Later chapters will address the distinctions in young people's assessments of school safety; here we examine the same survey measures with students' school racial composition as the component of classification (in contrast to the use of students' race as the classifier in figure 2.1). The lines in figure 2.2 represent the responses of all students who attended a given type of school, regardless of their individual race-ethnicity.

Once again, it is quite clear that a strong majority of students attending

Figure 2.2   Chicago High School Students' Perceptions of Insecurity, by
School Racial Composition, 2001

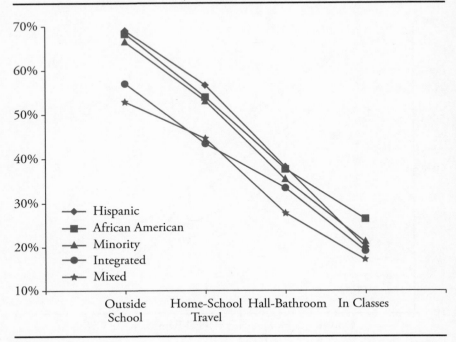

Source: CCSR data, 2001.

schools that are predominantly (more than 85 percent) African American or
predominantly Hispanic feel unsafe outside those schools and when traveling
between home and school. There must be decisive factors shaping the environments around these predominantly minority schools and students' passages
from home and school for them to be deemed very unsafe. In contrast, there is
a significant difference in perceptions of insecurity for young people attending
schools that are formally classified by Chicago Public Schools guidelines on
school racial composition as mixed (15 to 30 percent White) or integrated (30
to 45 percent White).

Gang activity, or at least the perception of it, is also critical to students'
assessment of school safety. Nearly half of surveyed students attending predominantly African American schools believe that more than 50 percent of
their peers were in a gang (see figure 2.3). Approximately one-third of the
students attending predominantly minority schools believe that more than
half their classmates are in a gang, in contrast to only one-fifth of those in
mixed-race and integrated schools.

These starkly different perceptions of their school environments raise an

Figure 2.3   *Chicago High School Students' Perceptions of Gang Population, by School Type, 2001*

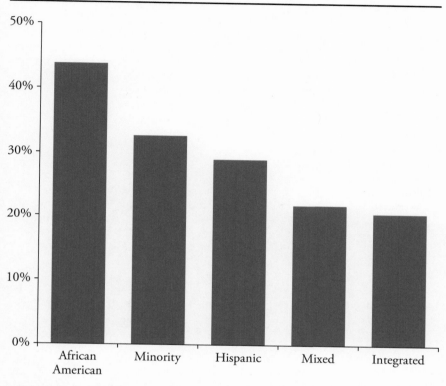

Source: CCSR data, 2001.

important question: what are the mechanisms and processes that shape students' perceptions?

Adolescent Geographies

Once young people begin high school, whether in Chicago or any other city, they enter a stage when they are venturing farther and farther away from home. This is the case not only because of the logistics of getting to school, but also because adolescents are in the developmental phase in which they seek exposure to more people and to varied experiences. Young people cross all types of boundaries to attend school—racial and ethnic boundaries, gang lines, and class barriers, to name only a few. What is more, the physical terrain they are asked to cross is governed by various social norms concerning where people should and should not go, how they should present themselves,

Table 2.3   Distance Traveled by Chicago High School Students Between Home and School, by School Racial Composition

	Segregated (Harper)	Predominantly Minority (Tilden)	Mixed (Lincoln Park)	Integrated (Payton Prep)
Short (less than two miles)	Keisha **Michael** TB David Rina Dewayne Hunter		Joaquin Louie Andre Gabrielle	
Medium (two to five miles)	Pink Chris	Jackson **Max** Juan Mike Dre Jasmine Terry	Billy Pilgrim Angelique Jane	Tasha Brianna Carmen
Long (five miles or more)		Jackson Shay Andrea	Boomer **Michelle** Janet	Angela John Amber Freddy Vanessa Darrell **Alex**

Source: Author's interviews and surveys, 2005.
Note: The names of the students whose journeys to school are highlighted in this chapter are in bold.

and how they should behave. These journeys have consequences. The very act of crossing boundaries—or just as important, *not* crossing boundaries—determines for my study participants the people with whom they interact, their experiences, and their perceptions of themselves and the world. A snapshot of their journeys to four very different educational settings introduces us to these consequences (see table 2.3).

FOUR JOURNEYS TO SCHOOL

A shrill alarm wakes Michelle every weekday morning. Grudgingly, she prepares for her trek to Lincoln Park High School. If she does not get a ride from her aunt, who nearly always has to leave for work before Michelle has finished her morning routine, Michelle uses the "El," the city's aboveground train system. She boards an eastbound bus that makes almost fifty stops, then gets the Brown Line train at Belmont to travel south on Sheffield Avenue through the tony, mostly upper-middle-class Lincoln Park neighborhood. Michelle does not look forward to her daily journey, which takes an hour and a half each way.

After attending a grammar school only a few blocks from her home in a Northwest Side neighborhood that has changed from ethnic-White to majority-Latino in the last two decades, Michelle misses her friends who continued on to the area's Catholic high school; she also deems Lincoln Park High unworthy of the long commute. She says, "I have to wake up at, like, 5:15 and then get out at 3:30 and then come home at, like, 5:00 PM. It's like a whole day . . . a waste." Her strong distaste for traveling all the way across the city for school is clear, but this ninth-grader has no choice in the matter. Michelle's cousin went to a top Ivy League school after graduating from Lincoln Park High, so her Filipino parents are adamant that their daughter will fulfill their immigrant dreams by following the same path. Lincoln Park acts as a guarantor of her successful future.

Much farther south, on the other side of Chicago, Alex wakes up early enough to leave his home by 7:00 AM. He begins his journey northward out of his African American middle-class enclave neighborhood of Beverly to arrive at Walter Payton College Preparatory High School, located just north of Chicago's downtown "Loop."

Once Alex got the hang of his commute early in his freshman year, he began refusing a ride from his parents. "I sort of like taking the train a little bit more than having my parents drive me everywhere 'cuz it gives me freedom and I don't have to be on their schedule," he says. "I can do things on my own without having to worry about, 'Oh, I have to hurry up, I have five minutes left to get out of the house.'" Alex relishes this small bit of freedom, but he is always aware that he has to be cautious about what he does and how he acts in certain areas. Alex never falls asleep on the train because he "sees everyone as a potential attacker," especially since one of his friends was mugged recently. The Red Line connects the more racially heterogeneous North Side of the city to the majority–African American neighborhoods south of the Loop, straddling the path of Chicago's Dan Ryan Expressway. Forty-five minutes later, Alex exits the Red Line train at Clark and Division streets and walks the few short blocks to his school, arriving just in time for first period.

Michael, an African American tenth-grader who attends Harper High School, located in the often maligned, predominantly African American and low-income West Englewood neighborhood, sometimes catches the bus when he remembers to bring his pass, but usually walks the twenty minutes northeast to school on the edge of his own neighborhood. He has the luxury of sleeping in until almost 8:00 AM, unlike his peers who commute to their schools on the North Side.

Michael describes his block as quiet, with no drug dealers or violence; the police are "around there every once in a while, but other than that, it's all good." He never worries about anyone trying to mess with him; after living in the area for five years, he mentions with obvious pride that he pretty much knows everyone. Several of his grammar school friends attend Harper, and they sometimes meet at the corner of Seventy-First and Wood Streets and walk together. He has a strong attachment to his school and looks forward to going each day. Michael adds that he would "rather go to school with people in my community than go to a mixed-race school."

Max, a ninth-grader with an easygoing demeanor, only needs about thirty minutes between waking up and arriving at Tilden Career Community Academy. He would normally have a twenty-five-minute walk to school, but getting a ride is much faster and safer. Max came to Chicago from Mexico a few years ago, and he lives with his aunt, brother, and two cousins in a disputed area between the territories of two warring gangs, the Black P. Stones, made up mostly of Black youth, and the Razas, who are largely Hispanics. His aunt began giving Max a ride even though he lives near the major bus route at Forty-Seventh Street, which would drop him one block away from Tilden, after his best friend was "jumped" (beaten up) by a number of guys at that bus stop a few times. However, classmates affiliated with the Stones have beaten up Max inside the school building. "By the bus stop is where more Hispanics get jumped," he tells me. "No, no, it's not more," he corrects himself, "it's where *all* Hispanics get jumped. I know two or three people that actually stopped coming to school because of that. They got too scared."

By the end of his freshman year, Max is not as worried about being beaten up, since he has gotten to know several members of the Black gangs—the Black P. Stones and the Gangster Disciples—as well as what he calls "my own kind" (Hispanics) in their respective gangs. Still, Max begins his day by stepping out of his aunt's car, waving good-bye, and letting her know whether he will need her to pick him up or will be taking his chances walking home with his girlfriend.

Young people's various journeys to school, like those of Michelle, Alex, Michael, and Max, expose them to different kinds of environments, raising their awareness of their own social position and that of others. Instead of opening up a new world of opportunity, traveling to a higher-ranked, better-resourced school may present a student with evidence that the world he comes from is worse than he thought. Instead of providing an escape from a bad area, the commute may subject the student to greater scrutiny, surveillance, and violence—either physical or symbolic.

Just as Michelle, Alex, Michael, and Max take different paths to begin their school day—and as we will see, in large part precisely because of those different paths—they will come to have very different understandings of the world around them and of their place in that world. Schools become "boundary objects," or "organizational interfaces," that make it necessary for adolescents to develop and maintain coherence across their social worlds.[53] Understanding how this works requires that they systematically catalog the "key mechanisms associated with the activation, maintenance, transposition or the dispute, bridging and crossing of boundaries."[54]

The boundaries that young people cross and those that they construct themselves give us insight into the few instances of agency they are able to enact. Keisha, a tenth-grader at Harper High, is adamant about keeping to herself. She recounted the following advice from a teacher and mentor at her school: "Ms. J. will be like, 'I told you everything will be all right, just stay to yourself.' She told me last year, 'Don't make new friends 'cuz they won't do nothing but get you in a whole lot of trouble.' And that's what I tried to do, I stay to myself."[55]

Keisha's words provide one portal to understanding how young people adapt to the settings they must navigate each and every day. Keisha has put boundaries up between herself and other people. She also thinks of "her neighborhood" as the two blocks around her house. She tells me, "There's nothing for me outside." Nevertheless, there are ways in which she transgresses boundaries via her language and behavior. Keisha enacts a form of "code switching"—that is, she approaches the distinct worlds of her high school and her neighborhood by varying her self-presentation and language to better negotiate these social worlds. Keisha believes that place is a causal mechanism behind much of the behavior she witnesses in both contexts, especially the bad behavior. She emphatically states, "These kids are still gon' act the way they act [bad]. This is Harper High, Englewood area! Kids are outrageous here!" When I ask if she thinks that kids would act better if they did not live in her area and moved to a different community, she replies:

> Well, basically if they [were] out in the suburbs where none of this ghetto-ness was happening, they'd be better. Or even if they was like me. (*pauses*) . . . I'm from the [housing] projects, but I don't show it, though. I could act normal in here, but outside the school, I'm a totally different person. See, in school I don't come to play. I just come to do my work and wait for the bell to ring and go home. Once the bell rings, I'm Ghetto-Keisha. I'm up outta here, for real. I'm just out.

Keisha seems to take pride in her ability to straddle both worlds, showing her serious, quiet side at school but also dealing with any issues in her neighborhood by adhering to local mores. Her "world" is the few blocks between home and school. In contrast to her thoughtful contemplation of others' worlds and experiences—"I need to go check out the suburbs and see how they treat them out there, and then maybe I can put two and two together to see what's going on" (see chapter 1 epigraph)—she is preoccupied with managing her own home and school worlds. When Keisha explains why she avoids the daily fights that occur at Harper High and also does not venture outside her home to hang out, the importance of her personal safety is clear: "I'm just worried about a bullet, 'cuz a bullet ain't got no name." Therefore, her strategy is to move from one context to the other as quickly as possible while avoiding personal danger as best she can.

Keisha is not the only student in this study who routinely goes home immediately after the bell rings at school, but this strategy has a different resonance for the South Side students than it does for those attending the North Side schools. When Boomer and Andre from Lincoln Park discuss the experience of the police telling them to move off school grounds, a listener does not get the sense that they are in any imminent danger. In contrast, the students attending Harper and Tilden have to understand the multiple dangers they may face after the school bell rings.

As mentioned earlier, Max feels that waiting around for the bus or hanging out on school grounds is unsafe for him and his fellow Hispanic students because they are in danger of being beaten up by Blacks. By contrast, Dewayne's caution about hanging around after school highlights the danger he might face from students who share his racial-ethnic background. "Like I say," he explains to me, "it's good for you to go home after school than go home *after* after-school." I ask him why.

> 'Cuz you can go home *after* after-school and get jumped on [because] all the kids is out of school. They won't get in trouble for jumping on you 'cuz they outta school [dismissed for the day]. It's outta the school's hands after that. They won't get in trouble for jumping on you. Now when the bell ring, they can get in trouble 'cuz, like, they still on school premises and they still in school until they make it home.

I cringe when I hear this. All of my interviews at Harper are taking place in a back office of the library *after school*. Once his interview concludes, Dewayne assures me that he will be fine, and he is in fact in class the following day. But his explanation demonstrates why the Harper (and Tilden) students' fears about remaining on school grounds once the dismissal bell rings are profound and complex. The resentment some of them hold for the school security guards and police officers who "hawk them" to go home (Dewayne's words) turns into longing if they are vulnerable to being "jumped on" once the school day ends. This fear is also the reason for the reluctance of students like Keisha and Dewayne to participate in after-school activities. They have thought about the danger of navigating from school to home during the off-hours, when they would lack the protection of the crowd of students leaving the school and the close watch of Chicago police officers, and decided that the risk is not worth it.

However, Dewayne does not leave Harper High every day just to sequester himself at home, as Keisha does. Instead, as he takes great pride in telling me, he ventures all over the city instead of putting up walls. In fact, crossing neighborhood lines has widened his perspective on how the world works and given him greater options for both self-perception and behavior. Dewayne has great disdain for the "bad kids" in his neighborhood. He knows that context matters, so he uses his agency to change his context. This comes out when I ask him whether he has any close friends, either at school or in his neighborhood:

> DEWAYNE: I don't get too close to 'em. Never get too close to 'em. 'Cuz they end up turnin' they back on you when you really need 'em. Can't trust your friends all the time. Ain't got no friends, got associates.
>
> AUTHOR: Since you live in the neighborhood, do those "bad people" influence you?
>
> DEWAYNE: I don't be around them. I travel. I get around. Out west, out east, out north.
>
> AUTHOR: By yourself?
>
> DEWAYNE: Yeah. Ride my bike [south] to like, 105th. I go to my auntie's house up north. Just ride and see . . . I wanna see Chicago. Picture the whole thing. Get around.

Like Keisha, Dewayne does not intimately associate with the other young people around him. However, his closed social network creates an even stronger urge in Dewayne to transgress the visible, durable, and salient spatial boundaries that constrain him and others who both live and learn in homogeneous settings.[56]

Unlike Dewayne and Keisha, the journeys of the students who travel every day to Lincoln Park, Payton, or Tilden have eye-opening, rather than insulating, effects that shape their perceptions of safety. But no matter whether students travel six miles or walk six minutes to attend school, safety is at the forefront of their minds. They understand the role of place in shaping their realities, but some do not have the benefit of using place to change their reality in a positive way. Traveling to a higher-ranking, safer school in a different neighborhood is one way of transgressing boundaries. But staying in your own neighborhood to attend school, even if that school is not deemed high-quality, can seem much safer than the alternative. The divergent paths and divergent outcomes of these young people reveal the great impact of physical mobility on social mobility.

Conclusion

Chicago's key structural institutions have long been permeated by deep racial and spatial divides. From the beginning of the twentieth century to the present, the city's segregated residential neighborhoods have both positively and negatively determined the life chances and outcomes of their inhabitants. Correspondingly, its schools have weathered the shifts of populations of racial and ethnic groups, both within and beyond the city's borders.

Chicago continues to be a "city of neighborhoods," but its schools are no longer neighborhood institutions. Schools need not be microcosms. Instead of mirroring a city's spatial concentration of poverty and inequality, schools can upend those conditions by providing a space where racial, ethnic, and class diversity is achieved. However, schools can also exacerbate existing stratifications by further cloistering the young people who attend their neighborhood school in segregated residential environs. This is why the large-scale transformations of Chicago's housing and educational stocks have made adolescents' adaptations to contemporary social realities even more intriguing to researchers hoping to understand their perceptions and experiences. Students now must incorporate new knowledge about neighborhoods and schools, as well as navigate new social and symbolic boundaries that may include shifting interracial residential boundaries or even intraracial gang boundaries.

It is imperative that students understand these social and symbolic boundaries if they are to achieve safe passage within and across neighborhood- and school-based borders. For them, the lines of demarcation are stark. When public policies—like school desegregation decrees and public housing demolition and relocation programs—do not recognize the social realities of the intended beneficiaries, these policies may make residents' lives more challenging and present them with greater dangers. The following chapter explores in greater depth how Chicago public high school students experience these institutionalized spaces.

CHAPTER 3

Of the Meaning of Progress

My log schoolhouse was gone. In its place stood Progress; and Progress, I understand, is necessarily ugly.

—W.E.B. Du Bois, *The Souls of Black Folk* (1903)

I heard a White man's yes is a Black maybe.

—Common, "U, Black Maybe" (2007)

In May 2010, I spent a few days simply observing the morning entrance routines at several Chicago-area public high schools. One Monday I was outside Tilden Career Community Academy at the northwest intersection of West Forty-Seventh Place and South Union Avenue, where I had a clear view of the north entrance. I saw the Tilden students, mostly Black and Hispanic, walking south on the east side of South Union Avenue into the school. They were dressed in either white or deep blue polo shirts; some walked solo, while others chatted with friends in clusters of three or four. On the west side of South Union Avenue, I saw White and Hispanic parents walking their grammar school–age children in the opposite direction, probably toward Graham Elementary School, located three blocks north of Tilden on the same street. Graham serves mainly White, Hispanic, and African American children from Chicago's Canaryville and Fuller Park neighborhoods. In 1999 Graham was approximately 55 percent White, but by 2010 it was predominantly minority, with a 38 percent White student body.

What I witnessed that morning were two different flows toward furthering education. Most of the kids heading to Graham were clasping the hand of a female parent or guardian and wearing maroon-colored school uniform shirts. They seemed quite subdued, in contrast to the animated conversations I overheard coming from the teenagers heading in the other direction toward Tilden. In this moment, the sidewalks of South Union Avenue served as a racialized, age-based divider. All was calm, but there was still a police presence observing, and perhaps even maintaining, these borders. Instead of a civilian crossing guard, there was a uniformed police officer with his squad car parked nearby directing traffic in the middle of West Forty-Seventh Street and motioning for students to cross or halt. This official police action was reminiscent of the earlier era when community members asked for more police to quell racial unrest inside and outside the walls of Tilden.[1] I saw that police were still serving as the mediators protecting the neighborhoods' residents from their fears of racial conflict, or perhaps even just rambunctious teenagers, but these officers might also have been providing a sense of security to those same students, predominantly Black and Hispanic, who were attending high school in an area known for its hostility toward racial outsiders.

Given their varied neighborhoods, racial composition, and residency patterns, the four schools discussed here—Lincoln Park High, Payton Prep, Tilden Career Academy, and Harper High—present different experiences of racial structure and culture to their students. Because race and place intersect at school, young people's physical mobility affects their understandings and expectations for their social mobility. This dawning recognition of different kinds of discrimination, with its accompanying sense of how they rank on the hierarchy of social and structural advantage, is a crucial component of their adolescent rite of passage. Let me reintroduce you to Michelle, Alex, Max, and Michael, featured in chapter 2, as well as some of their peers, to take a closer look at how their movements from home to school and back again shape their attitudes about race, opportunity, and justice.

Mixing and Matching

Michelle has a pretty good chance of getting into a well-respected college. She attends Lincoln Park, a top-tier school in Illinois that is consistently named one of the top 100 schools in the nation by *Newsweek* magazine. Michelle is Filipino American, but at Lincoln Park she is not part of the majority. Lincoln Park has no majority: in 2005, when I conducted the initial interviews, African Americans were the largest group of students at Lincoln Park, comprising 35 percent of the population, with Whites the second-most-populous group at around 30 percent. Hispanic students were underrepresented at Lincoln Park (20 percent) in contrast to their overall numbers in the local school district (around one-third of the population). Conversely, Asian and Asian American students were overrepresented at 15 percent, more than triple their proportion of students in Chicago public schools at that time (around 4 percent).

I was curious to hear how Lincoln Park's students see, or perhaps did not see, race operating in their school. Knowing that the lunchroom is a classic space for observing the social topography of any school environment, especially when racial diversity is up for discussion, I ask Gabrielle, a White ninth-grade student at Lincoln Park, whether she sees any racial divisions in her school lunchroom.[2] She describes the chaotic scene in one of the lunchrooms in the freshman building:

GABRIELLE: Yeah. It's like, somehow they've managed to form cliques according to their race, so there's, like, the Asian kids, the Hispanic kids. The Asian kids are always speaking their own little language, and so are the Hispanic kids, they're all speaking Spanish to each other. There's some, I think they're Russian, so there's a few people who *only* speak in Russian and they *only* talk to each other. And if anyone tries to break their little circle, it's like chaos.

AUTHOR: And African American students?

GABRIELLE: African Americans, of course, there's those groups, but African Americans blend in a little bit more. It's mostly African American at this school, I think. They're the majority.

AUTHOR: If someone was to say, "Lincoln Park High is so integrated and so diverse . . ."

GABRIELLE: It's diverse, but definitely not integrated. (*laughs*)

AUTHOR: Do you think it should be?

GABRIELLE: Yeah. I lived in a suburb for most of my life, and it was, like, all White people. There'd be, like, four or five Black people in my graduating eighth-grade class. And it was just ridiculous. I hated it because there was nobody out there to talk to who was not like you. It really bothered me that it wasn't diverse at all. So, I came here and I was very happy, but it's not nearly as . . . I mean . . . you'll always catch different races talking to each other. It's not like everyone . . . I don't know, I can't really put it into words. There're definitely cliques.

AUTHOR: So you can see people interacting, but you can also see cliques?

GABRIELLE: Right.

Gabrielle's comment that Lincoln Park is "diverse, but definitely not integrated," is a succinct and accurate description of the school in light of the overall racial composition of Chicago Public Schools. Statisticians, policymakers, and others who are preoccupied with the representation of different racial and ethnic groups within and across schools might miss the larger importance of Gabrielle's observation. Although members of different racial and ethnic groups walk down the same hallways and sit beside each other in class, they do not necessarily relate to or interact with each other. Instead, they stick to their own.[3]

This paradox of increasing racial diversity but diminished social integration also comes up in comments from Louie, a biracial (White and Black) ninth-grader.[4]

> LOUIE: Yeah, I see kids here that only hang out with Black kids, and when they see some White kids they make fun of them and things. I've seen White kids do that to Black kids and Black kids get mad, and they both end up fighting big fights. . . . It's really stupid, 'cuz they should all know that you can't change who you are.
>
> AUTHOR: What about the Hispanic and Asian students? There seem to be sizable amounts of each group here?
>
> LOUIE: The Asians? I've seen the Asians group with everybody. And then the Hispanics, you can't really tell if they're mixed or not, so nobody really cares. They just hide in with anybody.

Louie seems to be suggesting that school replicates the sorting that occurs in residential domains, as covered in chapter 2. The difference, however, is that school presents a reason for these groups to come together physically even if they are not socially integrated. The race- and color-based sorting that takes place in schools allows us to see the strictures of racial identification made manifest in social situations (who hangs out with whom), but it also allows for an analysis of transgressions across these same boundaries. The lines themselves can be quite blurred: as Louie says, Hispanics can "hide in with anybody" because of their varying skin tones and racial ambiguity (at least to outsiders), and his remarks also point to the permeability of boundaries for Asian students.[5]

In response to the same question of whether he sees divisions among groups at his school, Joaquin, a Filipino American student, answers affirmatively:

> JOAQUIN: There's definitely some clear divisions between the groups.
>
> AUTHOR: What about students who live in the neighborhood of the school and those who don't? Can you tell?
>
> JOAQUIN: You can tell, 'cuz Lincoln Park High is a neighborhood school for the Cabrini-Green projects . . . and you have lots of the population of the school coming from higher-class Lincoln Park homes, so you have a clash there. And it also brings out the diversity of the school.
>
> AUTHOR: So when you say "a clash," is it antagonistic or just different?
>
> JOAQUIN: No, it's just when I say "clash" you can see it. When you look out at the crowd after school, you can sit there and you can see the groups moving as, like, two different species of people almost.

Joaquin's phrase "two different species of people" may seem overstated, but his point comes across clearly. Observing school dismissals on several days, I cannot help but see the distinct clusters of students. Some groups congregate, typically in large numbers, at the bus stop outside the school, waiting to head west on Armitage Avenue to the Brown Line "El," which will then disperse this disparate bunch across the city. Others walk to North Halsted Street to catch a southbound bus, typically heading toward the (now-demolished) Cabrini-Green housing projects. And still others, nearly all White and mostly alone or in groups of two or three, walk to their homes on surrounding streets.

Those who are able to walk to and from home benefit from great privilege, even if they are uncomfortable claiming it. By the most recent estimates, just over half of the student body at Lincoln Park High School qualifies for free or reduced-price lunch.[6] By contrast, the Lincoln Park neighborhood itself has a median household income that is double the $41,000 income cap to qualify for free or reduced-price lunch.[7] In 2007 *Forbes* named the residential block directly across from Lincoln Park's entrance at North Orchard Street and West Armitage Avenue one of the "most expensive blocks in the U.S."[8]

Although Andre, an African American sophomore, lives in the Lincoln Park neighborhood with his mother (who "does something with lawyers and real estate") and his three siblings, he disputes any claim to being rich. Andre says, "You're not rich, you just live there." Gabrielle, who also lives in the neighborhood, says that she has never heard anyone bragging about how much money they have. She explains, "There's a lot of people who are like, 'You're so lucky, you can walk to school. I have to take the train. It's awful.' But then they just kind of blow you off because they think you're rich, and I'm not." She then laughs. The fact that she lives in the neighborhood actually makes Gabrielle feel that she fits in *less* at school since so many people take the train.

> If you live in a bad neighborhood, you're respected more, which I don't understand. People say, "I live in this awful neighborhood. I can't walk outside." Or they say, "I live on the South Side, an hour away." And everyone responds like, "Wow! You must be a great person." Who cares? It's like your bus pass is a badge of honor.

Clearly, the sense of belonging to the school and the sense of belonging to the neighborhood of Lincoln Park differ vastly by race, gender, and appearance.

Other students find great relief in Lincoln Park's residential diversity. Boomer transferred to Lincoln Park in tenth grade from a large, all-Black vocational school on the South Side. He complains that his previous school lacked diversity. Even though all of the students were members of the same racial group, his schoolmates "picked on him" every day, he says, once they found out that he lived on the West Side of Chicago. Boomer explains how his neighborhood affiliation was disclosed:

> BOOMER: One of my nephew's friends came to my house and was like, "You live on the West Side." And I'm like, well yeah. And he was like, "Well, we ain't cool with that." I just didn't pay it no mind. So the next week I got to school, and everybody was like, "You the one from the West Side." And I was think-ing, *There are other people here from the West Side, so why would you pick on me?* But, you know, I guess they thought I was scary [scared] and that I wouldn't fight. I got into it almost every day. And then they found out I wasn't in a gang . . . so, like, they really tried to get an advantage over me. But I wouldn't let them do it. I just told my mama that I didn't feel comfortable being there any-more, so they transferred me here.

Asked about the differences he sees between Lincoln Park and the vocational school from which he had transferred, Boomer has a one-word answer: "Ev-erything." Then he adds:

> Lincoln Park High is a very diverse school. We have all ethnic backgrounds here. At [the other school], it was nothing but Black people. I didn't even see White teachers, and that's just being honest. If they were there, I never seen 'em. But here [at Lincoln Park] I have every race here, every ethnic background here, different sexual preferences here. You have everything here. My mom felt as though it would be a good experience for me to see the diversity in schools and stuff like that. So this is why she really wanted me here.

Boomer's experience is unique in that he was *passing* in his former neighborhood-based school, but he was not transgressing boundaries of race in the conventional sense of the phenomenon. Instead, Boomer was passing by crossing boundaries of place as a resident of the West Side. For Boomer, Lincoln Park High is a welcome contrast—a portal through which he can see many different facets of diversity: race, ethnicity, neighborhood, class, and sexuality.

Joaquin, too, is passing. Although he identifies as Filipino, others always perceive him, he says, as White Hispanic. Despite his comment that the stu-dents at Lincoln Park segregate into "different species of people," he believes that the student body is accepting: there would be a place for him at Lincoln Park whatever his racial self-identification and external racial ascription.

> Normally this school wouldn't be as diverse without the IB [International Bac-calaureate] program. Like, I'm Filipino American, my girlfriend is Jewish Rus-sian, a friend of mine, he's Indian. It expands. It's very diverse. [Before Lincoln

Park,] I went to a Catholic school that was predominantly Caucasian and Hispanic, and since I went to a Catholic school, I didn't think about it too much. But I [now] realize how isolated it was at Catholic school. And coming here, and [seeing] how diverse it is, it's really cool. I didn't realize I was isolated until I came here, because it was so diverse. We didn't have any other Asians at the Catholic school. We didn't have any Blacks, you know, no Jews or anything.

Joaquin's comments highlight how an individual's context can dramatically shape his or her perceptions and experiences. He had no idea how racially homogeneous his world was until he started attending Lincoln Park High. The diversity at Lincoln Park has been eye-opening for him.

At Payton Prep, students encounter a student body that is similarly diverse, but similarly divided. The diversity was one of the things that appealed to Alex, a freshman who identifies as African American. Like Michelle at Lincoln Park, Alex has a cousin who also graduated from Payton. He and his parents checked out the school, and he was especially interested in attending once they figured out that he could get the same education at Payton that he was receiving at his current school—a prestigious and expensive private school on the South Side.

Asked what he likes most about Payton, Alex says, "I like the diversity, I guess. I like how there are students from every single race, and then every single different interest. I like the building. The area's decent. I mean, it's not the best and it's not the worst. So that's good too. I like the facilities, of course. I guess that's pretty much it." With regard to race, Payton is a grand contrast to Alex's grammar school, which he describes as "predominantly Caucasian and, like, a few Asians." Alex says that going to that school taught him how to hang out with all different races. He now is very open about his diverse group of friends: "I can go and, like, talk to White people, Asian people, Mexican people. . . . I just talk to whoever I share the same interests with."

In an echo of Joaquin's comment that there is a "clash" between parts of the student body at Lincoln Park, Alex says much the same about the physical location of Payton. In describing the neighborhood, Alex says that there is "sort of a weird contrast with Cabrini-Green, and then on the other side, you have downtown, Water Tower [a mall], and all those big restaurants." Census tract–level data corroborate Alex's characterization of Payton as straddling two worlds with regard to income. Census tract 8383, just south of the aptly named Division Street, which includes the school, has a median household income of approximately $35,000. North of Division Street, census tract 803 has a median household income of just over $89,000.

Payton is the most diverse school in my sample, so the topic of racial composition is particularly salient. Each of the eight students I interview at that school repeat, in one way or another, Alex's succinct analysis: "Even though it's diverse, it's divided." Students "mix in with everybody," but their closest friends are usually members of their own racial group. Consider, for instance, Amber, an African American ninth-grader from the West Side, who says that she does not feel "uneasy" at Payton, since there is an "even number" of all races there, but that her friendship circle comprises primarily African Americans. Amber also mentions that she would "really feel uneasy at Northside College Prep," another selective high school in Chicago, "because it's probably, like, two Black people there."

Amber's figures are not entirely accurate, though the perception of racial evenness at Payton and the lack thereof at Northside is valid in itself. Payton is 40 percent White in a district that is approximately 8 percent White; African Americans are the next largest group at the school, at 28 percent. Although there are considerably more than two Black students at Northside College Prep—in 2005, 71 students out of its 990-member student body (7.2 percent) were African American, and in 2010 Blacks were 5 percent of the Northside student body—Amber is correct in surmising that Black students are greatly underrepresented at Northside in a school district that is majority-Black.

John, a White ninth-grader at Payton, almost whispers to me, "There are a lot of cliques, and to be honest, they're almost completely race-based. It's bad, but it's sort of inevitable, I think. People feel comfortable with people in their own race." Deciding which clique to join can be quite a challenge for students who identify as multiracial (Brianna) or for students who identify as Hispanic because they speak the language and identify with the culture (Vanessa, Freddy, and Carmen). Carmen dislikes having to explain her Hispanic ethnicity to her classmates at Payton; she resents being seen as the authority, simply because of her accent, on the various Hispanic-themed celebrations in the city, and she does not appreciate other students finding it so hard to understand the type of music she enjoys. She explains why being Hispanic at another high school would be easier:

> That's why I also like Von Steuben High, because they're pretty much like a quarter of each, so then you get to kinda pick who you want to hang out with. 'Cuz you have a lot of Hispanics and the Hispanics know what you're talking about. And then the Black people that hang out with the Hispanic people know what you're talking about too. And then, so you kinda assimilate.

Carmen uses the word "assimilate" in an unconventional manner. "Assimilation," in her usage, is not a matter of having your particular culture erased (if you are not White), but instead, being able to not have your culture define you as a person. She also does a much better job than Amber of guessing the racial composition of Von Steuben High School, which she toured during the high school selection season: It is 30 percent White, 29 percent Black, 22 percent Hispanic, and 18 percent Asian, which is about as racially balanced as a school can be in a district that has fewer White and Asian students than these numbers would suggest.

The other two schools in this study, both on the South Side, are more segregated. Max, a ninth-grader who identifies as Mexican, makes it clear that he did not *choose* to come to Tilden for high school. He tells me that he was accepted into two other schools, but did not return any of the paperwork to lock in one of those choices; therefore, he was "sent over" to Tilden. Max's grammar school was over 90 percent Hispanic (primarily Mexican); going to Tilden was a huge change for him. The racial composition of Tilden in 2005, when I conducted my first interviews, was fewer than 2 percent Asian and Native American, 5 percent White, 32 percent Hispanic, and 60 percent African American. Max adapted to Tilden's diverse population by honing his skills as a "cultural straddler"—that is, making friends across and within racial *and* gang lines at the school.[9]

Unlike Max, his schoolmate, Shay, an African American tenth-grader, chose to go to Tilden instead of her neighborhood school. She travels to Tilden from her housing project just over three miles northeast of the school. Shay explains that "the people that go to my neighborhood school like picking fights, and I wanted to explore more by meeting new people instead of being around all the people who act bad. Even though I know every place is bad."

Shay's estimation that *all* places are bad reflects a particular brand of cynicism that was rather common among students in my two South Side schools. She goes on to provide details about the bad behavior she witnesses at Tilden. There is the general expectation, according to Shay, that the boys at Tilden will "act bad because they're in a different neighborhood, a much different neighborhood." She likes the neighborhood, however, since "it's quiet most of the time. But they got Kings and Latins [Latino gangs] around here." Shay corroborates Max's descriptions of the clashes between the Hispanic gang members and the Black gang members:

SHAY: Everybody talks to everybody. Latinos talk to Blacks 'cuz we got some Latinos in the Black gang! They talk to each other. They interact with each other. But you know, when it's really time to fight, they'll probably, you know, flip sides or something, just 'cuz of they skin color.

AUTHOR: Do you think your school is pretty diverse racially?

SHAY: What you mean by "diverse"?

AUTHOR: Like a lot of different races.

SHAY: Uh huh [yes], 'cuz we got Chinese, Puerto Rican, Mexican, Latino, Black, Hispanic. I like it. Because one of my friends is Mexican, and he learn a lot from us and we learn a lot from him. He teaches us stuff, we teach him stuff. So, basically we been friends for so long, we know about each other past. Well, you know, we don't dwell on our past; we look at the future and try to help each other go towards a good future and whatnot.

As Shay reveals, the climate at Tilden is not always peaceful, but the divisions between students are not invariably drawn by race. Gang affiliation, neighborhood, and even language can play a role. For instance, two students describe disagreements that escalated into fights because one group thought another group was "cussing them out" when they spoke in their native languages. (Chinese and Spanish were the examples given.)

Although the cross-racial affiliations may be tenuous, other students at Tilden describe positive interactions with students from different racial backgrounds and different neighborhoods. Jackson—a sophomore at Tilden who lives in a majority-Black neighborhood minutes away from the University of Chicago but a world away in reality—says that he "wants to see different color people and what they like to do, how they have fun." Simply stated, he just gets "tired of being with the same people."

That thought is a point of both disagreement and agreement with students a few miles south at Harper High School. Michael, a sophomore at Harper, says that his adjustment to high school was quite easy. Harper is "basically the same": since his grammar school serves as a feeder institution for Harper, Michael made the transition from eighth to ninth grade with the same people. Despite the easy transition, Michael had fervently hoped to go to a different school because he did not think Harper was "gonna be challenging enough."[10] After his first year, Michael was invited to join the Construction Technology Academy within Harper, because he reportedly was "too smart for the regular classes," and that has made him happier to be at Harper, since this is a more challenging track.

In contrast to Shay and Max, who crave a broader student body at Tilden, Michael says that he would not choose to attend a school with more Whites or Hispanics. This feeling carries over into his preference for his neighborhood's racial composition. Michael states that he does not go outside often, so "it don't really matter what neighborhood I'm gonna be in, as long as I'm safe. I like my neighborhood just fine because it's quiet. It ain't been no shooting or nothing over there."

His schoolmate Rina also considers her safety when I ask whether she would go to a different school if given the opportunity. She wants to be a lawyer and would transfer in a heartbeat to a school with a program to prepare her for that career. But Rina does not want to travel to another school because she would not feel safe. She explains:

Harper is right around my house, and I don't have a problem because I know people here. Most of my friends I grew up with are here, and I don't want to start over at another school, even though it would be fun. I wanna get to know other people. I like to make friends. It don't matter what race you are. And I'm not really hard to get along with, because I love to talk.

Rina's statement may give pause to readers who care about children's aspirations and know something about what helps them achieve their dreams. Rina, a petite tenth-grader with an open personality and an easy smile, sees herself as trapped in both a school that is not that great and a neighborhood that is limiting because she is too afraid to cross borders. She does not want to push at the geographical boundaries of exclusion by leaving Harper, even if crossing those boundaries would take her out of a low-resource school and a disadvantaged neighborhood and enable her to see and experience different things. Rina and some of her peers have a palpable fear of the unknown that has a simultaneously protective and detrimental effect.

Rina is quite clear, however, about the consequences of staying at Harper. She believes that there is "nothing but problems" in an all-Black school, with "people going against each other for no reason." Rina especially dislikes the gangs. Her schoolmate Chris shares her concerns. He complains about the fights that occur "mostly every day" at Harper. He says that friends would describe him as "kinda smart, and one who don't get down with all that bad stuff like smoking and drinking or talking back to grownups," even though he hangs out with "some bad and some good" kids. Chris estimates that most people at the school are in a gang, and he worries that if someone who is in a gang tries to fight him, he'll "get jumped on by that person and all his boys."

Chris especially worries that when he gets off the bus in the mornings at Sixty-Ninth and Wood something will happen to him during his four-block walk to school; he worries even more about the walk back to the bus after school, since "that's when all the drama starts!" Instead of the two or three police cars he sees outside after school, he would prefer to see "ten to fifteen cars" surrounding the perimeter of the school. Chris's descriptions of his experiences in his immediate neighborhood make it all too clear that he cannot stop worrying about his safety, even on his own block. He describes his neighborhood as clean, but says, "The people around there are just bad. Once you walk outside, you'll probably see a group of boys come up to you, and try to jump [fight] you or take something out of your pockets. It happens right on my block, but they don't live on the same block." He wants to move to what he believes would be a nicer environment, a place where "you don't hear a lot of gunshots, it don't be a lot of gangs, and people don't get jumped on and robbed." Chris would also rather go to a school "that got Black and White, or even Mexican, as long as it's not all-Black."

Of the nine students at Harper in the study, none are primarily concerned about race; safety and the presence of gangs loom larger. Race, however, is always present. Three students are vehemently opposed to going to a school that is more diverse, one simply does not want to leave Harper and accepts that it is all-Black, two are neutral on the question of racial integration, and three want to go to school with other ethnic groups. The responses of Keisha and TB particularly surprise me. Keisha justifies her strong anti-integration position by telling me about an experience she had in second grade while attending a racially mixed grammar school.

KEISHA: A little White girl snatched the rope and made me get smacked in the face. I pulled the rope back and I smacked her with it. So she went into the office, and the security guards came out there and told me I was finna [about to] be expelled. By me being little, I'm [confused,] saying, "Expelled?" I go in the office, and the next thing I know my mama walk in the door. She mad, cussing me all out. I'm tryna tell her, "Wait, Mama, that little girl she tried to take my rope and made me get whacked in my face, so I took the rope and whacked her back." So I didn't get a whipping, but I got hollered at, 'cuz my mama told me what I should've done. I should have went to tell an adult, but I took it in my own hands. I remember her name was LaShelley; she was around about seven or eight, just like me. She could've said, "Well, Keisha, can I play with y'all," or something like that, but she didn't say nothing.

AUTHOR: So even in high school, you don't think you'd be ready for more integration?

KEISHA: Naw.

AUTHOR: Would you want to go to an all-Black college?

KEISHA: See, Kennedy King College is all-Black anyway. (*laughs*)

AUTHOR: That's real interesting about how you say you can't go to school with White people. What about Hispanics?

KEISHA: That's about the same as Mexicans and Chinese and everybody else. I mean, I can get along . . . but I ain't finna be around 'em. . . . If I have to, I will. But until then, I won't.

I conducted my interview with Keisha at the beginning of April, only a few days after the date marking the anniversary of Dr. Martin Luther King's assassination. In the 1960s, Chicago's hostile racial climate was too much even for Dr. King. He came to the city in 1966 to spur the burgeoning grass-roots movement against de facto segregation in schooling, employment, and housing. During a march through an all-White neighborhood on the West Side in August of that year, bottles and bricks were thrown at Black participants, and Dr. King was "felled by a rock." The *Chicago Tribune* reported that King stated afterward, "I have seen many demonstrations in the south but I have never seen anything so hostile and so hateful as I've seen here today."[11]

Perhaps Keisha's encounter with LaShelley was a different version of racial turmoil in the post–civil rights era. In our interview, I also surmise that the resultant threat of expulsion is still strongly influencing her take on mingling with other races. I therefore ask her point-blank: "What do you think Dr. Martin Luther King would say about you not wanting to go to school with other races?" She laughs, then gets a bit more reflective: "I don't know. . . . He'd be upset, but in a way, he might be understanding. 'Cuz that's what happened to him; they was with the White and we see how they was treating the Black people. I don't think he'd have that much to say about it."

Keisha's anti-integration stance may just be a defense mechanism, one that plays out in a racialized way. Asked to describe herself, she says that she is a hard worker and on the honor roll, but that she is not a sociable person. As she explains, "I don't talk to any and everybody. The people I know is the people I socialize with." The very limited spatial area that Keisha roams determines her social circle, and she is quite unlikely to encounter many Whites outside of teachers at school or police on the street.

Keisha lives slightly less than two miles from Harper. She tells me that her after-school routine is to go home, fix herself something to eat, and then lie down to rest. "Basically, that's it. There's nothing outside for me." This is Keisha's world. If she ventures outside, it is to go see her boyfriend who lives only a few minutes away in the same neighborhood, "chill over there with him, and then come back in." Her goal is to get a nursing degree from Kennedy King Community College (which, as she points out, is majority-Black and less than two miles east of her home and high school) and start a family. Keisha's "guy" of four years has told her that it would not be right for her to go out of town for school if they want to start a family, so she intends to stay in the area.

My conversation with Keisha is by turns intriguing and frustrating. When talking about anyone except African Americans, much of what comes out of her mouth seems blatantly racist and reveals her lack of knowledge about other groups. But even if I find it remarkable that a single incident from second grade could color Keisha's inclination to be around others who do not share her racial-ethnic identity, I am also reminded of how normal this feeling can be. Keisha is truly more comfortable being around "her own kind," in a different way than her schoolmate Rina, who fears the unknown for reasons of safety but is otherwise open to crossing boundaries of race and place. To be fair, I must add that later in our conversation Keisha is quite insistent that she draws boundaries around herself to keep almost *everyone* out, no matter their race, because she is a self-proclaimed "antisocial person." Keisha's de facto segregated life on the South Side of Chicago is unlikely to change, and the same is likely to be true for her perception of other racial and ethnic groups.

What emerges from my detailed interviews in all four schools is the central role of race and place in shaping the students' worldviews. While some of them find their homogeneous world claustrophobic, others find it comforting. But whether or not these students realize it, the breadth or narrowness of their frame of reference will have profound consequences for both their experiences and their interpretations of those experiences.

Place and the Perception of Injustice

In parsing the physical worlds in which these students live, and the boundaries they must cross, we gain great—and sometimes depressing—insight into the lived reality of the next generation of America. A long-standing and far-reaching "racial-spatial divide," as termed by Peterson and Krivo, anchors their divergent social worlds, especially in the realm of education.[12] Even those students who attend relatively integrated schools return home to neighborhoods profoundly separated by race. Together, these two spaces—school and home—play enormous roles in developing adolescents' sense of self, and both of these institutions are deeply rooted in place. Their *perceptions* of the world are indelibly shaped by their *place* in that world.

It is clear, both from Chicago's school desegregation travails and the many thoughts expressed by the teenagers quoted in these pages, that the racial composition of a school is of vital importance to the resources teenagers can access, their future opportunities, and their perceptions of inequality.[13] But what, then, is the best racial balance in schools for our children to provide both access to resources and exposure to diverse arrays of people and perspectives? In a city as segregated as Chicago, attending a school with a sizable population of White youth might arguably lend youth of color one of their only opportunities to compare their personal experiences with those of their White peers. Unfortunately, instead of providing opportunities, spending time with people of different races more often seems to leave youth of color perceiving themselves as "deprived" or "subordinated" relative to White youth. Youth of color attending segregated schools experience structural discrimination on a daily basis, but they lack the opportunity to make between-race comparisons on a daily basis. Students who cross boundaries, in other words, are more likely to *see* discrimination than those who do not make these journeys.

Differential awareness of discrimination and injustice has been documented in African American men. In a study of young men (ages eighteen to twenty-four) on the Near West Side of Chicago, for example, the sociologist Alford Young Jr. found that his subjects' levels of social isolation framed their understandings of mobility processes. When questioning men he categorized as "extremely isolated" (because their social world was limited to Chicago's Near West Side), Young noted a remarkable pattern of silence concerning their particular life outcomes in comparison to others.[14] In his words, "These men, who had virtually no sustained social exposure outside of their community, were unable to register a strong sense of how race or other factors operate as social [stratification] forces."[15] At the other end of the continuum were the men who were "provisionally connected." Their "increased exposure to social conflict," primarily as mediated through their encounters with authority figures, left them with a "more conflict-based view of social stratification in American society." Whereas the extremely isolated men attributed social stratification to individual failings, the provisionally connected men perceived race and class to be key contributors to social inequality.[16] A third category of "marginally connected" men fell in between the other two categories, both in terms of their social isolation and their perceptions of social and economic inequality. The students I met a decade later, also in Chicago, displayed similar patterns.

Each of the four schools provides different levels of social and racial isolation and therefore different levels of awareness of discrimination and social injustice for its students. Racial-ethnic identity is still the main driver of an individual's perceptions of social injustice, but place can amplify or mute its effect. Figure 3.1 illustrates my assessment of each school's placement in a matrix of social and racial isolation and the provision of resources and opportunities. Harper High, positioned high in racial homogeneity and low in resources and opportunities, is an exemplar of a stagnant racial order reminiscent of years past, since all of its students are African Americans from mostly low-income backgrounds. The students who attend Harper reside in the school's racially and economically homogeneous neighborhood of West Englewood. The racial-spatial divide serves as a mechanism that further concentrates and exacerbates the limiting effects of both residing and learning in the same low-resource area.

Next in terms of resources and racial-ethnic homogeneity is Tilden Career Community Academy. Tilden caters to a racially diverse group of students, though they are predominantly Hispanic and African American and the racial-ethnic and language divisions are glaring. Students' perceptions of social injustice and their awareness of their placement on the racial-spatial divide often hinge on whether or not they are attending Tilden by choice. The African American students in the study chose Tilden because they saw better opportunities at the school than at their neighborhood schools. Many of the Hispanic students I interviewed, in contrast, arrived at Tilden because it was their neighborhood's default choice. Tilden's placement on the racial-spatial divide by race-ethnicity and place makes it a step up for the African American students but only the default—or perhaps even a step down—for its White, Hispanic, and Asian American students.[17]

Figure 3.1   Racial and Social Isolation and Resources and Opportunity at the Four Chicago High Schools

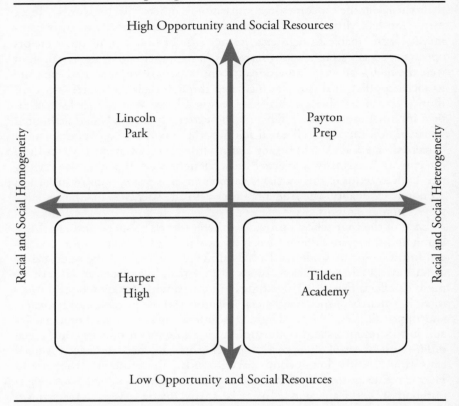

High Opportunity and Social Resources

Lincoln Park

Payton Prep

Racial and Social Homogeneity

Racial and Social Heterogeneity

Harper High

Tilden Academy

Low Opportunity and Social Resources

Source: Author's assessment of each school's placement on the matrix of isolation and resources and opportunity.

In a place on the matrix that denotes greater racial diversity and high levels of resources and opportunities is Lincoln Park High School. Because of its racial composition (which includes 30 percent White), Lincoln Park is officially classified by Chicago Public Schools as a "mixed" school. This school's position on the racial-spatial divide illustrates the great opportunities and extensive resources available at Lincoln Park, with its rigorous, highly ranked curriculum and its location in one of Chicago's toniest neighborhoods. However, some of the students attending Lincoln Park must navigate formidable boundaries. Race and place serve to split the school's students, with many of the low-income enrollees coming from less-advantaged neighborhoods such as (the former) Cabrini-Green housing projects and the Austin neighborhood on Chicago's West Side.

Another important mechanism shaping the social divisions at Lincoln Park is the school's highly tracked curriculum. Lincoln Park has a curriculum stratified by rigor: the International Baccalaureate program, Advanced Placement courses, double honors courses, regular honors courses, regular courses, and so on. Each pole of the curriculum continuum shows greater homogeneity, with Whites and students of Asian descent on the higher end and Hispanics and African Americans at the opposite pole.[18] Lincoln Park students, particularly the students of color I interviewed, have a clear sense of their relative placement on the racial-spatial divide by virtue of their attendance in a high-ranking school, but they are also aware of the great stratification beyond their own experience that affects their racial counterparts at the school.

Finally, the wealth of resources at Payton Prep, the most racially diverse school, earns it a place at the far end of the spectrum of racial diversity and resources and opportunities. Because of Payton's selective enrollment status, entry to its hallowed ranks is available only to students who pass its admissions test. The school website emphasizes that "diverse students from across the city of Chicago" are attracted to Payton "for its diverse staff and student populations," which inverts the traditional social order of the city's racial-spatial divide.[19] But schools like Payton also reinforce race and class stratification by further advantaging the students who already have access to great resources and opportunities. For students of color, Payton, like other similar schools, presents both opportunity and an exposure to inequality, in that it provides them with an expanded frame by which they can assess and confirm advantage and disadvantage, discrimination and favoritism—whether it happens personally or vicariously.

This alignment of each school by racial and social isolation and by resources and opportunities explains why schools are so important—even more important than neighborhoods—in shaping students' perceptions of injustice. Students cross boundaries on a daily basis (or choose not to) because of the opportunities that schools offer (or do not offer). Moreover, the admissions policies and default geographic boundaries of schools can either subvert or reinforce the reigning racial-spatial order. Policy, procedure, and, when possible, students' and parents' preferences determine how these forces combine to influence young people's perceptions and outcomes.

One of the more compelling students in my study is TB, an African American ninth-grader from Harper High on the South Side of Chicago. He, like Keisha, is satisfied with his way of life. Asked whether he would move to a different neighborhood if he had the choice, he responds: "I'll probably stay in the neighborhood where I am." He finds it just as unlikely that he would choose to go to a different school, because his friends are at Harper and he "prefers to stay around my own kind." In response to the survey questions that deal with social injustice, he disagrees with statements suggesting that members of his race face racial discrimination in hiring and residential choice.

In short, he sees the playing field as level. TB explains, "You can find a nice house where you want to live, and most African Americans are successful in what they do." TB attends a racially segregated school virtually devoid of resources. He lives just north of Harper in Englewood—a neighborhood that is as poor and racially segregated as his school. Although he tells me that he sees "lawyers, assistants, and accountants" doing well in his neighborhood, empirical data from his neighborhood belie his perception: according to census estimates, only 53 percent of the population age sixteen and older are in the labor force, and only 35 percent of those individuals are actually employed, predominantly in sales and service occupations.[20] Even so, TB is confident in his vision of the world.

TB and his neighbors live in an "extremely isolated" environment, as Young would characterize it. He is at an extensive disadvantage just by virtue of where he lives, one of the dilemmas of place that has been documented in several important sociological works.[21] Individuals in segregated communities are sequestered from job opportunities and housing choices, to name just two of life's necessities. But alongside this grave disadvantage, youth like TB are also sequestered from continuous, unequivocal evidence that they are likely to receive inferior treatment simply because of their race. In other words, because TB lives in a world of so little diversity, it may be easy for him to think that most Black people are doing well; he does not see enough concrete evidence of Black mobility to realize how immobile his world really is. And though some may find this distressing, I would argue that there is a protective element to this lack of confirmed disadvantage. In the same way that "ignorance can be bliss," less knowledge about structural inequality may be more enabling than paralyzing in the quest for social and economic mobility.

Consider, in contrast, the "privilege and peril" that Black middle-class Chicagoans encounter on a daily basis. As the sociologist Mary Pattillo and others have documented, members of the Black middle class are able to gain education and skills, but they still usually operate in the same social circles and spaces as their less-advantaged racial counterparts. The families she studied—and the children in particular—have to reconcile their race and class positions with their social and physical geographies.[22] Nor is this phenomenon limited to those who have actually attained middle-class status: it is especially true for young people who attend more integrated, better-resourced schools but whose family incomes and social status would not be classified as middle-class.[23] For these young people, attending better schools may put them on a more upwardly mobile life trajectory compared with their peers left behind in racially segregated, disadvantaged educational institutions, but there is still, to use Pattillo's term, "peril" along the way. Straddling the class fence actually increases adolescents' perceptions of injustice and their sense of relative deprivation.[24]

Consider the following account from Alex, the African American ninth-grader at Payton Prep. His response exemplifies the dubious distinction of being exposed to multiple worlds. Alex is privileged because he is at a good school where he has a diverse set of friends, but he is also disadvantaged because he not only encounters differential treatment in public spaces but can actually confirm it. When our interview turns to the topic of discrimination, Alex reveals a wide variety of thoughts on how discrimination operates in various facets of life. In discussing teacher interactions, he strongly disagrees with the survey statement: "Discrimination makes it harder for people from my racial group to get good grades in school." Alex elaborates: "Well, I can't really speak for every school, but for this school, it's all pretty much strictly by the book. And like, when it comes to, like, borderline grades, the teacher pretty much gives you a grade on how much effort you put into it. 'Cuz for the most part, I don't know any teachers who are really racist in any way at this school."

Alex also has strong impressions about criminal injustice, especially as it concerns police unfairly stopping members of his race. He has never been personally stopped by the police, but reports, "It's happened to my dad several times while I was with him, especially in, like, certain suburbs." Again, place matters. When I ask Alex about whether racial discrimination is a problem for him or other African Americans, he states, "You just can't blame everything for being Black, but sometimes it is because you are Black." He is quite aware that race and racial discrimination are not the only reasons why people have differential opportunities and divergent outcomes. I therefore ask him: how does he know when racial discrimination is to blame? Alex responds by describing vicarious experiences of discrimination. He also gives the following personal account of discriminatory treatment in the Water Tower Place, a mall located in downtown's Magnificent Mile:

ALEX: When I went to the Water Tower this year, I was with my group of friends. I normally hang out with a diverse group. So I was with Black, White, Asian people, and a Mexican. And one of my friends, he went inside a store and he picked up something, [but] he didn't want it. He walked out. Big Black guy, really big, had a big shirt on. He walked out, and all of a sudden the lady, she like, stops him and she's like, "Oh, you [looking at Alex's Black friend] stole something." So then, like, the security guards at the Water Tower come, and then they pretty much kick all of us out, like, all the Black people out.

AUTHOR: So not your whole group?

ALEX: No, not the whole group. They actually said, "You, you, you, and you (*pointing to all of the Blacks in the group*), get out." 'Cuz I don't know, maybe they didn't know we were together, but I doubt it.

Although Alex lives in an all-Black South Side neighborhood, he has made friends with a racially diverse group of friends during his first year of high school. Although he tells me that he has heard about discrimination mainly from others' experiences, he also has personally encountered discrimination, as this account makes clear. Alex's peril comes from seeing discrimination operate directly in front of him instead of simply knowing that it exists.[25]

I am especially curious to hear from Alex how class intersected with race in the resolution of his experience at the mall. How did his friend react to the store clerk's accusation and the security officers' racism?

> AUTHOR: What did your friend say? The one who was specifically targeted?
>
> ALEX: He was quiet about it, and then he was, like, "Oh." At first he didn't know what was gonna happen, so he called, like, his mom and then he called his mom's lawyer. I don't know . . . he called, like, a lot of people.
>
> AUTHOR: Does he go to Payton Prep too?
>
> ALEX: Yeah, he's a freshman.
>
> AUTHOR: So he was able to call people and let them know what happened?
>
> ALEX: Yeah, he had a cell phone. I don't carry a cell phone, but he had one.
>
> AUTHOR: And what about your friends of other races who were there? How did they process that experience?
>
> ALEX: I don't know . . .
>
> AUTHOR: Did you ask them . . .?
>
> ALEX: I didn't really ask them about it.
>
> AUTHOR: Did they stay in the mall?
>
> ALEX: Yeah, they stayed, got something to eat, and then left later.

I was also interested in how the students who were not ejected read the episode, but Alex did not discuss it further with them at the time. He only knows that they used their own (racial) privilege to stay in the mall, have a meal, and then leave the premises on their own volition. Alex is only a ninth-grader, so this experience may be the first of many in which he is treated differently because of his racial identity—and in which he *recognizes* that differential treatment.

Conversely, there are others who become aware of differential resources and opportunity primarily in retrospect. Jackson, an ambitious sophomore at

Tilden when I first interviewed him in 2005, had become much more cynical and dismayed by the education he received in a Chicago public school by the time I reinterviewed him five years later. When he participated in a school exchange program his junior year, in which he visited a public school in Chicago's south suburbs for a day, Jackson had immediately noticed the differences in facilities, students' academic abilities, and their resources. His overall assessment is that Chicago's public education system "sucks."

> They was taught a lot different, they was even much smarter than us. Compared to the city of Chicago public school, they was actually on college level compared to where we stand. And I was kind of upset about that because our education system—it sucks. It really sucks. The teachers, like, some of the teachers are there to teach you, but they can only teach you so much. And you want to become much smarter, you know what I'm saying, and be successful in the world, but you can't. Because of the crappy textbooks that you get, there's not that many programs, and there's not that many job opportunities compared to what other youths can get. And I guess that's the reason why that some students are not successful. I mean, even when we did tests on math skills, English skills, and science skills . . . some of that stuff we didn't even know. I felt ashamed. I'm serious, like, how come we don't know some of this stuff? How come we not being taught some of this stuff? I think our education system need to improve. I'm not gonna lie. I felt ashamed. I felt like my school wasn't nothing compared to theirs 'cuz they was being taught better than we was.

For Jackson, as for so many others, school has been the primary reason to cross the physical and social boundaries that have so vastly influenced his perceptions, attitudes, and experiences. Had he not been given this explicit comparison between schools, would he have been more optimistic about his life chances and more content with the resources and opportunities he had been given? The concept of "relative deprivation" suggests that Jackson might be more satisfied had he not acquired concrete evidence that others have it much better than him.[26] By traveling from his racially homogeneous community in the Grand Boulevard neighborhood to the predominantly White and Mexican American area around Tilden, Jackson has crossed race, gang, and, to a certain degree, class lines, but he has not been exposed to the different academic experiences of other young people attending schools rich in resources, both within the Chicago Public Schools system (like Payton Prep and Lincoln Park) and outside that system.

Thus, social isolation as Young defines and studies it cannot alone capture the various ways in which students understand their experiences and the ways in which their experiences shape their perceptions of injustice. Students experience diversity in the city in numerous ways, and their interpretations of those experiences clearly hinge on their placement on the racial-spatial divide.[27] Namely, the confluence of race-ethnicity, economics, and residential segregation has created and reinforced mechanisms of inequality that become differently imprinted across racial-ethnic groups in local settings (for example, variations in crime rates by neighborhood). Where students fall on the racial-spatial divide clearly affects how they understand opportunity and injustice.

Alex, TB, and Jackson have some things in common, but they live very different lives. They are all young, Black males who reside on Chicago's South Side; however, Alex travels outside of that world for school and sees things that TB may never see and might interpret very differently if he did. Their different locations on the racial-spatial divide tell us a great deal about how those factors collide to shape our attitudes and the ways in which we all read our various experiences. The primary reason Alex has to cross racial boundaries is to attend Payton Prep. Conversely, the more I talk with TB, the more I realize that Harper keeps him cloistered in a world that he does not even realize is a stark contrast from the worlds of those with a different hue, class, gender, or zip code. And Jackson's naïveté concerning equality and opportunity has been shattered after aging five years, moving outside of Chicago for several months, and experiencing his share of educational and occupational successes and failures.

For young people, an awareness of differential opportunities can only come from crossing boundaries, seeing different people, and experiencing different things; in essence, they must be able to reflect on the lives of others to better understand their own lives.

Living With and Learning About Social Injustice

Adolescents' answers to the CCSR survey questions on social injustice, combined with the interview data, provide enormous insight into their beliefs about their chances for upward mobility. Their elaborations on the history of racial discrimination, specifically along the dimensions of employment and housing, align with the sociological literature that focuses on the attitudes and experiences of adults. African American and Hispanic students perceive greater social injustice than their Asian American and White counterparts, a finding similar to that for adults.[28]

As depicted in figure 3.2, students' perceptions of social injustice vary significantly by race with regard to two out of three measures. Approximately 20 percent of the students agree with the statement that it is difficult for members of their own race to get good grades. Most students, whether Black, Hispanic, Asian, or White, do not believe that teachers discriminate when assigning grades to students. In contrast, the majority of African American and Hispanic students in the Chicago Public Schools system agree with the

Figure 3.2   Students' Perceptions of Social Injustice, by Race, 2001

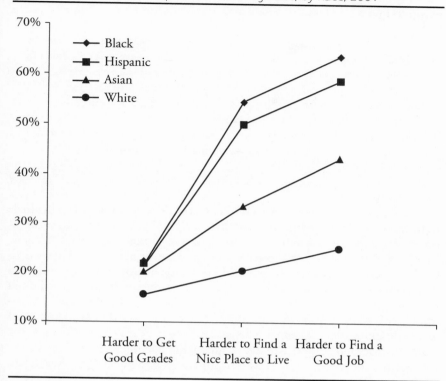

Source: CCSR data, 2001.

statements that it is harder for individuals of their race or ethnicity to find a job and harder for them to find a nice place to live, compared to well under half of Asian American and White students who agree with those statements.

In my interviews, students' assessments of discrimination in housing and employment also run the gamut from strong agreement to strong disagreement. These differences must be understood, in part, by the students' placement on the racial-spatial divide and by their awareness of their relative advantage or disadvantage with regard to the larger hierarchy of inequality, both as an individual and as a member of a racial-ethnic group. These varied understandings of history and the present shape their perceptions of their own opportunities.

Some youth invoke their knowledge about past unequal treatment to explain inequality in current times. For instance, Shay, the African American student at Tilden, on being asked on the survey whether she agrees with the statement that "discrimination makes it harder for people from my racial group to find a good job," responds:

> I think that because Black people been through so much, you know, slavery and stuff, different races think that Black people don't have no experiences in anything. So other races think that they are better than Blacks because [Blacks] weren't really much [as] slaves and whatnot. Just because you are richer than that person don't mean nothing. Also, I think it's hard for our Black men [with] the drama they go through, because they catch them selling drugs, catch them doing anything that's against the [law], but they gotta look at the fact that you won't hire them, so what else are Black men gon' do?

I ask Shay, "So you think that's what drives them into selling drugs?" and she says, simply, "Yeah."

Shay believes that the legacy of slavery has tainted the minds of individuals in power to the point where they are less likely to be fair in their determination of Black people's worth. Asked how she knows this, she replies, "Experience." Shay then tells me about her uncle to prove her point. He used to work at a fast-food restaurant, but his bosses and coworkers would "treat him like a nobody, and he just quit [the job] and went to sell drugs." Although Shay reveals that her uncle subsequently "got caught," she obviously sympathizes with his predicament and holds fast to this vicarious experience of discrimination. Her account of her uncle being subjected to a demeaning work environment experience also aligns with documented studies on the frustrations and setbacks faced by African Americans in the low-wage urban job market.[29]

David, another African American student at Harper High, gives his vicarious impressions concerning the impact of racial discrimination on his family members' attempts to secure employment. David even goes so far as to mention the (in)visibility of Blacks in media depictions of myriad occupations as more evidence for his conclusion that Blacks encounter employment discrimination. He elaborates on his strong agreement with the statement that "discrimination makes it hard for members of my racial group to find a good job":

> 'Cuz it ain't mostly Blacks in the world. I watch stuff on TV, I don't see no Blacks. I see mostly Whites in movies and stuff. It never was a Black president.[30] And then when my aunt, my grandma, and them [are] trying get a job, most of the people that be the managers or the CEO [are] White or Mexicans or Puerto Ricans. You ain't gon' find Blacks . . . they got ownership in only a few places.

The belief that prospective employers give preferential treatment to prospective employees of their own racial-ethnic background is in fact backed up in the literature on labor discrimination.[31]

Jackson also believes that African Americans have a harder time finding a job, and he bases this assertion on an experience he had in the South Side neighborhood of Hyde Park. Jackson says that he asked a White male clerk for a job application at a Walgreens drugstore and was told, "We don't have applications." Jackson continues: "So the next thing you know, when a White guy approached him and asked for an application, he gave him an application, and he didn't give me one at all." Incredulously, Jackson says, the clerk did this right in front of him. Beyond the racial slight, Jackson believes that the White applicant had the extra advantage of age. He describes this "guy" as older and believes that Walgreens would also be more likely to turn away a Black sixteen- or seventeen-year-old than a twenty-one- or twenty-two-year-old. Whatever the manager's motivation, Jackson easily recalls this experience when he is asked to elaborate on his perceptions of social injustice. Although his placement on the racial-spatial divide is near the racially segregated and lower-resourced end of the spectrum, based on his residence in the poor Grand Boulevard neighborhood, he still moves across racial-spatial borders to have interactions with Whites and other racial-ethnic and class groups at his school (Tilden) and while visiting nearby neighborhoods (Hyde Park).

Several White and Hispanic students at the two North Side schools also believe that Blacks are treated badly when it comes to the distribution of employment and housing opportunities and even police treatment. Angelique, a Lincoln Park High student of Puerto Rican and Mexican descent, has a distinct racial hierarchy in mind when it comes to understanding racial discrimination in America. She firmly believes that Hispanics are subjected to discrimination. However, she qualifies her statements by stating that Hispanics and Latinos are not targeted as often as African Americans for discrimination and that the duration of her group's mistreatment has been much shorter than that of African Americans. Gabrielle, one of Angelique's Lincoln Park classmates, also disagrees with the statement that discrimination makes it hard for members of her race (White) to find a good job. She does not think that anyone would judge her based on her race if she sought a job. However, when asked whether other races encounter employment discrimination, she emphatically answers, "Definitely."

When Jane, a Chinese American student also attending Lincoln Park, answers my query about the impact of discrimination on employment, she references her personal comparative frame and puts that in the context of the broader racial strata of those targeted by discrimination. Moreover, Jane's immediate reaction is to state that she does not have an opinion about discrimination because she believes that she and members of her family have not experienced racially disparate treatment.

> Well, I don't really have much of an opinion of that because most of my siblings, they already have, like, a stable job. So I don't really feel like there's much

discrimination. But maybe if you were like African American or something. . . .
African American people, they always think that people are discriminating
against them. Like, sometimes it's true, but other times, there's not much of
that.

Jane validates the existence of racial discrimination for African Americans,
but at the same time insinuates that perhaps members of this group are over-
estimating the degree to which it happens. The issue that each of these quotes
illuminates is that students believe that race and racial stereotypes have a negative impact on African Americans' opportunities for mobility.

John, the White ninth-grade student at Payton Prep, realizes that he and
other Whites are not usually negatively affected by race in their quest for
employment, a sentiment similar to that held by Asian American students. In
our discussion, John points to the centrality of race, whether conscious or
subconscious, in evaluating others. In response to the question of whether he
thinks members of his racial group are subject to discrimination when looking for a good job, he replies:

> Not negatively. I think, like, really everyone has judged people on race. . . . I
> don't think it's bad, but if you treat someone badly because of their race, con-
> sciously, that's of course horrible, but subconsciously. . . . I think that's why
> people hang out with people of the same race, they just feel comfortable. So if
> whoever is hiring you is of the same race as you, you're gonna have an advan-
> tage in most cases.

John believes that most business owners in Chicago are White, and he expresses his understanding of stratification by race, class, and gender in a very
straightforward manner. He knows that the power brokers who share his skin
tone and gender will be inclined to look upon him more positively than his
non-White peers when and if he needs their assistance in getting a job.

Another student at Payton Prep, Vanessa, who is Puerto Rican, also believes that most of the employers in Chicago are White and are much more
likely to "stick with" members of their own race when making hiring decisions. Asked whether she has been personally discriminated against, Vanessa
says no, but she believes that it is "common knowledge" that racial preferences have an impact on hiring decisions—unless "Hispanics are all they
have applying. Then employers don't have a choice." Vanessa also understands
where she stands in the racial hierarchy and believes that racial "favoritism" is
widespread.

Amber goes deeper than skin tone when discussing potential impediments
to employment. In response to the job discrimination question, she states
that her "ethnic" African American name (not Amber, which is a pseudonym)
could be a serious obstacle to her attempts to even get a job interview.

Say I went to a job interview and they didn't see me, but they saw my name. They'd be like, umm, "What does this say?" 'Cuz my real name is [ethnic name]. They would be lookin' like, umm, "Next! I can't even say your name." And then, I think you never see a really high-powered Black person, especially in the neighborhood or nothing. You never see that.

For Amber, a "shadow discrimination" looms over her prospective career search. She believes—correctly as it turns out—that there are unintended consequences for Blacks with unique or ethnic names, including the ability to even get in the door to achieve high positions in the employment sector.[32] Amber is bridging the racial-spatial divide by commuting from her low-income neighborhood on the West Side to Payton, where she receives a top-notch education, but the same cannot be said about others from her neighborhood (some of whom have similarly distinctive names) who attend neighborhood schools.

Neighborhood profiling is another means through which racial and ethnic profiling plays out in job searches. Hunter, a politically astute ninth-grader at Harper High, says that potential employers sometimes attribute negative traits and behaviors to job applicants simply because of the neighborhood where they live. Moreover, he believes, employers use neighborhood residence as well as race when making preferential decisions.

Now everybody over here is gangbanging, but you got 10 percent that's not. But you go out in the workforce and [employers] see what everybody over here is doing, they automatically gon' think, "Since you live over there, you gotta be affiliated [with a gang] somehow." . . . 'Cuz they'll be like, "All them people over there, they gangbangers, and you from over there, you live over there all your life, you must be gangbanging or something, so we can't hire you." But soon as you got another person come up and then they from that person's neighborhood who's hiring, he be like, "Well, you came from where I came from, we probably went to the same school, yeah, why not." They gon' choose that person from [their] own neighborhood before they would choose somebody from over here. You're not from the same neighborhood, or it seems just 'cuz you look like everybody else, they don't wanna hire you.

It is, of course, a form of prejudice to assume that a person is affiliated with a gang simply because he or she comes from a neighborhood with high levels of gang activity.[33] Moreover, anecdotal evidence (gleaned from personal observation as well as from the students) suggests that White individuals who reside in areas undergoing gentrification do not suffer from these assumptions, even if gangs are still active in their neighborhoods.

In sum, old-fashioned discrimination and prejudice have an effect on the lives of these young people, who are likely to recognize this even if they live in and attend school in racially homogeneous, socially isolated neighborhoods. Their perception of structural discrimination is more uneven, however, if they attend segregated schools within their own segregated communities.

Place Matters

There is a huge difference between what we recognize as some people's acts of prejudice and discrimination, which involve individual beliefs about and negative behavior toward members of negatively typed groups, and structural discrimination or inequality, which persists beyond the individual and is deeply embedded within social structures and social processes, especially in the realms of education, employment, and housing. Residential housing inequality is an extraordinarily powerful example of structural inequality. One residential area can bring its inhabitants immense gains in terms of access to resources and quality of life, and another can create and reproduce disadvantage. Those gains and losses endure across generations.[34]

Neighborhoods, in particular, are the driving mechanisms that perpetuate racial stratification.[35] Chicago is an extremely segregated city, and neighborhood disparities are marked by the intersections of race and place.[36] High levels of unemployment for people of color in urban areas, perceived and actual job discrimination, housing discrimination, wealth and income inequality—all have an impact on an individual's "choices" about where to live.[37] The young people in this study have much to say about the racially marked residential boundaries they recognize, reconcile, and *sometimes* cross.

Louie, who identifies as mixed (his father is Black and his mother is White), believes that self-selected segregation explains Chicago's racially segregated residential patterns. He believes that people choose where they want to live, but he also implicitly suggests that the response of prospective neighbors has an impact on individuals' housing choices.

> I think people choose to be segregated. There's White neighborhoods, there's Black neighborhoods, there's other neighborhoods. . . . If you choose to be the same as everyone else, then. . . . (*voice trails off*) Like, say you're Black and move into a Black neighborhood, and then you wonder why, "Oh, I don't see any White people around here?" But if you're White and move to a Black neighborhood, then everyone has a problem with you and vice versa. So I think it's the people who choose whether they want to segregate or not. It's all a person's choice, not anyone else's.

Louie's ideas about segregation are individual-oriented; he may not yet realize that structural forces also shape the decisionmaking and behavior of those who move into neighborhoods as well as of those who are there to receive them as neighbors. Louie resides in the majority-White neighborhood surrounding his school, Lincoln Park. He encounters more racial diversity at school than in his neighborhood, but as discussed earlier, Lincoln Park is not necessarily socially integrated.

Several of the students I spoke with believe that structural forces constrain one's residential choices much more than racial-ethnic prejudice or discrimination. Carmen, a Puerto Rican student at Payton Prep, believes that if people are able to pay the rent, their racial or ethnic category does not matter. Recognizing that her neighborhood is in the midst of vast demographic change, she concedes that gentrification is "putting people out, but that doesn't mean they can't rent another apartment. It'd just be more rent. So I don't think that people are screening anymore to see if you're Puerto Rican or if you're Mexican." This sentiment is also held by two of her African American schoolmates, Alex and Darrell.

Another one of Carmen's classmates disagrees, however, and recounts some of the stereotypes that Whites may have about Hispanics and the impact of those stereotypes on their assessment of members of this ethnic group as potential neighbors. Freddy, who is Puerto Rican, believes that Whites see his group as "a bad influence" because they assume that Hispanics "do drugs, deal drugs, or shoot guns" or might have an affiliation with the Latin Kings and "mess up the whole neighborhood." The Hispanic students quoted here clearly understand that their ethnic classification can affect their mobility, whether in the realm of employment, housing, or general treatment by other groups. Their opinions represent, however, only a slight majority within both the larger and smaller research samples.

Other students insist that both personal and structural discrimination can be overcome through hard work, perseverance, and personal responsibility. Four African American male students, for example, think that "presentation of self" is the key to attaining a job, and they discount the impact of skin tone in producing racially stratified occupational outcomes. Two of these young men state that some Blacks simply make it hard on themselves by misunderstanding dress and behavioral codes for job interviews. Boomer, a student at Lincoln Park, recounts the following experience:

> Like, I went for a job interview at Wendy's [restaurant], and it was three other guys with me. I was the only one who had a shirt, a tie, and pants on. Everybody had on blue jeans with gym shoes and jerseys, and stuff like that. And I feel as though, if you gon' be ignorant to the fact of the proper way to go into an interview, you holding yourself back. And it's sad to say, but African Americans are really ignorant of the way you supposed to carry yourself in society.

Boomer blames African Americans' difficulty procuring jobs on their lack of "cultural capital"—such as not knowing how to properly present themselves in society. He adds that he knew he should put on a nice shirt and pants for his interview at Wendy's, but his mother also made sure that he put on a long-sleeve button-down shirt *and* a tie. He got the job. The other three job candidates may not have had access to the same information—the same cultural capital—to compete for a position in that workplace.

Louie also speaks of the importance of appearance. He believes that you have to "present yourself all business-wise, then [employers are] gonna take you seriously and know that you're there to do something." He thinks that discrimination is not a huge issue and that job opportunities are "all based on the person." Darrell, another Black student at Payton Prep, says: "I haven't really even seen discrimination based on careers or whatever. I got a job and it was really easy." Darrell helps out at a barbershop on the North Side (where he lives with his dad during the week) and is interested in pursuing that as a trade instead of going to college. He says that the owner has already promised him his own chair once he gets a barber's license. This is a tangible career path for him, albeit an unconventional one, since he and his peers at Payton, with its rigorous curriculum, are being groomed for college.

These three students' belief that it is *not* necessarily harder for Blacks to find a good job puts them in a minority in my sample, at least among students of color. Two of them bring up the notion of "professionalism"—the need to "get it together" in order to present oneself as a suitable job candidate—and the third concentrates on results instead of the process. Darrell interprets his easy procurement of a job at the barbershop and as a summer clerk with the school as proof that discrimination may not be to blame for Blacks' higher rates of unemployment. Darrell would agree with TB, the fourth African American male I interviewed on the subject. A student at Harper High, TB has a low perception of social injustice and says that he sees successful Blacks working as office assistants, as lawyers, and in other professional jobs. He thinks that employment chances "depend on the skills that you got and your attitude . . . like the mood that you in once you go to work."

But where do those skills come from? At least a few of the students offer explanations of employment discrimination that recognize the structural barriers to "equal opportunity." Rina from Harper High, for instance, makes the connection that an individual's potential social capital—the skills, self-presentation, and confidence that Darrell, Louie, Boomer, and TB refer to—is related to his or her economic capital.[38] And if Blacks are poorer, they are more likely to lack these important attributes and will still be subject to stiff competition from other minorities in securing the available low-skill jobs.

RINA: Because most Black people come from a low-income family. And when they want a job, [employers] look at lack of skills. . . . If you don't have the skills, they don't want you. . . . But like the Mexican person come in, they'll hire them, and most of the Mexican people don't know how to speak English, but they know how to do the work. But if you can let a Mexican do the work, all you have to do is teach the Black person and they'll know what to do. They can do it, but that's how it is.

AUTHOR: So have you seen that happen personally, or do you just think that from . . .?

RINA: I haven't seen it, but I see, like, Mexicans everywhere I go. And I be like, that coulda been me that had that job. . . . They doing what I could do. It's not really that hard, all I gotta do is learn.

Rina's belief that employers more readily hire Mexicans who may not even speak English contradicts the belief of the Hispanic students quoted earlier, who think that their ethnic status and English-language barriers complicate their job searches. Rina's hostility toward the "Mexicans" she sees working in jobs that, as she says, "I could do," is quite apparent; it also does not bode well for her ability to see the similarities in the discriminatory treatment that African Americans share with other people of color. Instead, Rina's "truth" highlights a major difference as she experiences it: *they* have jobs and *she* and her racial counterparts do not.

Michael, a Black student at Harper High, believes that a slowdown in public-sector hiring impedes Blacks' search for employment. Although Michael does not mention it, he is absolutely correct in thinking that, in Chicago and elsewhere, public-sector employment has historically been a reliable path to the Black middle class.[39] Cutbacks in public services, combined with Blacks' lack of social networks, limit these opportunities.

AUTHOR: What about not just you but other African American people in general? Do you think it's hard for them to get jobs?

MICHAEL: Umm, yes, because the state ain't hiring too many people nowadays. You gotta know somebody in order to get somewhere you wanna be. Like a manager or a supervisor or somebody that can get somewhere quicker. . . . If anybody else try to get a job at my age, they gotta go through a lot . . . gotta keep calling the place and making sure that the application is still in. Or sometimes they won't even call you back after you fill out an application.

AUTHOR: So how does that make you feel about your chances looking for a job in the future?

MICHAEL: Right about now, I don't even care no more. 'Cuz I said if I can't get no job, I'd rather go to school . . . after high school, I'd rather go to school.

Like Jackson, Michael realizes that his age may be an impediment to getting a job, but he also knows that social networks—another form of human capital—matter in getting a response to an application. For now, he claims, he would rather pursue higher education than get a job after high school. We are left to wonder, however, what he will think if he has trouble finding a job *after* he has gained his education.

The students also notice that their housing opportunities are limited by how they look "on paper"—another reference to economic capital. For example, Boomer believes that more Blacks have bad credit and that this diminishes their attractiveness as home buyers and renters.

> But I mean, as far as homes and houses and stuff like that, my mom went for a home, and her credit is not bad, but it's not great, and they denied her. And for a lot of African Americans, from what I see, they have bad credit. So, I'm not gon' necessarily say just [because] you're Black, well, you're not gonna get a house, but you know. I feel as though they would accept a White person with bad credit before they will a Black person with bad credit. That's just my opinion.

As Boomer sees it, not only are Blacks more likely to have bad credit, but Whites with the same bad credit are accepted for home loans and lease agreements when Blacks are turned down.

The manifestation of discrimination "on paper" is also clear to Amber. She and her mom were trying to leave their segregated West Side neighborhood and looking for a home in the integrated middle-class western suburb of Oak Park. Asked why discrimination might affect their ability to find a place to live, Amber recounts the sense of "unease" and isolation she felt when navigating a mostly White section of Oak Park with a White friend from school:

> Zero White people live in my neighborhood. And it's not like in all neighborhoods, but when you go, like, in *certain* neighborhoods like Oak Park, and it's, like, people staring at you and stuff. And when we was gon' move out there [to Oak Park], my mother checked the prices on the houses. She [found out] what the man was trying to sell it for, but he offered another White person a lower price than what he [offered] my mother. . . . And when I went out to my friend's house [in Oak Park] . . . she's White, they was, like, uneased for me to be out there or something. And I was uneased too. Just to be out there by myself . . . the only Black person in that area.

What Amber is saying is that even Black people who can afford the homes in Oak Park will probably feel isolated there and sense the "unease" of the Whites in the neighborhood reacting to their presence.

Several of the African American males in the sample believe that having money—having economic capital—would be enough to buy them access to higher-quality, more racially diverse neighborhoods. Alex from Payton Prep thinks that your job, more than your race, determines where you live and the size of your house. He believes that "you can buy a house anywhere. The community [members] where you live may not want you there. . . . But as far as buying the actual house, if you have the money, they'll take it. Money is money." Mike and Terry from Tilden Career Community Academy agree that, if you have the money, you can get the house you want in any neighborhood. But Michael from Harper High—who has not moved beyond the earlier discussion of the difficulties encountered by members of his racial group in attempting to secure a job—believes that getting a good house is hard because "you gotta have a job for one." He cannot even consider the question of how discrimination affects homeownership.

Students' future opportunities may also be limited by their contacts with the criminal justice system—and when I interviewed these students, they were all too well aware of this. David, a student at Harper High, made a direct connection between physical mobility and his chances of securing legitimate employment. While elaborating on why he believed that members of his racial group do not have equal chances for jobs, David stated, "Naw, I don't think they have a fair chance, 'cuz, like, every time I go out . . . a couple of days ago I was just walking down the street and the police pulled me over and checked me for no apparent reason." We were not even at the point of the interview related to police contact and perceptions of criminal injustice, but David brought it up, spontaneously, in reference to employment discrimination.

People of color are disproportionately under the control of the criminal justice system—yet another strike against minorities seeking jobs. Moreover, race can supersede criminal or felon status in importance in job interviews, furthering the disadvantage faced by African Americans and Hispanics in the job market compared to Whites, with or without a criminal record. In a racial audit study, the sociologist Devah Pager sent Black and White testers to fill out job applications with identical criminal history and job experience information, then assessed the differences in callbacks for low-skill, entry-level jobs. Pager found decisive evidence that any contact with the criminal justice system, whether for nonviolent or violent offenses, had a negative impact on subsequent employment prospects for Blacks and Whites. However, the *degree* of the harm was significant by race. Specifically, Black applicants with no criminal record were less likely to get a callback than White applicants who reported a history of criminal justice system involvement.[40] As

Pager puts it, "The fact that a criminal record severely limits employment opportunities—particularly among Blacks—suggests that these individuals are left with few viable alternatives."[41]

Remember Jackson, the Tilden student who could not get an application at Walgreens? This is precisely the kind of legitimate entry-level employment that *should* be available in the areas where these students live and go to school. Andre discusses his experience seeking employment at Walgreens in Lincoln Park, the middle- to upper-class neighborhood where he both lives and attends school.

> Like, when the majority of Black guys go [to] find a job, the first question [employers] ask is, "Have you been convicted of a felony?" Most African Americans are felons, and that's making it even harder for them to get a job. I used to apply for jobs at Walgreens. They asked me if I had any criminal [history], and I responded back in a very . . . a high tone. "So do I look like I've been a convict?" And they said, they ask any people, if they're applying for this job, if they've committed a felony. So, I was like, well . . . okay.

Despite being African American, Andre was at least given an application (unlike Jackson), but he was upset about being asked whether he had ever been convicted of a felony. Pager also documents this racialized "salience of employers' sensitivity toward criminal involvement." She reports, "On three separate occasions, for example, Black testers were asked in person (before submitting their applications) whether they had a prior criminal history. None of the White testers were asked about their criminal histories up front."[42]

There is consistent evidence that employment is the greatest predictor of crime desistence, and it is worrisome that Blacks as young as fourteen have already experienced employment discrimination or perceive that they have less opportunity than Whites to secure gainful employment, purchase a home in their preferred neighborhood, and stay out of the criminal justice system because of their race, residence, gender, and age.

Conclusion

The students in this study frame their understandings of social inequality through personal experiences, vicarious experiences, and their knowledge of social and structural hierarchies. Race and ethnicity is the predominant lens through which these young people see the world, but it is not the only one. Their location on the racial-spatial divide further illuminates their perspectives and affects how likely they are both to perceive and to experience discriminatory treatment in education, employment, and access to quality housing. In particular, the African American students differ in how they connect racial discrimination to lower employment opportunities, but they all acknowledge that "race matters." Some also believe that a Black person's skills, appearance, and demeanor must triumph over the limitations their dark skin color may present when they compete for employment. What is striking is that the African American students who cross more racial and class boundaries, whether to attend school, search for a job, or hang out in public spaces with friends, have a keener sense of these social injustices than the students who do not. *Where* and *how* students figure out the workings of structural inequality are critical. As we shall see, students' uneven levels of dawning awareness of structural barriers to social mobility have a major effect on their socialization toward the legal system and their perceptions of criminal injustice.

Young people have ideas about important issues that are likely to endure as they grow into adults. Their transgressions across boundaries of race, class, and neighborhood combine to influence their sense of opportunity—both for themselves and for those who are like, and unlike, themselves. Their school's placement on the racial-spatial divide, as denoted by its racial composition and its resources, is critical to shaping their perceptions. Understanding the minds and lives of urban youth requires that we determine where they are located in place, how they move within and across social settings, what happens to them in those various spaces, and how those experiences affect their perceptions of injustice.

The next chapter deals more directly with the extracurricular education that Chicago youth receive, both within and outside of their school environment. On top of lessons about inequality, schools teach legal socialization and put students in a constant relationship with authorities ranging from teachers to city police officers. The symbiotic relationship between the school system and the criminal justice system is apparent in what students say about their relationships with authority figures and about the impact of those relationships on their attitudes about injustice.

CHAPTER 4

The Universal Carceral Apparatus

A guard sits at his elevated desk intently surveying the six camera screens in front of him. To his right is an orderly procession of teenage boys who are told to place their belongings on the scanner while they step up to be patted down for weapons and other prohibited items before passing through metal detectors. Once they are searched and scanned, the young men pick up their belongings and proceed to the main concourse.

This is neither an airport nor a prison; it is a public school located on the South Side of Chicago—the juncture where the technologies and imperatives of the criminal justice system have penetrated our public school system.

Contemporary urban youth are exposed to police contact more frequently and at earlier ages than their predecessors. Schools—and for those who live in public housing, even some homes—have begun to resemble correctional facilities. Metal detectors, surveillance cameras, and other mechanisms designed to monitor and control inhabitants are now standard equipment in American urban schools. Youth who must navigate these spaces are inevitably at high risk of police contact, which may lead to frustration, disengagement, and delinquency.

A number of scholars, from Patricia Hill Collins to Jonathan Simon, have made polemical and conceptual arguments about the "merging of the school and penal system," but these arguments have lacked empirical substance.[1] In providing both qualitative and quantitative data on youth experiences in Chicago's schools, this book explores how pervasive prisonlike practices have become in our educational system and—just as importantly—how students interpret their daily encounters with metal detectors, pat-downs, and police. As more and more aspects of "youthfulness" have been criminalized, students' beliefs about whom the police "serve and protect" changes. This chapter examines young people's conflicted attitudes toward the police and security guards patrolling their hallways and classrooms.

Urban public high schools are simultaneously places where attendance is compulsory until a certain age and places where one must submit to being scanned and scrutinized, which is very similar to the processes of entry and

Photo 4.1   Main Entrance to Tilden Career Community Academy, Chicago

Source: Photo taken by Carla Shedd, August 26, 2010.
Note: At the entrance to Tilden, the sign CHILDREN FIRST! MAIN ENTRANCE: BUILDING FOR THEIR FUTURE is posted side by side with the sign UPON ENTERING BUILDING YOU MAY BE SUBJECT TO SEARCH.

enmeshment in overtly carceral institutions (see photo 4.1). Despite the fact that they do not always feel welcome there, high school is also a place designated for adolescents. Although police officers and judges are generally cited as the "two key points of public contact in our legal system," I argue that we should look at the legal authority that is manifest in the schools that serve our children and the law enforcers embedded within that space.[2]

In fact, the modern public high school is the extension of our larger "disciplinary society."[3] We can see that there is a coercive apparatus, what I term the "school disciplinary superstructure," that students must navigate after they traverse the vast physical and social terrain to even get to school (see photo 4.2). Young people have yet to learn how to discipline themselves; the role of surveillance is both to supervise them and to teach them to surveil themselves.

Through their routines, schools are sites of socialization that set students' expectations for their behavior and their perceptions of how others treat and receive them. Schools are also sites of compensation, providing experiences that cannot be replicated or reproduced in the home, in the workplace, or in

Photo 4.2   Main Entrance to Harper High School, Chicago

Source: Photo taken by Carla Shedd, August 26, 2010.

the wider social world. It is critical to understand the processes and mechanisms at work within these institutions. In these sites, certain "routines and rituals" compete with academic pursuits, putting some students squarely on the path to a heightened perception of criminal injustice and/or greater police contact.[4]

The first section of this chapter provides baseline information about urban adolescents' interactions with the legal system, both nationally and in Chicago. To fill in the picture, I then present the experiences of the young people I interviewed for this work. This chapter demonstrates that the prisonlike conditions created when schools implement a universal carceral apparatus in the name of safety have unintended consequences for youths' attitudes toward criminal injustice.

Frequency and Severity of Youth Contact with Police

Each year the fatal encounters of Black adolescents with police grab headlines as tragic symbols of the institutionalized racism inherent in "law-and-order" policing, but how representative are these events of the general experience of minority youth? On the one hand, as the criminologists Francis Cullen and John Paul Wright have warned us, it is important to not overstate youths' encounters with the police.[5] At the same time, we must put the annual figures in the context of cumulative, or lifetime, risk of contact with the juvenile justice system and recognize that the impact of the justice system is "socially concentrated."[6] A small percentage can still represent a substantial number of cases. Thus, the specific numbers regarding adolescents' police encounters need to be put in the context of a justice system that disproportionately arrests, detains, convicts, and imprisons people of color.

In 2011 alone, U.S. law enforcement agencies made approximately 1.5 million arrests of individuals under age eighteen, out of a total population of more than 70 million Americans who were eighteen or younger.[7] This number actually represents an improvement over previous years: juvenile arrests for both violent and property crimes have been declining since they reached their peak of nearly 2.8 million arrests in 1994.[8] However, racial and gender disparities remain in juveniles' official contacts with the justice system. Black youth are overrepresented in juvenile arrests: while they are only 17 percent of the population, more than half (51 percent) of all juvenile arrests for violent crimes in 2011 involved Black youth. Arrests of White youth (who include juveniles of Hispanic ethnicity) made up 62 percent of those arrested for property crimes, with Black youth again overrepresented, this time at 35 percent. Females accounted for nearly 30 percent of all juvenile arrests in 2011.

Although these national figures are helpful in understanding the larger trends for youth arrests, juvenile arrest rates demonstrate great geographical variation within and across states, particularly in Illinois. Thus, it is necessary to look closely at what is happening in the state's largest engine for crime statistics—its largest city.

The patterns of juvenile contact with police in Chicago are similar to nationwide trends. In 2009 Chicago police arrested 20,664 juveniles age sixteen and younger. The most frequent offenses were narcotics violations, simple battery, and disorderly conduct.[9] Between 2003 and 2009, the arrest rates of five- to sixteen-year-olds declined by 25.7 percent, with the largest reduction occurring between 2005 and 2006—the years I was embedded in Chicago public high schools collecting data.[10] For all five years, juvenile arrests constituted between 11 and 12 percent of all arrests. Out of this population, nearly 70 percent of all arrests involved youth age fifteen or sixteen; fourteen-year-olds were the next-most-numerous group, representing nearly 18 percent of all arrests. With regard to gender, males accounted for just over 83 percent of all juvenile arrests in 2008 and 2009, and Black youth were disproportionately represented, comprising nearly 80 percent of all arrests.[11]

Place weighs heavily on these statistics. The number of arrests made on public school grounds in Chicago increased significantly between 1999 and

2004. In 1999, 21.7 percent of juvenile arrests occurred on educational properties, compared to 26.5 percent in 2004 (total arrests: 28,132), with 98
percent of those arrests on public school grounds. The remaining arrests in
non-educational settings occurred "on the public way" (43.5 percent), on
residential properties (11 percent), and in retail sales or service establishments
(7.7 percent).[12] In the latter half of the 2000s, those arrests began decreasing
in number. In 2010, 5,500 arrests of young people age seventeen or younger
took place on Chicago Public Schools properties, and that number declined
to 4,287 in 2012. Black youth were still disproportionately represented in
this population, accounting for over 75 percent of school-based arrests while
comprising only 42 percent of CPS students. Males were more likely to be
arrested on school grounds than females (68 percent versus 32 percent), and
the majority of the offenses were classified as misdemeanors (84 percent).[13]

The majority of Chicago public high schools have two police officers assigned to them, so youth encounter these officers daily as they perform their
regular duties.[14] Arrests made by officers assigned to the public high schools
are included in the arrest figures cited here. The fact that private, parochial,
and charter high schools are *not* required by the Chicago Board of Education
to have police officers present almost certainly explains why 98 percent of
those arrests were in public schools.

The potential problems raised by the presence of police and security guards
in Chicago public schools have elicited growing public comment in the last
ten years. A landmark report by the Advancement Project, *Education on
Lockdown: The Schoolhouse to Jailhouse Track,* highlights these concerns.[15]
This report analyzes the evolution of so-called zero-tolerance policies at
schools in three cities (Chicago, Denver, and Palm Beach, Florida), the disproportionate impact of these policies on students of color, and the changing
role of police in schools. Zero-tolerance policies were originally used as a
drug enforcement tactic, but in the early 1990s, after a few highly publicized
incidents of violent "rampages" in schools, these policies were widely adopted
in schools across the nation. The zero-tolerance approach is generally defined
as the use of severe penalties, primarily suspension and expulsion, for both
major and minor violations of a school's code of conduct.[16] These changes in
both policies and practices began to reflect what I term a "universal carceral
apparatus" that undermines the educational functions of these institutions.

Both the report and activists claim that students who misbehave are increasingly encountering criminal penalties either instead of or in addition to traditional school punishments. In the report's words, "even non-violent acts are
now subject to citations [tickets] or arrests and referrals to juvenile or criminal
courts."[17] Such punitive policies were nominally put in place for the safety of
students, teachers, and administrators. It has become clear, however, that strict
zero-tolerance policies and a highly visible police presence have not translated
into safer learning environments or less disruptive student behavior.[18]

Around the same time, the *Chicago Tribune* reported on the work of Blocks Together, a West Side community group that surveyed neighborhood youth on the issue of student arrests in school. They found that many students "complain about overzealous security guards who escalate conflicts" rather than making them feel safer.[19] Moreover, the presence of police officers on school campuses has resulted in greater numbers of students being arrested or referred to the courts for infractions that were formerly handled by school personnel.[20] A lack of hard data, however, left Blocks Together relying primarily on anecdotal evidence.

The writers of the Advancement Project report also lamented the difficulty of tracking the trends in suspensions and expulsions that have resulted from "infamous" zero-tolerance enforcement because Chicago Public Schools refused to provide these data to advocates. During that same period, however, the school system provided the Chicago Police Department with information on student infractions.[21] In the last two years, several organizations—most prominently, the Chicago Student Safety Act Coalition, led by Mariame Kaba of Project NIA—have gained momentum in their push to get Chicago Public Schools to make school discipline data more transparent and publicly accessible. The example of the largest school district in the country helped immensely: with the passage of the Student Safety Act in 2010, New York City's schools began sharing school discipline data.

After more than a decade of filing FOIA reports and persuading local news and education-focused media outlets to highlight the dearth of public data, Project NIA and their supporters won their battle. In December 2013, the school system's CEO, Dr. Barbara Byrd-Bennett, endorsed an agreement to make timely and reliable data tracking the number of school-based arrests, suspensions, and expulsions available on the Chicago Public Schools website. In February 2014, CPS published school discipline data on its website for the first time.[22]

It is critical to look at the antecedents to this victory. Over 8,000 CPS students, ages five to eighteen, were arrested in 2003.[23] African American students, who make up just under half of the students enrolled in Chicago public schools, accounted for more than three-quarters of those arrests.[24] This racial disparity was similar for school suspensions and expulsions by race, with Black students comprising 76 percent of suspensions and nearly 78 percent of expulsions.[25] From 2003 to 2009, the total number of juvenile arrests (ages sixteen or younger) declined by 25 percent. In 2009, 4,597 youth were arrested at public school locations. The most frequent offense was simple battery (a fight in which no injuries or minor injuries resulted), followed by simple assault and larceny-theft.[26]

These numbers do not necessarily reflect the number of fights that occurred on school property, but only the instances of simple battery that resulted in official contact with police. "Juvenile arrest has a *random* component," according to the criminologists David Kirk and Robert Sampson, as "numerous factors beyond the control or background of an individual influence whether a given criminal act will culminate in an arrest."[27] The current CPS school code of conduct identifies simple battery as an offense for which the school may use its discretion in notifying police about the incident.[28] After police are notified of the offense, the officers on the scene have considerable discretion as to whether to proceed with an actual arrest. These numbers quite likely, then, substantially underestimate the number of fights taking place on school grounds.

The most recent CPS data release shone necessary light on a new problem: differences in disciplinary action between traditional public schools and charter public schools. The initial data lacked information on arrests at charter schools, but it did make clear that students attending charter schools were "11 times more likely to be expelled" than students attending traditional public schools. Just 193 students out of 353,000 attending traditional schools were expelled, while 306 of the 50,200 charter students were expelled.[29] With the expanding number of charter schools in the CPS system, this is the new battleground for all parties interested in full information on disciplinary trends in all types of Chicago public schools.

Getting Hassled and Moving On

This discussion of arrests is important, since an arrest record can severely limit a youth's opportunity, but it is incomplete without fuller attention to the broader range of contacts that urban youth have with the police, both in school and elsewhere. There are indications that frequent police contact, even of a *minor* nature, has a great impact on the perceptions of minority youth. This section addresses the broader range of youth encounters with police in Chicago, based on ninth- and tenth-graders' responses to the large-scale Consortium on Chicago School Research (CCSR) survey and my interviews with students at Lincoln Park, Payton, Tilden, and Harper.

The 2001 CCSR survey included a self-reported measure of students' personal contact with the police, asking how often in the past year they had been "told off or told to move on by police," "stopped and asked questions by the police," "searched by the police," or "arrested by the police." The data reveal that adolescent contact with the police—ranging from the low-visibility, relatively minor experience of being "told off" or "told to move on" through the official and therefore more statistically visible contact of being arrested—is quite substantial. The raw frequencies, by level of police contact and race, are shown in table 4.1. Figure 4.1 displays this same information in terms of percentages.

At the lower level of severity, 45 percent of White students, 49 percent of African American students, 43 percent of Hispanic students, and 23 percent

Table 4.1   Chicago Ninth- and Tenth-Graders' Contacts with Police, by Race and Level of Severity, 2001

	Told by Police to Move On	Stopped by Police	Searched by Police	Arrested by Police
White	1,324	1,387	866	353
Black	4,699	4,775	3,588	1,818
Hispanic	3,907	4,225	3,140	1,231
Asian	271	278	136	54

Source: CCSR data, 2001.

of Asian students have been "told off" or "told to move on" by police. At the more severe level of sanctioning, arrests of African Americans were greater than for other racial groups: whereas only 5 percent of Asian youth, 12 percent of White youth, and 14 percent of Hispanic youth had been arrested at least once in the previous year, 19 percent of African American youth had been arrested.[30]

Figure 4.1   Percentage of Contact with Police for Chicago Ninth- and Tenth-Graders, by Race and Level of Severity, 2001

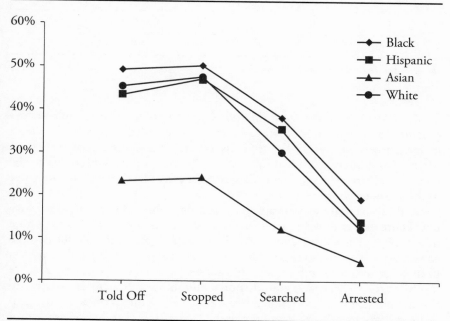

Source: CCSR data, 2001.

Figure 4.2   Chicago High School Students' Contacts with Police, by Race and Level of Severity, 2005

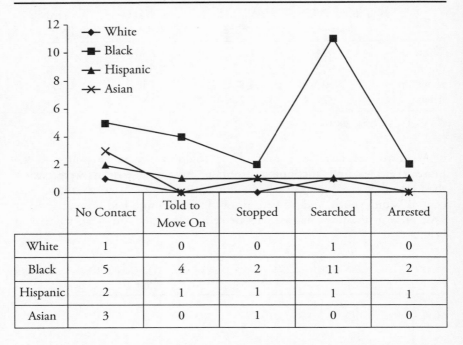

	No Contact	Told to Move On	Stopped	Searched	Arrested
White	1	0	0	1	0
Black	5	4	2	11	2
Hispanic	2	1	1	1	1
Asian	3	0	1	0	0

Source: Author's interviews and surveys, 2005.

My study of students from the four Chicago public high schools uncovered similarly high levels of African American youth contact with the police in 2005 (see figure 4.2). The majority of the African American students I surveyed and interviewed had experienced "severe" contact with police in the past year. (Thirteen respondents had experienced at least one search or arrest in the previous year.)[31]

As always, certain caveats apply to data on police contact. Students may not report that they were arrested, although the survey's confidential nature might mitigate their reticence somewhat.[32] Estimates are equally likely to be conservative, because students who have had contact with the police are less likely to be in school to fill out a valid survey.[33]

Other researchers have found similar numbers with analyses that reveal the significance of race, age, gender, and place in police contacts. In a pioneering study by Warren Friedman and Marsha Hott on Chicago youth, for example, 71 percent of students reported having been stopped by the police, with 62 percent of African American students who were stopped feeling that the police had been disrespectful.[34] Additionally, Arthur Lurigio and his colleagues' study of Black and Latino high school students in Chicago found that individuals in both groups who had been stopped by police *and* felt disrespected during the interaction were less willing to aid police and less likely to believe that the police cared about their neighborhoods.[35] Nor are such high levels of racially skewed police contact confined to the city of Chicago. A survey of Cincinnati residents found that "nearly half (46.6 percent) of African Americans said that they have been personally 'hassled' by the police, compared with only 9.6 percent of Whites."[36]

Police harassment of suspects, moreover, produces a vicarious effect that differs by race. Even if a young man has not personally experienced harassment, witnessing others being harassed affects his feelings about the police.[37] In the aforementioned study of Cincinnati adults, Sandra Browning and her colleagues also reported that 66 percent of African Americans said that they had felt vicariously hassled, compared to only 13 percent of White respondents.[38] The criminologists Rod Brunson and Jody Miller surveyed and interviewed forty African American adolescent males (ranging in age from thirteen to nineteen) in St. Louis, Missouri, and found that the vast majority of them reported having experience with police harassment, whether personally (83 percent) or vicariously (93 percent).[39] The CCSR data and other studies reveal that being considered a suspect is its own form of punishment. This effect is especially problematic when a young man believes that those who are supposed to be legitimate representatives and enforcers of the law have wronged him.

Having data on young people's contact with police, from the least to the most severe outcomes, is important. Acquiring data on stops, searches, and arrests, however, is only part of the story. The frequency and severity of personal contacts with police do not account for the important role played by vicarious contacts in shaping adolescents' perceptions about the attitudes, behavior, and mission of the police.

What Makes a School Safe?

The official mandate of the Chicago Police Department is to serve and protect, and the CPS Office of Safety and Security (OSS) pledges to "support CPS in providing a safe and secure environment that is conducive to learning."[40] The stated mission of Chicago Public Schools, in turn, is to offer its 400,000-plus students a "world-class education for the twenty-first century . . . to ensure that every child is on track to graduate prepared for success in college, work, and life."[41] Looking at the mission statements alone, it is clear that these institutions should be providing services that help students, not harm them. This begs the question of how youth are able to manage the extensive contradictions they face each day, particularly when they see or experience adultlike consequences (such as arrest and prosecution) being meted out for adolescent behavior. How, in other words, do these contacts with the police shape youths' expectations about the police and other authority figures?[42]

Students should not only be safe but feel safe at school.[43] Urban schools have a bad reputation for student safety, but no one wants safe schools more than the students who actually attend them.[44] Unfortunately, politicians and school administrators often implement "get tough" policies, such as increasing surveillance and policing in schools, instead of developing solutions that could address the roots of "inappropriate" and "disruptive" behavior. It is becoming increasingly clear that these policies, with their resulting suspensions, expulsions, and arrests, have negative repercussions for students, schools, and communities alike and have contributed to the development of a universal carceral apparatus.[45]

The Chicago Public Schools administration has begun to take activists' and scholars' criticisms of these punitive policies seriously. In 2006 CPS started to incorporate procedural justice and restorative justice principles into its disciplinary procedures. In July of that year, the Chicago Board of Education approved changing the title of its disciplinary policy from "The Uniform Discipline Code" to the "Student Code of Conduct (SCC)," based on the recommendation of the Community School Justice Task Force and the advocacy efforts of the Advancement Project, the West Side–based group Community Organizing and Family Issues (COFI), and Voices of Youth in Chicago Education (VOYCE).[46] The policy was additionally "modified to clarify the purpose of the policy and to reinforce that discipline should be instructional and corrective, not punitive."[47] But critics lamented these changes as nominal at best and continued to seek deeper change in both the culture and practice of school discipline.[48]

One highly promising alternative to punitive disciplinary procedures is the philosophy of restorative justice.[49] The principles of restorative justice aim to prevent or address conflict before it escalates and to guide the response or management of conflict and misbehavior after it occurs. Both the Chicago Board of Education and the Illinois Criminal Justice Information Authority have sought to appease their critics by giving school personnel practical strategies aligned with restorative justice philosophy to reduce the need for juvenile justice system involvement and for excluding students from school for misconduct in school.[50] The three main goals of restorative justice are accountability, community safety, and competency development.[51] More specifically, these programs (1) provide opportunities for "wrongdoers to be accountable to those they harmed" and enable students to attempt to repair the harm they caused; (2) implement strategies to build relationships and empower the community to take responsibility for the safety and well-being of its members; and (3) offer opportunities to increase the "prosocial skills" of those who have caused harm to others.[52] The Board of Education encourages principals and administrators to implement restorative justice philosophies and practices as outlined in the revised Student Code of Conduct.

The "disciplinary gaze" of the new SCC is far-reaching in time and space. According to the document, the SCC governs students' behavior under the following conditions:

> The SCC applies to students at all times during the school day, while on school property, while traveling to and from school, at any school-related event, on any vehicle funded by CPS (such as a school bus), and while using the CPS network. The SCC also applied to student behavior *outside* of school if: (1) a student engages in a Group 5 or 6 behavior, and (2) the behavior disrupts or may disrupt the educational process or orderly operation of the school.[53]

The consequences for first and second infractions include "skill-building in-school suspension up to three days"; a third infraction might result in additional in-school suspension, out-of-school suspension, or some combination.[54]

Although the SCC remains a disciplinary document, its subsequent development includes two important changes. First, the most recent version of the SCC (2014) places stronger limits than previous versions on the use of suspensions and emphasizes restorative, corrective, and instructive responses to student misbehavior. These tactics include redirecting inappropriate behavior; gathering information from all involved parties when conflict or misbehavior occurs; restoring student participation in the school community after school exclusion; and peer juries, mediation, and conferencing as approaches to resolving conflict. These practices have been shown to enhance the school environment, stimulate prosocial development and learning in students, and promote positive relationships, inclusion, respect, and safety.[55] But perhaps the most important change relates to the relationship between in-school disciplinary infractions and the carceral apparatus: policy notification is no longer mandatory for all infractions, only for certain violations of criminal law.[56] This revision also notably includes a statement that CPS's chief executive officer or designee will systematically monitor and publish disaggregated student discipline data.[57]

At least on paper, then, the situation has improved, and the carceral apparatus in Chicago's schools has been downgraded rather than expanded even further. But while much of the language around "zero tolerance" has been removed, students, scholars, and activists still question whether the district has truly transitioned to restorative justice by, for instance, providing more resources to restorative justice programs than to traditional district policies that are still based on the zero-tolerance philosophy.[58] Given that the entire purpose of a disciplinary code of conduct is to ensure a safe and productive learning environment, we need to understand the kinds of crimes that are occurring inside schools, whether the current approach is effective, and the impact of the school disciplinary superstructure on students.

During my time in the field conducting interviews with students in each of the four selected public high schools, a small majority of Chicago's high schools saw a rise in violent incidents. According to the *Chicago Sun-Times,* in the first five months of the 2005–2006 school year, "a school-by-school analysis shows more high schools reported increases in violence than decreases, with forty-four showing hikes; thirty-four showing decreases, and nine with no change."[59] The *total* number of violent incidents in Chicago high schools, however, was on the decline (1,724 total incidents in 2005–2006).

The approximate rates of change in violent incidents at each of the four schools studied here varied most by local area. The documented violence levels for Lincoln Park and Payton Prep, north of downtown, were similar: the figures for both schools remained in the single digits. Lincoln Park experienced a slight decrease in reported violence (seven incidents in 2005–2006 versus eight incidents the prior year), while the number of violent incidents at Payton Prep more than tripled, from two to seven incidents. The South Side schools' overall rates were much higher. Tilden Career Community Academy had a total of eighty violent incidents, which exceeded the numbers at all other public high schools in the city. (Fenger came in second with sixty incidents.) Harper High had a 14 percent increase, but the school's level of reported violence, at thirty-three incidents, lagged far behind the rates of its South Side counterpart.[60]

The major theoretical and policy question, then, is whether an increase in security would have a substantial impact on levels of violence in schools. The current climate of fear in America's urban schools persists, even though, according to the educational anthropologist John Devine, students who attend urban, lower-tier academic schools automatically associate education with uniformed security guards, police tactics for hallway surveillance, and weapons searches with high-tech scanning devices.[61] My experience in studying Chicago's schools leads me to agree with Devine's contention that schools' reliance on guards, police, and sophisticated equipment conveys an impression that these spaces are out of control. In this "new panopticon" of urban education, the gaze of supervision is no longer omnipotent.[62] Instead, teachers' preoccupation with students' minds is counterbalanced by the use of security forces to police the bodies of inner-city students via physical patdowns, metal detector scans, and more.[63] But perhaps more to the point, most of these interventions do not leave the students feeling safe.

A False Sense of Security?

My discussions with students suggested that the presence of police is not making them feel safer. Instead, it makes them feel imprisoned. Students from each of the schools discuss school security protocols using the terminology of policing and prisons, referring to "cells," "interrogation rooms," "hall sweeps" (anyone caught outside a classroom when the bell rings is automatically sent to the "police office"), and "pat-downs," or physical searches (which occur daily upon entering Harper High School). They also routinely see students handcuffed after a fight, and much more.

Dewayne gives the following example of why students feel "trapped" at Harper High:

> Harper feels like a prison, to tell you the truth. 'Cuz you have to stay in the classroom, use the bathroom when they tell us, eat lunch when they tell us, it's like a jail. . . . Security guards ask, "Well, what's your ID number?" when you're in the hallway. Just like in jail, you gotta say your ID number and not your name. It's no different than jail; it's just that we up in here for six hours a day, every day. That's why kids act bad. They feel like they trapped in here.

The extensive presence of and reliance on "school safety officers" is moving students' significant interactions with adults from teaching staff to security guards—especially since teachers are increasingly under orders to avoid any disciplinary actions with students.[64] In contrast, security guards have the leeway to both perform their assigned duties and potentially cultivate emotional ties to students, for better or worse.[65] In what follows, I present a summary of students' perspectives, separated by school, on the effectiveness of school security.

Students at Lincoln Park High mostly agree that the school is relatively safe; however, several of the sophomore students perceive an increase in both disorderly behavior and the number of security guards. Angelique, who identifies as Hispanic, reports a noticeable upsurge in the number of gangs, fights, and suspensions at Lincoln Park, which was once known as one of the best high schools in the city. She is "very surprised" that this is happening, but she attributes it to both the "new principal and to schools closing down and kids coming in from the West Side." Billy, who also identifies as Hispanic, agrees that the new principal may not be getting the respect she deserves, and he also mentions a rumor about the new "outsider kids" starting trouble. He leans in and almost whispers, "Someone was telling me that some other schools had closed and a lot of people from those schools . . . some troublemakers from there had come here. Last year there wasn't as many fights as this year, and I think that is [why]." Jane and Janet, both Asian American sophomores, believe that the school "seems more hectic" (Jane) and that "security [guards] are much more watchful this year" of students (Janet). Boomer, a Black student who transferred from a large South Side high school to Lincoln Park, disagrees with the latter point. He sees the security as "more lax," but he feels safer at Lincoln Park than at his former high school.

On several occasions I observed teachers and security guards at Lincoln Park requesting that students place their identification badges around their necks. However, I never witnessed any fights or other disturbances during my visits to the school campus.

The students are willing to acknowledge some moderate level of effectiveness of the security guards, but they scoff at the metal detectors. Each time I walked into the main entrance of Lincoln Park High School, the metal detector would beep (most likely because of the audio recording devices I was carrying), but the guards never checked me when it went off, even before they recognized me as a frequent visitor to the school. Not all of the school's doors have metal detectors, and Gabrielle (who identifies as White) and Jane tell me that they believe the metal detectors are "just there as a front"; they suspect that the machines may not even function. Gabrielle sees them as using up financial resources that could be allocated to repairing the school's water fountains, buying new books, and handling the rodent problem. "It's ridiculous to waste all this money that we could have used for important things instead of our false security," she says. Both Jane and Michelle (whose parents are from the Philippines) see it as normal when a metal detector beeps but the security guards do not make additional checks of the person who set it off. Janet and Louie (who considers himself mixed-race) suggest that security guards should consistently use the metal detectors by actually checking people, but Joaquin (who also identifies as Filipino) discounts the feasibility of stricter enforcement because it would "take too long."

In contrast to the students at Lincoln Park, all Payton Prep students agree that their school is very safe. One African American student, Amber, thinks that there are too many security guards who do not have anything to patrol, and she wants them "to back [off]" and give students "some breathing room." She even wishes for more "fights and excitement" at Payton Prep, since she was used to that at her predominantly Black grammar school on the West Side. Carmen, who identifies as Hispanic, complains about "feeling trapped" because she is required to both scan in her school identification card upon entrance and wear the card around her neck at all times. Carmen agrees that there are too many guards whose main job seems to be ordering them to wear the identification, which she does not think is "a life-or-death situation." She suggests that the guards are focusing on the small things because there is nothing else for them to do.

The majority of students at Payton Prep believe that the use of metal detectors is unnecessary, not because the machines are useless, but because the school is safe. Carmen likens the presence of the machines to being at the airport and "just needing to show them that you don't have anything." I conducted the majority of the interviews at Payton during the month of June, at different times of day; most students had a "free" period in the morning while others were interviewed during the afternoon "enrichment" period. No matter when I visited, the halls at Payton Prep were very orderly when students traveled between periods and rather empty during class sessions. The guards stationed at different posts throughout the school were essentially, as Amber sardonically puts it, "patrolling each other," because the students were usually where they were supposed to be. But even so, visual patrols were ever-present. Security guards relied heavily on surveillance cameras to monitor students both inside and outside the school. The students deem this unnecessary, as there is no visible disorder in their school, which none of them perceive as unsafe.

A carceral apparatus consisting of security guards, cameras, and metal detectors may be deemed out of place in a school like Payton, where students' educational pursuits are foregrounded and violent crime is a rare phenomenon. Payton students are not the usual "captive audience" (like those who attend neighborhood schools or schools of last resort), having instead chosen to attend the school. The universal carceral apparatus does not need to be "activated" in this space, since the threat of violence is almost nil. Instead, its passive presence conveys the even stronger message to students that the "disciplinary superstructure" is necessary even though students are not in physical danger.

The situation at Tilden Career Community Academy could not be more different. The majority of the students I speak with report feeling unsafe both inside and outside the school, even with the extensive use of surveillance cameras. And in contrast to the Payton Prep students, they want *more* security guards to patrol the classrooms and hallways inside the school and to ensure their safety on their way home from school. Shay and Terry, both African American, express concern that security guards and teachers have been "jumped" or overpowered by students in the past, but Terry takes comfort in knowing that guards are trained in "how to keep kids off of them."

Jackson, who identifies as African American, and Max, who identifies as Mexican American, offer detailed assessments of security guards' effectiveness as well as suggestions for increasing both the *perception* of safety and *actual* safety in the school. Jackson describes in great detail the particular angles and placements for surveillance cameras that he believes would best capture images of students attempting to set off a false fire alarm or start a fight in a remote, unsecured hallway. Max specifies the number of guards stationed at the entrance and exit doors who are needed to watch students more intently to prevent them from bringing weapons into the school. Nevertheless, he says, tighter surveillance at the doors would not help that much because students would fashion weapons out of school-approved items instead, such as locker padlocks and pencils. These comments by Max and Jackson demonstrate that the aims of the school disciplinary superstructure have been achieved: these two students are participating in their own surveillance by suggesting refinements or improvements in the school's surveillance processes.

In contrast to the two North Side schools, the security guards at Tilden Career Community Academy rely heavily on metal detectors. I routinely saw students being thoroughly checked if the machine beeped, indicating the presence of a metal item. Paradoxically, most students believe that the metal detectors are effective, even if the use of the scanners fails to allay fears about safety in school. Terry explains that he knows the metal detectors work because he himself had to spend five minutes getting "fully checked for leaving my belt on" while going through the detector. The guards are also fastidious about processing new visitors to the school (though I was often able to bypass the metal detectors once the guards became familiar with me). Between classes, guards and staff members have a visible presence in the hallways and outside the boys' bathrooms, but unlike at Payton Prep, the students I interviewed at Tilden are generally comforted by their presence.

Despite Tilden's relatively high levels of officially reported violence, I did not witness any fights or other serious incidents of disorder during my visits to the school. This may have been an artifact of the timing of my visits: I usually conducted interviews during midday lunch periods. According to official reports and interview responses, most fights occur after school. This would also explain why there was a much heavier police presence outside the school during those times.

Shay offers a particularly vivid description of the police presence surrounding Tilden:

> The polices be on it at school! The polices at school, they out here to help you. I think the police at the school is really nice, 'cuz when you get out of school they say, "Go home, go home, go home." If you in a big crowd, they break you up instantly. Like on Halsted, they consider Halsted a part of Tilden. You can't fight on Halsted. You can't fight down on Forty-Fourth and Union. You can't fight down there 'cuz the police going way down there just to protect you 'cuz you came from this school. I like the polices here 'cuz last year they had a shooting in front of our school, a boy got shot, and ever since then . . . they been following up on they job. Polices' paddy wagons be here before school, after school, during the school . . . all the school hours. They be here soon as school starts at, like, six o'clock. Soon as you come in, it's a police car right on the corner and then it's a paddy wagon right down the street. It's so many polices over here I can't even. . . . It's too many polices over here. . . . Sometimes I feel safe, but sometimes I don't.

Thanks to the extensive police coverage outside the school and her trust in the police, Shay feels less safe in school than she does outside it. "I feel safe coming to school," she says, "'cuz I know the police gon' be right there on the corner. Now in school, I'm sorta shaky. I feel safe sometimes, but I be kinda scared because I know people will try to sneak up on you, but you gotta watch your back."

Shay's use of the word "polices," pronounced *po-leeces,* is striking. I notice that she adds the *s* to "police" when she is the first to use the word (that is, I do not prompt her with a question that includes the word "police") and also when she becomes excited while answering an interview question. That she and six additional African American students use the term "polices" may reveal that, for these young people, the singular form of the word, though it normally is the plural form as well, could not begin to encompass the ubiquity of their presence.[66]

Jackson, a tenth-grader at Tilden, wishes for an even heavier presence of police for safety reasons and even suggests that the officers should "do foot patrols instead of just staying in the cars." Mike also likes having the police present at school. Asked his opinion about their effectiveness, he states, "When they leave, I'm like, damn!" Recall Max's remark that, "when the police leave, that's when the [Black] people jump Hispanics and stuff like that." His description of the dangers that students face because "bad kids" have learned the officers' routines when they patrol the streets after school is even more poignant.

Harper High students are also concerned about their safety; like the students at Tilden, they are not convinced that the security guards are as effective as they should be in maintaining order. Hunter, an African American student with an easy grin and a twinkle in his eye, literally laughs in my face when I query him about the security guards' efficacy. He complains that they "are too fat and talk too much stuff" to students to be able to assert their authority over them. Hunter boasts that he relies on his fists for personal safety; as far as the security guards are concerned, he says, "I don't trust 'em and I don't need 'em."

Students' estimations of whether there should be more or fewer security guards are more varied at Harper High than at the other three schools. The girls I interviewed at Harper, Pink, Rina, and Keisha, believe that there should be more guards because they have seen security guards "get stole on" or punched during fights between students. David and Chris also speak of students "jumping on" security guards, police officers, and even the principal at their school. Pink, a sophomore, notices that the security guards have gotten stricter since her first year, when they would "be nice and give out candy." Now, she says, they are much more serious about patrolling the hallways inside the school and the grounds outside the school doors.

Dewayne, in contrast, is annoyed by the "security guards constantly hawking people to get off the school grounds" and feels that there are too many of them. He also notes that many of them "are nothing but off-duty police officers," which makes the school "feel more like a prison or something."[67] David, an African American student, is strongly opposed to the daily pat-downs upon entering Harper. He says, "I feel they shouldn't do that to all kids 'cuz most kids are innocent and I don't like them securities touching on me! They checking to make sure everybody is safe, but man, they ain't gotta pat us down like that. They can use the metal detector or one of them wand things. That's all I gotta say." His frustration is palpable; it is striking that he feels so strongly about this issue at such a young age, but these pat-downs are part of David's daily routine.

The Harper High students disagree on their desired levels of police patrols outside the school. When asked how many police cars surround the school after dismissal, most students estimate that five to six cars surround the school for at least twenty minutes after dismissal each afternoon. The majority of students are satisfied with this number, but a couple of them think that "there are too many out there as it is." Chris, an African American student, is the one exception: he fears that kids might be able to overpower only two to three officers and would feel safer, he says, with "ten to fifteen police cars outside the school." When I probe further, Chris tells me that he has never seen any kids "jump on" the police; still, he worries that it could happen one day. His classmate David does not think more police are needed either inside or outside of Harper. David believes that the extensive number of police surrounding the school reinforces the perception "that Harper High is one of the worst schools in Chicago. . . . But when I came and [saw] for myself," he adds, "Harper is not really that bad."

As at Tilden, the guards at Harper rely heavily on metal detectors and camera surveillance. Students are physically "checked" every day as they enter the school. Girls have one entrance, where they are searched by female guards, and boys another, with male officers. Students do not complain about the time it takes to go through this process because this system has always been in place during their time at the school. Although David complains about having to endure the guards "touching on" him, his schoolmate Dewayne acquiesces to the searches in the name of efficiency. Dewayne argues that, since the metal detectors go off for innocuous metal objects (such as zippers and belts), "they might as well get patted down." Chris even suggests that security be intensified. He says that he would feel safer if the guards used the book bag scanner more often, just in case a student brings in a weapon. Like Max from Tilden, Hunter reports that students at Harper High also use weapons fashioned from school objects if necessary for a fight, instead of smuggling a knife or gun into the school. It is no surprise to hear Rina complaining about the guards not paying attention to students' "approved" metal objects; for instance, she says, they once allowed a girl to bring a pocketknife affixed to her key chain into school.

As this discussion should make clear, students' opinions on the effectiveness of the security apparatus vary significantly, and once again, place matters in these variations. It appears that Lincoln Park may be changing for the worse as more fights take place and general disorder intensifies, even with the hiring of additional security guards. While Payton Prep's safety climate has not changed in students' assessment, the increased intensity in surveillance strategies (identification checks, security patrols of halls, and so on) does not match the context. Students at Tilden believe that the metal detectors, security guards, and police officers in their school are effective, and their trust in these crime control measures is evidenced in their requests for more intense screening and more guards and police. Even so, the Tilden students remain concerned for their safety. Finally, even as Harper High students seem to endure the most extreme surveillance measures, including physical pat-downs, they are calling for more officers to guarantee peaceful classrooms and corridors.

In the two North Side schools, the use of metal detectors and a larger force of security guards has not made much difference in the school's safety climate, for better or for worse, lending credence to Gabrielle's belief that the only result of these strategies is a "false security." In contrast, the South Side schools are still deemed unsafe, even with their extensive use of security guards, metal detectors, and video cameras. The next section moves from focusing on the disciplinary control of teachers and security guards to examining how the presence of Chicago police officers and their relationships with students affect youth perceptions of injustice.

Defiance and Compliance: Perceptions of the Law's Legitimacy

Adolescents' attendance at urban schools, which forces them to navigate and reconcile a school's carceral apparatus on a daily basis, accustoms them to being viewed from a "criminal gaze" that operates not by force, but through three nonphysical practices: hierarchical observation, normalizing judgment, and examination.[68] The mechanisms of social control instituted by policymakers and administrators, in particular, operate from a deterrence or instrumental approach to achieve compliance. In the words of the psychologist Tom Tyler, "people are viewed as shaping their behavior to respond to changes in the tangible, immediate incentives and penalties associated with following the law."[69] Thus, by searching all students and exhibiting unilateral suspicion of groups of youth, particularly males, the carceral apparatus is structured in a way that presumes, not that youth are compliant by default, but rather that they are criminally inclined and deviant. This instrumental perspective sees compliance as a response to external factors and punishments, and it puts great pressure on the enforcers of the law to observe, influence, and police public behavior.

In contrast, the normative approach to procedural injustice posits that people comply with the law when they believe it is proper to do so.[70] They do not act primarily out of self-interest. Instead, there is a "connection between normative commitment to legal authorities and law-abiding behavior."[71] Moreover, people evaluate the justice or injustice of their interactions with the law and assess how legal directives are given independently of the outcome. It is clear that the *manner* in which directives are given and rules are enforced is especially important to the youth in this study, and that it shapes their sense of the legitimacy of the rules and their determinations of whether the outcomes are just.

Perceived injustice is a measurable phenomenon that powerfully captures adolescents' attitudes about social and structural disadvantage, as informed by their personal and vicarious interactions with authoritative institutions and their representatives. The measure of perceived criminal injustice I use in this study hones in on students' attitudes regarding the legitimacy of police action. I define their assessments of criminal *justice,* which can be studied both quantitatively and qualitatively, as congruence between their expectations about key agents in the justice system and their perceptions of these agents' behavior, while defining their assessments of criminal *injustice* as the gap between the same. The confluence of personal identity, experiences, and social contexts shapes the expectations and perceptions of the young people in this study and invariably determines what they perceive as normal and legitimate.

Chicago public school students' reactions to and interactions with authority figures display racial and spatial stratification, both within and outside school walls, and are also differentiated by space and place. This finding extends the argument made by both Robert Sampson and William Julius Wilson that social context—especially neighborhood—shapes an individual's ideas about what behaviors and practices should be considered normative.[72] The distinctive social context of each student's school and neighborhood environments influences his or her ability to perceive an interaction with security guards or police as just or unjust.

Map 4.1, based on CCSR data, depicts the distribution of students' perceptions of injustice in police behavior toward members of their own race, toward young people, toward poor people, and toward males, with the darker shadings representing a greater intensity of the more negative perceptions. The community areas with moderate to high perceptions of injustice are also community areas with a greater concentration of African Americans and Hispanics. These findings of race and place effects on perceptions align with the

Map 4.1   Chicago High School Students' Perceptions of Criminal Injustice, by
Race, Gender, Class, Age, and Neighborhood Area

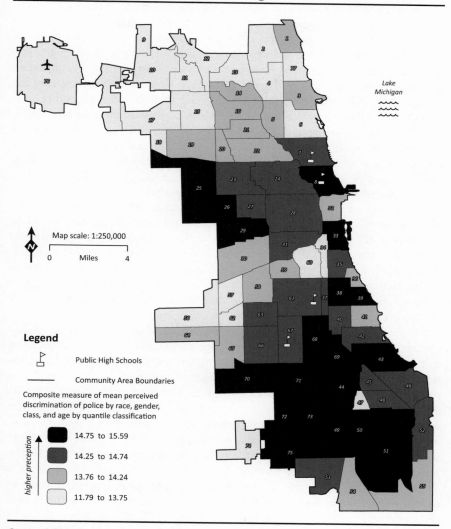

Source: CCSR data.

general findings in this subject area for both adults and adolescents and support the idea of a racial gradient for perceptions of injustice, with Blacks at the higher end of the scale and Whites and Asians at the lower end.

Map 4.2 displays youth contact with police by neighborhood now overlaid onto the map of perceived criminal injustice (map 4.1). As map 4.2 makes clear, many of the neighborhoods showing a light shading for low perception of injustice—that is, police are more often perceived as just than as unjust—also have a very large circle, which denotes high police contact. Other neighborhoods have low levels of police contact but high perceptions of injustice—that is, police are more commonly regarded as unjust. These "off-diagonal," or unexpected, results are rather compelling. The low perceptions of injustice in some neighborhoods with high police contact might be explained as a consequence of changing normative landscapes: perhaps attitudes around policing and perceptions of justice change significantly when individuals who have frequent contact with police become concentrated in particular neighborhoods. Individuals with extensive police contacts (particularly those who have been stopped and searched multiple times without an arrest) may not perceive these incidents as injustice because they are the "experience of the expected" for individuals who look like them and reside in their neighborhoods.[73] Alternatively, those same individuals with extensive police contacts could begin to see a racial pattern in policing that they perceive as discriminatory, especially if they are able to confirm that not all groups are subjected to such a pattern.

In contrast, individuals who have no police contact may have a higher perception of injustice because they judge race-based police discrimination from a wider vantage point—that is, from a distance. They may note the patterns of policing that affect others in their racial group, but they may also realize that they have some means by which they escape such contacts themselves (means based on class, gender, appearance, or some other characteristic or behavior). The perceptions scale used in the CCSR survey combines race, age, gender, and class to encapsulate individuals' feelings about how these various identities combine to disadvantage or advantage people like themselves in interactions with police.

The focus on the racial indicators lends even greater insight when contextualized by school location and police contact. The responses from the thirty-six students I surveyed and interviewed similarly display a wide variety of attitudes toward criminal injustice by race and by school, but a pattern starts to emerge when both their experiences with police and their school context are taken into account. The two White students and the four Asian American students rate as having a low *racialized* perception of injustice. This makes sense, because the exclusion of age, class, and gender leaves the focus on the remaining two questions, which ask whether they believe that members of their own race are "treated worse" and are "more likely to be stopped

Map 4.2   Chicago High School Students' Contact with Police, by
Neighborhood

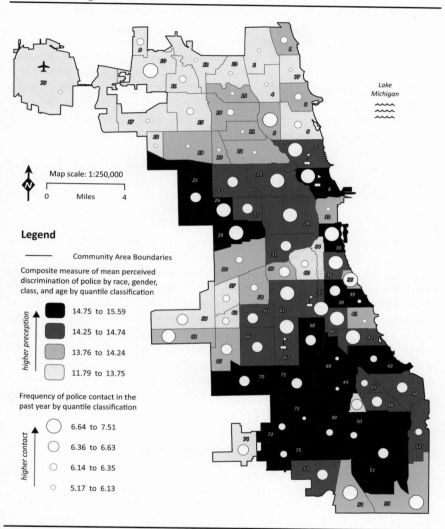

Source: CCSR data.

and searched" by the police. None of these students see their racial group as being at a disadvantage on these two measures in comparison to other racial groups, such as African Americans, Hispanics, and even Muslims.

Two Hispanic students have a low racialized perception of injustice and three have a high racialized perception of injustice. Only one Hispanic student, Max, has experienced the most severe form of contact with police—arrest. Two have had no contact, one has been told to move on by police, and one has been searched. The perceptions and police contact survey data are much more challenging to reconcile for the twenty-five African American students (two of whom self-identify as biracial or multiracial but say that most people perceive them as Black). Most of these students (72 percent) have a high perception of racialized injustice: they believe that members of their race are more likely to be "treated worse" and "stopped and/or searched by the police." They are well represented in both of the "off-diagonal categories"—that is, high perceptions of injustice and no police contact, and low perceptions of injustice and being searched. (No arrested students have low perceptions of injustice.)

Several factors have shaped these students' perceptions of criminal injustice: their personal and vicarious contacts and interactions with police, the frequency and substance of those interactions, their neighborhood context (particularly its safety and the level of disadvantage associated with it), their school context (again, especially in terms of safety and disadvantage), and their frames of comparison (shaped by their mobility across these various contexts).

Table 4.2 provides just a glimpse into these young people's varying degrees of clarity and ambivalence about their interactions with authority figures, their perceptions of criminal injustice, and their perceptions of themselves. Getting a sense of the full story requires sitting down with them, talking to them, and capturing their perceptions and experiences.

Making Sense of Injustice: Students' Perspectives

Of the female students at Lincoln Park High, five have low perceptions of racialized criminal injustice and have had no police contact in the past year. None of these students are Black, and all have generally positive perceptions of the police, at both the individual and group levels. Angelique, the sole Hispanic female at Lincoln Park, has a slightly more complex perspective in that she believes that Hispanics *are* treated unfairly by the police, but not to the same degree as African Americans and individuals of Middle Eastern descent. Jane and Janet, both Asian American, declare that they continue to have positive perceptions of the police because they have had no personal "association" with police officers that had a negative effect on their perceptions. Jane wonders whether the invisibility of the police and the visibility of school se-

Table 4.2 Chicago High School Students' Racialized Perceptions of Criminal Injustice, by Level of Police Contact

	No Police Contact	Told to Move On	Stopped	Searched	Arrested
High perception of injustice	**Boomer** and **Andre** (Lincoln Park); **Freddy** and **Brianna** (Payton); **Pink** and **Rina** (Harper)	**Angela** and **Alex** (Payton); **Shay** (Tilden)	**Amber** and **Carmen** (Payton)	**Vanessa** and **Darrell** (Payton); **Andrea, Jasmine,** and **Mike** (Tilden); **Dewayne** and **Hunter** (Harper)	**Max** (Tilden); **Keisha** and **Michael** (Harper)
Low perception of injustice	Gabrielle, Michelle, **Angelique,** Jane, and Janet (Lincoln Park)	**Louie** and **Billy** (Lincoln Park)	Joaquin (Lincoln Park); **Terry** (Tilden)	John, **Dre,** and **Jackson** (Tilden); TB, **Chris,** and **David** (Harper)	

Source: Author's interviews and surveys, 2005.
Notes: Names in bold are those of students who self-identify as Black, multiracial, and/or Hispanic. N = 36.

curity officers translate into positive opinions of the former and negative opinions of the latter.

> AUTHOR: You stated that the security guards are sometimes inconsistent in enforcing the rules. What do you think about police officers and their enforcement of rules?
>
> JANE: Yeah, 'cuz I don't really see police officers. Well, I see them in the school and stuff like that, but I never really had to encounter them. But since I have encountered the security guards, I guess, I don't have good feelings [about] security guards.
>
> AUTHOR: In general?
>
> JANE: Just with some of them, the ones that actually are inconsistent. 'Cuz I know some of them are pretty nice and stuff like that, but I don't have anything against them, it's just the one on one.

If Jane were to ever personally witness inconsistency or unfairness from the police, her positive perception of the police could be corrupted. Her opinion about security officers is negative because she has "encountered" them "one on one." Jane's ninth-grade classmate Michelle also complains about guards' inconsistency or favoritism toward certain students but goes "on the record" about her disdain only with me, not with school authorities. Michelle says that she would never challenge the guards because "they are the authority."

This seemingly impenetrable barrier between authorities and their subjects is not always as formidable as it seems, but perhaps it should be. Students hold various opinions about whether security guards should establish an emotional connection to students or whether they should maintain a strict authoritative relationship with them to maintain order in the school. Janet has never attempted to cultivate a close relationship with any of the security officers; her opinion of them is based on an early interaction with one guard, which she recounts:

> I've been at this school for two years, and I have never been close to security guards. I remember there was one incident when I was a freshman in the other building. I didn't know that you were not supposed to open the locker after the bell rings because I was tryna get my lunch money. And I opened it, like, a minute after and that security guard was really mean, like, "Close your locker now!" I was like, "Hold on, let me get my money." "Close it now!" I was like, "Whoa!" So I guess if they were all nice and really close to kids, then no one would listen to them. So, yeah, I'll just have to get used to it.

Here Janet reveals that she shares Michelle's feeling of resignation. Even though she dislikes the way the guard addressed her during this encounter, she is getting used to what she deems their brusque manner of maintaining order in the hallways of the school.

Janet's schoolmates Gabrielle and Andre are much more critical of the guards' rude behavior and believe that it would be better for guards to treat students with respect rather than yelling at them. Gabrielle, who identifies as White, mentions a female security guard who was "really nice" to students. "We just followed her completely," she says, "because she was, like, so nice. And then we got these mean, awful people, and no one listens to them." Gabrielle believes that students are much more likely to comply if security guards are nice to them. Andre, who is African American, speaks of an additional benefit when students and guards establish an amicable relationship: "If you interact with students, you get a better [understanding] of them. You know what they're gonna do. You can see if they're telling the truth to you or not." In a sense, guards can perform the positive duties envisioned in Devine's "new panopticon" by using their connection to students' minds to ensure that their bodies are compliant with school rules and regulations. There is still a chance, however, that students will resist establishing friendly relationships.

Almost all of the students complain about the recent "strict" enforcement of the rule that they must wear their school identification cards around their necks, even while in class. The official policy requires that students wear ID "at chest level and visible to school personnel at all times during school hours and events, especially when you enter and exit the building." The reason behind the policy is not explicitly stated in Lincoln Park's rules, but other CPS high schools that enforce this rule say that it deters trespassing and unauthorized access to the school property. Lincoln Park sophomore Billy concedes that it is a "pretty good idea to be somewhat strict," but adds, "They're kinda pushing it with, like, giving detentions." In general, the students are bothered not so much by the requirement itself, which makes sense to them, but by its uneven enforcement, which strikes them as unfair.

Billy's classmate Janet, also a sophomore, speaks to the changes in the enforcement of this rule since she enrolled the previous year:

JANET: I think the police officers and the principals do really well, especially enforcing security. But I think it's a bit too tight, though.

AUTHOR: Really? Tell me why.

JANET: I don't know, it's good to be that tight, but it's just kinda creepy sometimes. It feels like someone's always watching over you. Like, "Put your ID on." I know it's good for us. . . . I agree with how [the principal] is enforcing codes and *laws,* no . . . codes and, like, *new rules. . . .* We'll adjust. I mean, last year we did have a lot of freedom, *complete freedom,* like no one cared. The security guards were just sitting there, and even if we were late, they wouldn't say anything. But now, they're like, "Tardy!" one second after the bell rings. We're just not adjusted to it yet. . . . I heard some rumors, like, if you don't wear your ID around the school campus, they will give you an in-school suspension. And I thought that was just kind of harsh, you know. I know they're trying to put forth a message to all the students to put your ID on, it's for your own good. Yeah, but it does work, though. Everyone's been wearing more IDs now.

The comments of Janet and her peers complicate the analysis of why students would comply with the more strictly enforced "codes and new rules" at Lincoln Park. Do they have a successful deterrent effect? Are students compliant because of a sense of procedural justice and (recent) legitimacy accorded to both the newly enforced rules and the enforcers? Or are we seeing students submit to the overarching school disciplinary superstructure that exploits the normalization of a carceral apparatus? Or is it—as I would argue—some combination of all of the above?

It is meaningful that Janet corrects herself, substituting "new rules" for "laws," but perhaps her first thought was apt. Most students at Lincoln Park state that they are annoyed by the "lack of consistency," since the biggest change for them has been that "laws" already on the books only started being enforced in the middle of the year. Several others resent the invasive nature of the codes and the enforcement. Michelle, for instance, notes that "you used to be able to go to the bathroom, and now you can't leave your class. You have to have a pass to go see your counselor. Or go to the library or the computer lab. I guess that's good in a way. But if you have to go to the bathroom, some teachers are like 'No, sit down, you can't go.'" Michelle concedes that "the principal's trying to make the school better in a way," but she still thinks that "she's going a little too far."

The fundamental role of bodily control in the school disciplinary superstructure is manifest in these students' testimonies, but many of them see the increased discipline as a justified means to an end (for instance, deterring fights, restoring greater order, or decreasing fears about unauthorized youth entering the school). Jane, a sophomore, echoes this point when she says that things were "hectic with, like, all these *enforced* rules. . . . But I guess since there were some fights going on, [and the principal] had to do something about it." Nevertheless, she adds, "No one likes the rule that she has about not using the bathroom during class."

When Gabrielle, a freshman interviewed in late April, is asked whether rules were more strictly enforced after the fall semester, she hones in on the dress code: "Actually, the dress code hasn't been made more strict. That's a lie! Everyone says it, but the truth is, all they did was retype the old dress code and start enforcing it." Hearty laughter follows. Again, the students do not seem to be reacting to the creation of rules, but rather to the activation of the *consequences* for breaking those rules, which thus become more meaningful and tangible to those subject to their enforcement.

Instead of relying on rumors, Boomer gives more details on the "heavy consequences" latent in the newly enforced disciplinary process. He refers to his personal experience when asked whether he has noted any changes at the school in rules enforcement.

BOOMER: Well, they've started coming down on kids that, like, cut class a lot, that are late and things like that. We have to have on our IDs when we're in the classroom. If you don't have an ID on, it's an automatic write-up, or you have to go get a "temp." If you don't have the money for a temp, you have to get an IOU, and you have to pay that back within a week.

AUTHOR: How much is the temp?

BOOMER: It's a dollar.

The student "Code of Conduct" (known at the time as the "Uniform Discipline Code") designates specific punishments for specific infractions. Classroom misconduct seems to be "ground zero" for the imposition of zero-tolerance disciplinary measures; it is also exactly the kind of situation that might be better addressed by the tenets of procedural and restorative justice, in large part because such processes assure students that disciplinary actions are not arbitrary.

Consider Louie's story. Louie, a tall, husky, light-skinned freshman who identifies as mixed (White and African American), recounts an incident in which he got in trouble with a teacher and ended up being pulled from class and physically searched by a school security guard. Louie, who describes himself as a class clown, has a playful glint in his eyes as he expounds on his survey answers on youthful rebellion ("Oh, I can't do that? Sweet . . . I'm going to do it"), respect for police ("If you give respect, then you receive it. . . . And you can't really expect it just 'cuz you have this shiny badge thingy"), and interactions with school authorities.

Asked to explain why he strongly agrees with the survey statement, "My teachers punish kids without even knowing what happened," Louie recounts an incident that began early in the spring semester. A teacher for one of Louie's "regulars" classes—which, he says, has some of the "worst kids"—knew that he and his friend Channing could make a very distinct chirping noise like a bird.[74] The teacher did not know, however, that another student named Donovan could make the same noise. Louie reports that he and Channing were "written up" before having an opportunity to profess their innocence.[75]

At that time, the Uniform Discipline Code had no provisions giving students the right to tell their side of the story before being punished.[76] Louie says that he felt the ramifications even several weeks after "the chirping incident":

> The first day I come back from my spring vacation and walk in the classroom, Ms. Miller proclaims that I threw something at her. I just came in and sat down. Then, the security guard takes our whole row and the next row to the left of us out in the hallway. [The guard] makes us empty our pockets, searches us, and is like, "Where's all the coins?" And oh, it's really funny. My friend Mitch is like, "If we had coins, we must have already thrown 'em." (*laughs*) It didn't make any sense to search us. And then the security guard is like, "Okay, if I hear of you guys throwing anything again, I'm gonna send you all down to the police room." And that was really pointless.

Interviewed in late April, just after returning from spring vacation, Louie's memory of the interaction is still fresh. Louie's favorite descriptor is the word "pointless." He uses it nine times in an approximately forty-five-minute interview, usually to describe situations in which he believes that another person's behavior does not align with his expectations. For example, he saw police telling students to disperse from the bus stop outside the school, then not letting those students board the bus once it arrived.

Louie indicated on the survey that he has gotten into trouble at school more than five times and that his parents have had to be contacted. Asked for more details, he rattles off the list of infractions, which include "that penny thing [being searched for coins by the security guard], not turning work in, cutting class, getting into arguments with teachers, ummm, not having my ID—now that was really pointless—and being caught off-campus for lunch." Louie sees only two of his violations, the "education things" (cutting class and not turning in homework), as disciplinary matters worthy of punishment. And although Louie acknowledges that he was wrong to leave campus for lunch (only seniors have open lunch), he can rationalize that incident:

> Like, the lunchrooms, kids are in there screaming, throwing food, squirting people with apple juice. . . . It's real pointless. Going out is much more peaceful. You stay clean. . . . And some of the security is just lazy. They watch the kids throw food, and they just sit there. And it's like, you're security—you expect to see our IDs and we expect to feel safe here and not go home with grape stains on our shirt.

Louie strongly argues that the security guards should focus their energy on "big" problems instead of enforcing the rules about wearing ID. In his words, "When there's people getting beat up, getting jumped, getting stuff stolen, getting books stolen, failing classes because their books are gone, and they're tryna get you for not having your ID on—so pointless." And as Louie's peer Andre laments, "When we don't get the point of it, they just say, 'That's just the rules.'" As a result, both subjects and enforcers of the rules must accept them in the name of safety, regardless of whether they believe the rules are reasonable and effective.

At Harper, where the entire student population is African American, students' observations of and interactions with police and security guards happen almost entirely before they even enter school. Hunter describes his frustration with trying to get through the door. He mentions an instance when a security guard denied him admission based on a strict adherence to the uniform policy. The students at Tilden and Harper have a dress code of plain white shirts (polo-style or button-down) and black pants or skirts, to minimize signaling of both socioeconomic status and gang or neighborhood affiliation. Hunter has found the guards' enforcement of the code uneven:

> They be talking about, like, even if you got some black jeans, if they ain't black enough, you can't get in the door. Or if you got stripes or something through 'em, you can't get through the door. And sometimes they won't even let nobody else in, but they sometimes got they little favorites, so they'll let them in or something and they can go past and others can't. And that be messed up. Some people walk ten blocks from they house just to get here, and you turn them around and somebody else do it and you let them in the door. That ain't right.

Hunter, who seems wise beyond his years, admits that his black pants were faded from many, many washes. But his comments also reveal that he is assessing the security guards' legitimacy by closely watching the people who are supposed to be watching him and making note when they inconsistently enforce the rules.

His schoolmate Chris actually made it past the guards and into class while wearing his faded black pants, but still got in trouble, twice. Chris reports that his teacher told him that he "had to go to in-school suspension because I didn't have no uniform on." Chris concedes that his black pants "probably had faded away or something," but he did not report to "in-school" as ordered. As a result, the teacher called Chris's mother, who gave him a "talking-to." He says, "My mama told me to just come to school with my black pants, don't argue with the teacher, just go to class." Chris never had to serve the in-school suspension for that offense.[77]

High school students have always expressed their dissatisfaction and disillusionment with their school's disciplinary apparatus; after all, questioning authority is part of the developmental process of being a teenager. But the application of the carceral apparatus to urban high schools has changed the outcomes. Students who "misbehave" at CPS too often find themselves in contact with the police.

At CPS, the Office of Safety and Security is the locus of school-based security services.[78] The OSS has many major responsibilities, from developing and managing all safety and security efforts in Chicago public schools to placing and training school-based security staff. The OSS also monitors *and shares* school surveillance feeds with the Chicago Police Department, proudly highlighting this service as the "24-7 hub of communications between Chicago Public Schools Administration, Chicago Public Schools, the Chicago Police Department and the Chicago Fire Department."[79] The OSS touts its responsibility for "supporting schools and principals in installing, maintaining, and troubleshooting 8,000+ cameras, 500+ alarm systems, 150+ X-ray machines, 300+ metal detectors, 400+ door entry systems, and 35 bus trackers."[80] Within the schools, the OSS employs both full-time and part-time "uniformed on-duty Chicago police officers to "support a stable environment" and provide a flexible response. Security guards (some of whom are off-duty police officers) carry out most security functions, but the police officers have arrest authority.

Although some Lincoln Park students mention that they have seen other kids handcuffed or arrested inside the school, none of them have ever had any "official" contact with school police—that is, none of them have been stopped, searched, or arrested in school. Janet's response highlights the unfamiliarity of the majority of the Lincoln Park students with school police. Generally, they know that school police exist, but they never have much interaction with them. "I've only seen a police officer like once or twice this year," Janet says. "I know there's a place that is kinda like a police office, like . . . if there was this one person that got in trouble or hurt someone really bad in a fight, they would just handcuff him until the other police officers came. I don't know. I just heard that there was like this cell here or something. I don't know."

This finding in itself suggests something about the sample, since the Lincoln Park students are a more racially diverse group than the students at the other three schools—that is, more White, Hispanic, and Asian American students attend Lincoln Park and are included in the study. It is noteworthy that the only two male students in this small sample who self-identify as African American have had unofficial interactions with school police officers.

Several blocks south, at Payton Prep, Darrell, an African American student, is quickly reminded of the police officers at his school when answering my initial query on his general feelings about police. Darrell believes that the male officer "does his job and everything, but doesn't make it feel like he's being unfair. But the other one, it just seems like she's corrupt or something." He then acknowledges that "corrupt" may be "too strong a word," but it is clear that this school-assigned officer has influenced his overall negative perception of police officers. Darrell recounts being stopped by her twice, once while inside the school and once outside for "making an exchange of money." Darrell says that both times he was only exchanging dollars for coins with a person of another race, but the police officer suspected him of selling drugs. After pondering this admission a bit, Darrell reveals that he understands why the school police officer could have been suspicious of his behavior. Still, he says, "it just didn't seem right to [search me], and I don't see that it would happen to all races." Darrell adds that attending Payton Prep has given him his first chance to see "police officers at school who are actually assigned to the school," in keeping with citywide CPS policy to have two officers assigned to each high school.

Jackson, who attends Tilden Career Community Academy, has also come in contact with the police at school, through a general weapons sweep. Jackson professes his innocence, telling me that he was comfortable with the extensive search because it made him feel safer. Not every student attending a school known for having "safety issues," however, feels more comfortable in the presence of police. Dewayne, for instance, describes an encounter with police he observed at Harper High that would shape his perceptions of police officers' fairness and legitimacy:

DEWAYNE: The police in this school, they jumped on one of my brothers. Put him in handcuffs. You know, they take him in the interrogation room, put you in handcuffs; they start gettin' uppity at the little boy. Soon as you say, "I didn't do this," they hittin' you, know what I'm saying. They talk to you like you one of them, like you a grown man or something, that's how they treat ya.

AUTHOR: And this is in school you're saying?

DEWAYNE: In school, in the interrogation room. Told you, they treat you just like it's prison. They got more police officers around here than they do security guards. All the security guards is off-duty policemen. Then you got security guards out[side] like this a prison or something. . . . I feel it's necessary and it's unnecessary. It's necessary in case a fight break out. It's unnecessary for the police to be hawking students like that, saying, "Get off the premises." Maybe people got after-school activities they gotta do, know what I'm saying.

In further discussion, Dewayne connects his brother's interaction with police inside the school to his own experiences of being searched by the police in his neighborhood (discussed in more detail in the next chapter). Both incidents have reinforced his strong perception of criminal injustice. And as the interview proceeds, it is apparent that Dewayne has been thinking about these issues for a long time. He has an air of maturity that stems from having experienced a lot in his young years, including, as a self-professed "demo" (demoted student), the experience of repeating ninth grade. It is clear that he has been thinking critically about much more than his GPA.

AUTHOR: So tell me why you're bored in school even though you say it's academically challenging.

DEWAYNE: Like I said, it feel like we in jail. We ain't getting more experience like back then when y'all was going to high school. Things was more fun. . . . Like, people said high school supposed to be your last experiences of school, and it don't feel like it's our last experience of school [like something special], it feel like another day to them. You know what I'm saying?

AUTHOR: So you mean people aren't made to enjoy it?

DEWAYNE: People aren't made to enjoy and learn at the same time. You come here to learn, but at the same time you come here to enjoy it. They try to make us learn more than we enjoy. . . . They too serious about stuff. They don't give the kids no leniency. If they gave them more leniency, the kids would appreciate the school, the test scores would be higher, and [kids] wouldn't be acting the way they act.

The current structure and culture of urban public education is socializing young people to interact with agents of the law inside their schools, thereby conditioning them to be ready to interact with police outside the schoolhouse doors, not as students but as suspects. The socialization process can also happen, however, in reverse. Keisha responds to a general question about security guards and police by describing her positive relationship with a school-based police officer that was a direct result of interactions with the same officer in her housing project:

KEISHA: The security guards? They straight here. It's like, I see 'em and don't see 'em. But the police officers, the lady, I know her from the [housing] project, so she real cool. She straight. I don't like police officers, though.

AUTHOR: Why? You like her.

KEISHA: 'Cuz they too strict. It's only certain people that I just like. I don't like too many people, and I'll let 'em know. I keep it real with 'em.

AUTHOR: Does your good relationship with the female police officer here have an influence on your ideas about the police in general?

KEISHA: Uh. (*shakes head, signaling "no"*)

Keisha describes herself as very antisocial, and it is most likely that it is only her contact with the particular female officer in two domains, both at home and at school, that has allowed their positive relationship to develop. However, that is where Keisha's kind words about the police end. The positive relationship she has cultivated with one police officer has not changed her general notions about the police (nor has the presence of the security guard).

Jasmine, a student at Tilden, gives a more detailed account of her positive relations with police in school and explains the impact of those relationships on her general assessment of the police. She calls one of the officers at school her "uncle" because he looks after her and keeps the boys from "messing" with her. Jasmine goes on to say that her positive impression of this officer makes her view other police officers more positively. This is not true for one African American male in my sample, who does not extend his positive interactions with specific officers to his general impression of police. Boomer sees the police officers at Lincoln Park High as surrogate fathers, even calling them "Pops," and he believes the same is true for many other students "who don't have fathers at home." He describes his relationship with these officers:

> BOOMER: I'm very close with them. I go in the [police officers'] office almost every day. And they ask, "Are you stayin' out of trouble?" "Yes, I'm stayin' out of trouble, I'm goin' to my class, I'm doing this and I'm doin' that." So they, like, really stay on me, like tough, and then they know my mom. And umm, I don't see them really hassle any of the other students, but they're more strict towards African American students than they are anybody else.
>
> AUTHOR: Are they African American?
>
> BOOMER: They are African American. And my only reason for saying that they are more strict with us is because they want to see us succeed. And they know we can't succeed without an education, so they really stay on us real hard. They roughed a couple of students up. I've been roughed up before by them, and I can take it. But some of the other students, they can't take it.

Boomer voluntarily visits Lincoln Park High's "police room" specifically to maintain his close relationship with the African American officers assigned to the school. He also describes their informal methods of discipline, which he believes they use to ensure that African American male students do not take a negative direction under their watch. If one of the officers thinks that Boomer (or any other African American student) is behaving badly, he will "rough him up" instead of formally disciplining him, through what I term a kind of "friendly fire"—between officers and civilians in this instance, rather than between officers. And in fact, Boomer's testimony is not surprising: other research reveals that most juveniles who have contact with police are diverted rather than arrested or taken into custody.[81] The research also shows that these diversions most often happen when the police officer shares the racial identity of the potential arrestee.[82]

Lincoln Park, with its diverse student body, provides an expanded vantage point from which Boomer can explicitly compare the school-based officers' stricter treatment of Black youth to their treatment of students of other races. He is comfortable with his assessment because he believes that the officers have a racially vested interest in seeing Black males like him succeed. At the same time, he believes that the police in general interact with civilians differently depending on their race:

> Not trying to sound racist, but I look at the Black police officers more differently than I do the White ones. I know I would connect more with a Black police officer before I would a White police officer. And not only because of the race, but my mom is an ex-cop, my father is a sheriff. So when the officers are talking to me, I can just see my dad doing that. And then [my parents] tell me about how the White cops were racist toward them when they were going through the academy and stuff like that. So I just feel like it hasn't changed today.

Although he treads lightly around the idea that he might be racist himself, we see that race definitely plays a role in Boomer's willingness to establish friendly relations with any police officer. His "connection" with the African American school-based police officers makes even more sense once Boomer shares that both of his parents worked in law enforcement. Boomer also takes pride in and is protective toward his relationship with the Black police officers at his school. He recounts the time he "got into it" with a White officer at the school who tried to stop him from just walking into the office, without knocking, to greet the Black officers, as he routinely did every day.

> We had a White cop upstairs, and I'm just used to walking in the police office. You know, no questions asked or anything like that. And he was sittin' at the officers' desk, and I walked in and he said, "What the hell are you doing?" "Coming to speak to Mr. J. and Mr. H." "Well, you know, you have to knock." And then Mr. J said, like, "Well, you know, he's cool, he can come in whenever he want." The White officer was like, "I don't feel that's right." Well, I can't help what you feel 'cuz this is not your office. And that's what I told him: "This is not your office." Now, if Mr. J or Mr. H told me to do other, I'd do other. But this ain't your office, so you really can't tell me nothing.

Boomer was able to ignore the directives of the White officer without suffering any consequences because he had established such a friendly, almost familial, relationship with the African American officers. Moreover, Boomer saw the Black officer overrule his colleague, and that interaction probably further diminished any modicum of respect Boomer had for the White officer. It is refreshing to hear about strong positive relationships fostered between school police officers and the students they "protect and serve"; at least in this case, however, that strong attachment has not yet moved across racial lines or beyond the school walls.

Any analysis of the development of youths' perceptions of criminal injustice must acknowledge this relationship between police officers and their function of providing a safe and secure environment. Students experience a "soft bigotry of low expectations" or "unilateral suspicion" that can precipitate their interactions with police in schools, even if they have not misbehaved.[83] Andre, an African American sophomore at Lincoln Park, has not experienced any official stops, searches, or arrests by police, but he still holds a high perception of racialized criminal injustice. On being asked whether he has ever interacted with the police officers in his school, he responds:

ANDRE: Yeah, like the one that's by my math room. Like, he's really cool. We just go there and we just say hi. He said, "How come you never get in trouble?" I'm like, "That's not me. I don't get in trouble."

AUTHOR: He said that?

ANDRE: Yeah, he said that. "How come you never get in trouble?" I don't get in trouble. I try not to get in trouble.

AUTHOR: Do you think having a friendly relationship with him makes your opinion about police more favorable in general?

ANDRE: A little bit more favorable. If you get along with that person, it's cool. . . . But I view him as an individual. On his personality, not other cops, 'cuz I don't think every cop's the same way.

Andre believes that he has been doing the right thing by staying out of trouble with the police inside and outside the school, but he still finds himself questioned by the officer about why he is *not* exhibiting non-normative behavior. Andre opines on the police view of youth: "Other cops, they seem to think, like, the kids today are gonna be in trouble or gonna get into trouble *soon.*" Since these police officers apparently see "trouble" as an inevitable destination for these youth, Andre looks like an anomaly to them.

The positive inroads that school-based police officers can make toward improving police-community relations are obvious. Nonetheless, it is distressing to see how their presence can also further marginalize, alienate, and criminalize young people.

Conclusion

Amicable informal relations between police and youth can increase rule compliance, decrease disciplinary action, and change students' assessments of police officers, even if they do not extend their more positive estimation beyond the individual officer. Negative interactions can make students cynical about the police and security guards and create a sense of criminal injustice, which varies by school and neighborhood.

The actual criminalization of the students in this study varies in important ways, particularly for those students on the tail ends of the racial-spatial divide. Students at the South Side schools are more likely to have had extensive contacts with police, but they are also better able to reconcile those contacts, both warranted and unwarranted (that is, contacts in which they were searched and not arrested), with their hope that officers will ensure their safety inside and outside of school. In particular, the students with low perceptions of injustice *and* experiences with police searches are African American and attend either Tilden or Harper (except for John, a White male at Payton). Their responses to invasive contact with the police range from indifference to incredulity about the possibility that police searches could be discriminatory. Conversely, the students who have had no personal police contacts but who do have high perceptions of injustice sometimes have had strong vicarious experiences. Their perceptions of injustice have been shaped by their experiences, both personal and vicarious, with police and security guards in their school environments.

A universal carceral apparatus in which all schools have police officers, legions of security guards, metal detectors, and so on, is not the best use of the scarce economic resources allocated to public schools. In the decade that I have been studying the Chicago public schools, the security functions have become more expansive and expensive. The 2014 CPS budget was approximately $5.6 billion, with the OSS spending $97.7 million on 1,200 positions.[84] Whatever its actual effectiveness in establishing school safety, it is abundantly clear that the presence of so much security in schools is socializing students to prisonlike conditions. Students perceive social control to be supplanting what should be a school's main focus: education.

Moreover, students' education does not stop at the schoolhouse door. These adolescents' ambivalence about the presence and purpose of police in their schools is quite clear. Some Harper High students are asking for more police officers, more security guards, more surveillance, and more protection, even when they recognize that these requests may very well put them in greater contact with police. At the opposite end of the continuum we have

Payton Prep, a school whose beautiful facade matches the safety and order within its walls.

There is great nuance in students' assessments of the jobs performed by security guards and police officers inside their schools, and there is also great variation in the relationships that emerge from these contacts. The following chapter will take us outside the schoolhouse to further explore young people's perceptions of injustice and their contact with police in their neighborhoods and in the public sphere.

CHAPTER 5

To Serve and Protect?

I think the kids feel like if they do something bad, they think they gon' get a whipping by their parents, but sometimes they get locked up by the police. This affects [their] life because they already have experienced what adults would experience. I think the child should have their childhood and not be having it taken away just by one little incident.

—Shay, African American ninth-grader,
Tilden Career Community Academy

The mission of the Chicago Police Department is prominently emblazoned in bright blue letters on the side of every police car: WE SERVE AND PROTECT. The Chicago youth in this study know these are the purported aims of the city's police force, but they differ significantly in their beliefs as to whether serving and protecting is what the police actually do. Terry trusts the police, wishes there were more of them in his Washington Park neighborhood, and would call them in a heartbeat if he felt threatened; Andrea, his schoolmate, thinks that the police are corrupt, racist, and best avoided at all costs. The variable of perceived injustice is a way of capturing these different attitudes.

These divergent attitudes toward police are not random, but rather are dependent on race, gender, class, and the combination of school- and neighborhood-specific factors. Students' perceptions of policing and surveillance inside their schools are directly related to their beliefs about the presence and strategies of police officers in their residential neighborhoods. As young people journey to and from school, across the racial-spatial divide, their various experiences with police inform their opinions about police. If they travel farther along the racial-spatial divide, their bases for comparison expand, and if they remain in their racially isolated residential neighborhoods for school, their frame of comparison remains limited. Either way, these vantage points reveal much about what Chicago youth think and feel about a critical organizing feature of their lives—the presence and practices of Chicago police.

To make sense of the historical, contextual, and spatial dimensions of the relationship between race, gender, age, and criminal sanctions, we must consider the treatment of young people and their reconciliation of their experiences, particularly with legal authorities, outside of school. These interactions matter because they may serve as a transition or "turning point" that has a negative impact on a young person's life trajectory. Being stopped and questioned, physically searched for drugs or weapons, or arrested for a legitimate reason by the police can spell an early "exit from adolescence." These experiences mark the "adultification" of young people—a process that transitions some of them to the realm of adultlike experiences, responsibilities, and consequences owing to their identity or behavior. The uneven experience of adultification along the racial-spatial divide demands close analysis. Research clearly shows that adolescents' experiences of physical violence catapult them into adulthood, with detrimental psychological and social effects, but it is also important to evaluate evidence on whether the experience of symbolic violence does the same.[1]

As we have seen in the previous chapter, urban youth are already experiencing significant contact with police in their schools. Many of them also frequently encounter police in their neighborhoods. What they see shapes their willingness to call, help, or even tolerate the police. This chapter discusses how youth evaluate police effectiveness; the spectrum of their perceptions of racialized criminal injustice; and finally, how adolescents' interactions with police socialize them to think like adults—specifically, like criminally compliant adults.

Assessing Police Performance: Effectiveness, Efficiency, and Equity

Police exist to protect people and property, at least in theory.[2] It is important that police perform these two duties in a manner that protects the legitimacy of the institution and satisfies the community. Police functions depend on citizen cooperation, and public cooperation depends on whether residents view the police as legitimate. My assessments of adolescents' perceptions of criminal injustice suggest that this is not always the case. There is a complex interaction between race, gender, school context, and community context that shapes citizens' perceptions of police.

Several students in the study simply have a jaded view of the police without ever having personally experienced contact with them (Gabrielle, Brianna, and Pink). These students see police officers as only interested in "getting a paycheck" or protecting and serving the public "when they have time to." Angelique, a Hispanic student attending Lincoln Park High who ranks low on the racialized perception of injustice scale, believes that police are sometimes guilty of abandoning their mission to serve and protect. Instead, she believes, "they do what they want because they have guns and can arrest you for little things."

Other students are more willing to give the police the benefit of the doubt. Three Payton Prep male students of color, Alex, Darrell, and Freddy, say that even though the police may not be performing the job at their best, at least they are doing something to "protect the community" and "make the streets safe." John, one of their Payton classmates, even rationalizes the police stopping and searching him and his friends the prior Halloween, after acknowledging that they were targeted only because they were teenagers. The interaction began, he says, when "the police said, 'What are you kids doing out so late? Why are you causing trouble?' Something like that."

AUTHOR: So, did they find anything?

JOHN: No.

AUTHOR: What did they say once they didn't find anything?

JOHN: "Go home. It's past curfew."

AUTHOR: What did you think about that? Or how did it make you feel?

JOHN: I don't know. I guess you can't really count Halloween because it's likely that we *were* carrying eggs (*to throw at people and homes*). I'm saying, like, police, they're not annoyed with the murders, you know. A good cop would want to find a murderer. But they don't want to waste their time with, like, kids throwing eggs. It's dumb. So I didn't mind it.

AUTHOR: Have those interactions with the police made your opinion about them more positive, more negative, or didn't change it?

JOHN: [Those experiences] didn't change it. Just family, friends, and TV.

John's opinions about police have been shaped more by the experiences of his family and friends, he says, and by what he sees and reads in the newspapers, than by his personal experiences with police, which include being told to move on while out past curfew in the encounter described here. Notably, John, a student at Payton Prep and the only White male in the study, was not stopped and searched by the police for drugs or weapons—the experience of the other students who shared his level of police contact. His one invasive contact with police, being searched for eggs on Halloween, did not strongly shape his perceptions of injustice. Even so, the experience did affect John's perception of police efficiency, since he thinks they were "wasting their time" searching for eggs when they could have been out doing real police work like "finding a murderer."

It is striking that students often recount seeing police who are not focused on what they are supposed to be doing and who sometimes do not follow the rules they are tasked with enforcing. Whether it is "roughing people up" in the neighborhood, as Keisha says happens "everywhere she goes" between home and school (although Keisha does not leave her neighborhood too often), or "corrupt" police "not doing [their] job by co-signing or flipping sides," as Shay recounts during her interview, students pay close attention to these abuses of authority. Multiple students note small offenses—such as police officers not following traffic rules or having nothing better to do than stop and search people for no reason in hopes of finding contraband—that diminish their legitimacy. Shay tells me that she has both seen and heard about one corrupt practice in particular: "Police be taking drug money from dealers when it's close to Christmas, letting them finish what they gotta do, taking the money and saying like, 'Oh, this [is] my Christmas money.'. . . Police supposed to take you *and* your money, lock you up, and turn that money in."

Police have great powers of coercion during encounters with citizens, ranging from the verbal to the physical.[3] When young people observe police using *and* abusing those powers, their perceptions of police effectiveness and equity are eroded. When asked why she believes that "police think 'all youth are bad,'" Rina, a petite, soft-spoken African American student at Harper High who wants to become a lawyer, responds:

> I see, like, every day . . . police harm teenagers my age. They even shoot 'em or just arrest 'em. Police, I think they crazy, because they know what they can do. They know with the authority that they have . . . they just take advantage of [their] authority, and that's not right. When you young, they think you need to be taught a lesson. Everybody needs to be taught a lesson, but that's not the way you teach a person a lesson, like, by beating [him or her] up or something . . . shooting at 'em. . . . You know? That's not right.

Although Rina brings up the potential of actual violence at the hands of police, her response should also be understood through the lens of symbolic violence. Students notice the authority given to police officers, in both their neighborhoods and their schools, and they either consciously or unconsciously recognize their potential domination by the police on the basis of their race, gender, and, increasingly, their age.

These kinds of situations in which the police seem to be exceeding their authority affect students' perceptions of police whether they happen inside or outside of school. When asked whether she has had any interactions with police, Rina recounts the following incident, which happened right outside Harper High. The incident did much to shape her assessments of police when she encounters them now elsewhere in public:

Rina: No, I just see 'em when they do what they supposed to [do]. Like when kids fight outside school, they break it up. One time a police just, like, really manhandled this girl, and I don't think they had to do all that. That's too much, but that's [their] job, and we can't say too much about it.

Author: What do you mean you can't say anything about it?

Rina: I mean, what we gon' say? "*Stop*"? We can't say, "Stop doing that to her!" We can't say that 'cuz who are we to tell them how to do [their] job?

Author: Do you think the police have a lot of authority?

Rina: Yeah, I really do. They run stoplights. They just pull us over for no reason. We got pulled over, like, last week—me, my mom, and my [female] cousin. The police say they stopped us because some people were shooting out of a blue car, but we were in a green car. And the police, the White man, he was like, "It's blue enough." How you get light green from blue? He says, "It's blue enough." And it was a White policeman and a Black one. And the Black one was like, "You know, well, since we don't know who did it, we gon' let y'all go." Why would we shoot? I'm riding with my mother, why would we . . . we don't even own a gun.

Pierre Bourdieu's explanation of symbolic capital and violence is instructive in understanding the plight of these students.[4] Police are granted symbolic capital by the authority imbued in their official uniform and badge. The most powerful component of this dynamic is that, as Bourdieu puts it, "objective relations of power tend to reproduce themselves in relations of symbolic power."[5] These young people are marginalized by virtue of being minors, and they become complicit in their own domination insofar as their "cognitive landscapes" are shaped by their place on the racial-spatial divide (or put more simply, by their social worlds). From the knowledge embedded in her system of meaning, Rina clearly condemns the wrongful behaviors of certain police, but she feels powerless to speak out against them.

Even as students can recount stories of police abuse, however, some admit that there have been times when they wanted the police to come—to defuse a situation, to provide security, or to stop a crime. Community context plays a major role in students' estimations of police responsiveness to their calls for help and the frequency of police patrols. A majority of the students at Harper, most of whom live within two miles of their South Side school, believe that most police officers, though not all, do not care about their neighborhood. They are particularly disappointed by how police fulfill the "protect" part of their mission to "serve and protect." Students at Tilden and Lincoln Park offer a mix of positive and negative assessments on police service; unlike their peers at Harper, many of them differentiate their school-based evaluations from their various residential neighborhood–based assessments of police. Students at Payton, whose population comes from across the city, exhibit no distinct pattern except that the African American students are less satisfied with police service. Students' recountings of having observed firsthand different levels of police patrols and service in more-advantaged neighborhoods are especially compelling and persuasive in understanding how these observations shape their perceptions of injustice.

John, the only White male in the study, thinks that police may respond more quickly to crime in his mostly White Northwest Side neighborhood in comparison to a predominantly Black or Hispanic poor neighborhood. I ask him whether police care about the neighborhood where he lives. He replies by noting that, since there is relatively little crime in his neighborhood, "there's not much for them to do. But if there was a murder or something serious in my neighborhood, because it's so unlikely, I think they'd be more willing to respond than in a worse neighborhood if there's like a gang shooting. . . . It goes back to the whole thing where initially police helped rich people because they were very corrupt." John, who is very class-conscious in his beliefs about Chicago's status hierarchy and in his answers regarding perceptions of injustice (he strongly agrees, for instance, with the statement "Police treat rich people better than poor people"), perceives himself to be privileged that police would be much more likely to respond to violence quickly in his mostly White neighborhood on the Northwest Side of the city than they would elsewhere.

In contrast, several students who live in more economically disadvantaged neighborhoods believe that they do not receive high levels of service from the police. Terry feels unsafe in his neighborhood because the police ride through it only once a day. Yet their constant presence at his school, Tilden Career Community Academy, makes him think that they care about the neighborhood that surrounds the school. Terry's wish for a more extensive police presence might seem surprising, but at Tilden he sees the police as a calming presence that prevents physical violence against him and other Black students. In fact, many other students—including Terry's Tilden classmates Dre, Jasmine, and Mike—share his wish, saying that they simply want the same level of service delivery in their home neighborhoods as they see in their school context.

Hunter shares the belief of some other students that the delayed response to emergencies in his neighborhood is confirmation that the police do not care about him, people like him, or even the communities in which they reside.

HUNTER: If you go in a White neighborhood, now you see all these White people and everybody walking, police gon' drive past. Now, you get two Black boys walking into a White neighborhood, you gon' have all the police right there around 'em.

AUTHOR: Have you seen that happen before?

HUNTER: Yes, I have.

AUTHOR: In which neighborhood?

HUNTER: Out west.

AUTHOR: So, if you wander into a White neighborhood . . .?

HUNTER: You gon' have a problem. You gon' have somebody peeking out the window like, "We got a couple of Black people out here. They probably start trouble. Betta' come get 'em." [The police say,] "Okay, we'll be out there." Call the police out here in my neighborhood. . . . You say somebody just got shot, it take 'em almost an hour.

To convey how he thinks the report to the police from the White neighborhood would sound, a very animated Hunter raises his voice several pitches to speak with a warbled tone, as if he were an elderly White woman making such a call. He also motions as if he were peering out of a living room window from behind heavy curtains. This is how Hunter conceives how, and for whom, police service requests are made and fulfilled in a place only marginally distant from him in actual miles but worlds apart socially.

Jackson, who lives in the Southeast Side neighborhood of Grand Boulevard, states that the differential response across types of neighborhoods "is not fair." He believes that if police officers truly cared, "they'd be in the neighborhood every ten minutes, 'cuz there's always something going on." Jackson's wish for more patrols in his neighborhood reflects his safety concerns and echoes his earlier calls for additional security and police officers in his school (Tilden). His sentiments are similar to those of other students who want more police inside and outside both Tilden and Harper High because of their fear of crime and violence in those settings.

As might be expected given their varied opinions on police reliability and effectiveness, the students are divided on the question of whether they would be comfortable calling the police for help. In the interviews, one-third of the students explain their level of comfort with calling the police for help at length. Only three of them—Angelique, Freddy, and Mike—are willing to call the police if they have a problem. The other nine students, all African American or Hispanic, give examples of times they called on police for help but ended up feeling that they were neither protected nor served in the manner they deserved. Harper student Rina has an instructive account of calling the police after someone shot into her South Side home:

RINA: I don't like the police. I don't trust them. Like when we call the police, they not on time. And they [are] the police, they supposed to be on time and they never on time.

AUTHOR: So have there been instances where you've had to call them for help and . . .?

RINA: Yeah, because somebody had, like, shot in our house or something. When we got home and called the police, it took the police like an hour [to get there]. And they kept calling like, "We on our way, we on our way." And when they get there, they wanna question us like they think we know the person who did it. Nine times outta ten we don't really know who would shoot in our house.

Rina is not comfortable with the thought of having to rely on police to help her because she has had the experience of police not coming when she needed them. She also did not like the way the officers questioned her once they did arrive. The police officers were probably asking questions they would have asked any other victims of a crime, but their tardy appearance may have negatively affected the way Rina and her family responded. Several other African American and Hispanic students tell stories of the police coming thirty minutes to three hours after they were called, a response that has made them less willing to call the police for help and to rely on police protection in the future. Amber, an African American ninth-grader at Payton who lives on the West Side and has been stopped by the police before, has become unwilling to call police for help in an emergency. She believes that police patrol her neighborhood, not to keep residents safe, but to "see if it's drug dealers there on the corner." In an emergency, she says, it would "take them forever to get there. You might call them at seven, they won't come till eleven." Questioned further, Amber says that this has in fact happened to her.

AMBER: Like when one time my uncle [and] them was fighting, and my great-grandma stay downstairs from me, and he was aggravating them, and they called the police on him, and they didn't come till like three hours later. He had been long gone by then.

AUTHOR: So how does that make you view the police in general?

AMBER: They do what they wanna do. What they feel is important.

AUTHOR: So when they say their motto is to "protect and serve," do you think they're accomplishing that?

AMBER: No. They protect and serve when they have time to.

I found a strong correspondence between students' comfort with calling on the police for help and their willingness to help the police. All of the students who have a low perception of racialized injustice—none of whom have ever had any personal police contact—state that they would be willing to aid the police if asked. That being said, external pressure in the form of the social prohibition against "snitching" on others might reduce the likelihood that these students would voluntarily help the police should a situation arise, no matter where they fall on the matrix of perceptions of injustice and police contact.[6]

Most of the ninth- and tenth-graders in this study are aware of the potentially harmful repercussions of aiding the police in identifying criminal offenders in their neighborhoods. For some, the nature of the offense in question would determine their cooperation. For instance, John states that he is willing to point someone out or help police if it is about something minor. But Darrell, John's schoolmate at Payton Prep, says the exact opposite. Darrell says that he would consider helping the police on a serious matter, but not if "it was like just some misdemeanor. . . . Plus, it wouldn't be right to point somebody out from your neighborhood." Other students are willing to help in what may be a "middle territory" for offense categories. For instance, Terry says that he once described a drug dealer who ran past him to police, and Keisha has described some boys her boyfriend "got into it with" to the police.

Several other students with high perceptions of injustice and/or some previous police contact speak at length about the possibility that if they helped the police, either the officers would tell suspected offenders that they had given up their names or other witnesses would see them talking to the police and tip the offender off. These students worry that the suspected offenders would discover their identity and that they would then be subject to harmful reprisals. Amber says that she was recently stopped and asked questions by police about a violent crime she witnessed in her West Side neighborhood.

AMBER: This girl got shot right in front of my house. And we was walking and looking to see what happened. Then the police was just like, "Go by, it ain't nothin' to see."

AUTHOR: Did they question you at that same time or was that a different time?

AMBER: That was the same time, because I was right outside when it happened. It was about two or three months ago. . . .

AUTHOR: So, were you willing to help them at that time, to tell them—

AMBER: (*interrupting*) Nope! Unn unn [no].

AUTHOR: You didn't tell them anything?

AMBER: I didn't know nothin'! I say I saw her get shot, but didn't see who did it. . . . 'Cuz in the neighborhood, things spread around, and it's best to leave yo' business yours, and other people's business their business. It's more like for your safety instead of telling everybody else business. [You] betta' keep your mouth closed and move on.

AUTHOR: Even if you had seen the person who did it, you wouldn't have told them anyway?

AMBER: Unn unn [no]. I would [have] kept quiet.

Like many other students with a strong racialized perception of injustice, Amber is unwilling to help the police, and after experiencing their slow response to a family member's domestic incident, she is not confident about calling them for help. The consequences of helping police, especially in a serious matter like a shooting, are too risky.

Jackson talks about the harm of snitching, not on alleged offenders, but on the crooked cops in his neighborhood. He tells me that he has observed the "police picking up hookers, but we can't call 9-1-1 on them. . . . If they find out you tricked [snitched] on them, they'll find any way to give you a ticket, arrest you, or tow your car." Jackson even attends community policing meetings in his neighborhood, but he has not revealed his information because he "can't tell who to trust or whether they a good cop or bad cop." He also wants to suggest to the city some additional locations in his neighborhood to install cameras (similar to suggestions he has given to his principal on where to place school security cameras), but he believes that they probably would not listen to him or accept his suggestions. Jackson's earnest attempts to participate as a fully realized citizen, in both his neighborhood and school communities, show the possible benefits of truly incorporating young people and their ideas into the decisionmaking on policies and procedures. The experiences and perceptions of all the young people included in this study also highlight the risk of incurring their disengagement and cynicism by ignoring them.

The student experiences recounted here have larger consequences for their understanding of justice and their relations with authority figures. These experiences with police have the power to transform their understandings of justice from something that is incident-specific into a more wide-ranging assessment of authority figures, from parents to teachers to future employers, as well as the laws they enforce. The impact of these contacts across each teen's life is fairly profound.

Perceptions of Police Officers' Racial Biases and Other Biases

The students have doubts in general about how effective the police are in protecting them, but they also have very specific opinions about how police behavior is affected by race, gender, and age—of both the suspects and the cops. Race is a particularly critical variable that affects young people's assessment of police officers' behaviors and interactions; indeed, they often identified an officer's race without prompt or inquiry. As we shall see, their personal and vicarious experiences reveal why they have good reason to be concerned about police officers' biases, racial and otherwise.

Several students told me that police operate with race-, age-, and gender-based stereotypes, a belief that leaves them feeling less empowered. Andrea, an African American ninth-grader at Tilden who lives in a housing project on the State Street Corridor in the Bronzeville neighborhood (one of the two projects still standing after the Chicago Housing Authority's "Plan for Transformation" was implemented), recounts several neighborhood- and home-based incidents that have shaped and reinforced her negative perceptions of police.

> AUTHOR: Tell me why you think that police are more likely to stop people from your racial group.
>
> ANDREA: In my neighborhood, like, if you have on some baggy pants, a T-shirt, and a do-rag, they'll think you a crackhead or a gangbanger. If you don't stay down there [in my housing project], they'll quickly arrest you for trespassing. Or if you drinking outside, they'll arrest you. Anything they see you doing wrong, they think they have to arrest you for it. . . . You could just be walking and they'll stop and harass you, asking you questions like, "Where you going? Who you ride up under?" and stuff like that.
>
> AUTHOR: Who you ride up under?
>
> ANDREA: Who you ride up under. Like, what gang you ride up under.
>
> AUTHOR: The police will ask that?
>
> ANDREA: Umm hum (*nodding head "yes"*).
>
> AUTHOR: Now, do you think if a White person was dressed in baggy clothes, would that person be stopped and asked questions? Do you think they'd be treated the same way if they were dressed in that manner?
>
> ANDREA: No.
>
> AUTHOR: Why not?
>
> ANDREA: They won't.

Andrea is quite resolute in her response. Further probing does not elicit further theories as to why this should be the case, but Andrea brings up both race (whiteness) and location (her neighborhood) when elaborating on her racialized perceptions of criminal injustice. Her vicarious and personal contacts with the police, including being searched but not arrested three to five times in the past year, perhaps explain her negative attitude:

AUTHOR: The survey shows you've been told to move on by the police and stopped and asked questions. What were the instances when that happened?

ANDREA: Like, okay, if there [have] been like a lot of shootings, police don't care who you are, you can be little, they'll tell, like, little kids stuff like, "Go find your mama and go in the house," or something like that. Or like, if you standing around while they arresting people, they'll tell you to "Get the [*expletive*] on or move out the way." They'll try to run you over, curse you out, throw you on the car if you say anything smart to them, they gon' take you around the corner somewhere and probably try to beat you up. Or they'll, umm, take you to, like, their jail and write you up, make you have a court date.

AUTHOR: So have you seen that happen to other people or has it happened to you?

This follow-up question immediately prompts Andrea to recount an incident when her mother, a Chicago Housing Authority maintenance worker, was stopped and searched by the police:

Like, one day my mama was coming from work, and she had on her uniform and stuff. [The police] thought she was a crackhead 'cuz she was coming out of one of the buildings and they made her put her hands on the car and they asked her where she just got through doing her dope. And by her working outside where we stay at [live], she had leaves and like little drug papers and stuff in her plastic bag. My mama tried to tell them that she wasn't no crackhead and that she was working. . . . Police [will] just harass any and everybody. They don't care if you a worker, a parent, a teacher, or nothing. They'll still curse you out. Like, just because they got a badge they think they higher authority. But if [police] want respect from other people, you gotta give respect and they don't show it.

Andrea's personal and vicarious experiences of unwarranted searches have unquestionably shaped her attitudes toward the police. Moreover, her low-level contacts with police (being told to move on while in and around her very own apartment building) have also been instructive. It is no surprise that she strongly registers her feelings on the survey and in the interview that she does not trust or respect police, that the police make her feel afraid, and that she believes that police do not care about her neighborhood and are not fair. Her schoolmate Shay, who also attends Tilden High, shares similar observations from her housing project, framed by her belief that police are only doing their job about one-third of the time:

SHAY: They supposed to serve and protect all the time. They only serve one out of three times. Serve and protect one out of three times.

AUTHOR: And what are they doing the other times? How would you describe that?

SHAY: The other times, if a woman gets hit by a man, they'll help you. Other than that, kids fighting, they'll stop and break it up, you know, tell them they can't do this or they'll be arrested. I personally think they treat the children like criminals more than they do the adults.

AUTHOR: Tell me why you say that.

SHAY: I say this because they are so quick and willing to, you know, lock the kids up, 'cuz we can't really defend ourselves. We can't really say nothing. People think kids are nothing, we ain't got nothing. They look at us like, oh, we don't have no rights. Children have rights too! I know we bad and all. We don't do everything we supposed to do, but we do have rights. We don't deserve to be getting handcuffed just because we was fighting somebody. I think we deserve just to get, like, a little talking to or a program. If you wanna do something, give us some extracurricular activities. I think that'll help us better.

Shay's comments echo much of what Rina and Andrea have to say about police abuse of authority. Indeed, these students believe that young people are less likely to be treated fairly by the police.

Max believes that contact with police is a pretty common experience for youth his age. Although he agrees that members of his race (Hispanic) are more likely to be stopped and searched by police than other races, Max thinks that age and gender trump race in police officers' determinations.

AUTHOR: Is it a normal experience for other guys your age to be stopped and searched by the police and stuff like that?

MAX: Yeah, all races, not just Hispanics, all races. Mostly police tend to stop mostly, like, teenagers and males, instead of, like, females.

AUTHOR: So it doesn't matter if you're White, Asian, African American, or Hispanic? Just if you're young and you're male?

MAX: Yeah.

Max qualifies this statement by mentioning that numbers matter too. He does not believe that police officers simply follow the practice of "they see you, they stop you." In fact, he believes that police do not even see you unless you are in a group of "two or three. . . . Then they kinda be suspicious and try to stop you and check you and stuff like that." He explains by giving the example of one of his multiple stops and searches in the previous year:

Yeah, like, if I'm by myself, usually, like, nothing goes down. Recently, I was walking with my brother and two other friends . . . and my brother, he dresses in, like, big [baggy] clothes, and we got stopped because of that. But nothing happened, though. The police said that they were looking for four young people that did something and they thought it was us. The [suspects] were Mexicans or Hispanic or whatever and we were too.

Although Max describes this search incident rather nonchalantly, he does not think it was justified. They were only walking through the park, he says, and "weren't doing nothing bad." Max acknowledges that they could have been seen as suspicious if they had been "looking all around or hiding and stuff like that," but he reports that they were simply walking in a group.

This incident and others like it may explain why Max respects the police but does not necessarily trust them or think they are fair:

MAX: The police are supposed to be fair. They have to *not* take one side of the story. Most police, if an older person stop them and tell them [a kid] did something, they just stop the kid and don't ask him [for] his [point] of view or nothing. They tend to prefer older people and not [people] our age, teenagers.

AUTHOR: That's why you think police treat young people worse than older people?

MAX: Yeah.

AUTHOR: What about the belief that they treat males worse than females?

MAX: Yeah, 'cuz you can be walking with your friends and be wearing, like, baggy clothes. . . . They right away think you gangbangers or something, and they be like tryna stop you or something and check and see if you got anything on you. And with the girls, they don't mess with them. They don't usually stop them. They just walk freely.

Max believes that females and adults have an advantage in their interactions (or non-interactions) with police. However, Max also recognizes that he could "disarm" the negative combination of his ethnic and gender identities by traveling solo, because he would then be less likely to be stopped and searched by the police. The adage that there is safety in numbers does not necessarily apply to young men of color.

Vanessa, from Payton Prep, also acknowledges that females are less likely to be stopped and searched by police, but notes that she has been searched several times while hanging out with her "guys." Vanessa believes that the "ganglike" appearance of her male friends exacerbates their negatively typed racial, gender, and age identities in the eyes of the police and makes them all susceptible to stops and searches by police. Thus, Vanessa does not expect to be "pulled over" by the police when hanging with her "girls," who "dress nice," but feels it is inevitable when she is in mixed-gender company.

The same cross-gender relations that compromise Vanessa's ability to avoid police contact can be protective for the young males in the group. According to Carmen, another Hispanic student who attends Payton Prep, some young people who are typed with negative group status identities know how to adapt:

CARMEN: And also, when I used to hang out with my friends, they'd be like, "Oh, you'll have to walk in front so they know we're with a girl so the cops won't stop us.". . . Because then, they [the police] kinda know if you're with a girl then you're not gonna do anything like a gang.

AUTHOR: So these are guy friends telling you that?

CARMEN: Yeah, they say, "You have to walk so they know that we're with a girl, then they're not gonna stop us, not gonna search us or nothing."

According to Carmen, her male friends recognize that the police are less likely to stop them if they are with girls, so they try to diminish their negative group status (male) by navigating public spaces with female company. This strategy is protective for boys, but it also makes girls more vulnerable to police contacts if police decide to stop and search the mixed-gender group. It is worth testing whether a male-female alliance would or would not diminish police officers' purportedly negative racial perceptions of Black and Hispanic youth—that is, if the mixed-gender group is racially or ethnically homogeneous.

Carmen also talks about having to escort her thirteen-year-old brother around her neighborhood and to the park. She explains, "By my house, if you have a hood on or if you're just hanging out on the corner, cops will stop you, especially if you're a guy at night. That's why my mom doesn't let my brother walk around out there." Both Carmen and her mother worry that the police will mistake her brother, who is nearly six feet tall, for someone much older who is in a gang. They also worry that the guys in her neighborhood will target him for recruitment into a gang. Although Carmen complains about having to take her younger brother to baseball practice and do other tasks with him, she is attuned to the protective force of her gender for both her brother and her peers.

There are others who, like Carmen, are worried about the impact of early contact with police on their younger siblings and peers. Shay believes that the least culpable are often the ones who are treated the worst. According to her, the "big boys" do the fighting and then "run and leave the little kids there" as "innocent bystanders" to deal with the police and ask, "Why I gotta move?" In providing some examples of these types of interactions with police, she speaks quite casually about seeing police coming into her project and pointing their guns at people (which she refers to as "gunning somebody down"):

SHAY: You want to stand there, 'cuz it's your building. You on your floor, playing or doing whatever. . . . Now, if problems occur on the other side of your hallway, you gon' get put off from your side! No, I say that's wrong, [police] supposed to stay on the side [where] something happened. Just let us finish playing; we ain't bothering you. You know what I'm saying?

AUTHOR: So that's happened a lot in your halls?

SHAY: Yeah, police will gun somebody down, don't want nobody to see it, tell us, "Good-bye, get out, get off the floor!" And we don't be paying no attention, not so much that they'll be gunning people down, they'll just be coming on the floor, "Bye, go this way, do this, do that." And you live on the floor! You could be in front of your house talking. "Go this way . . . you don't supposed to be on this floor." Uh, my mama do pay rent here. I deserve rights too, just like you. I don't believe you want any Black policeman to tell your child to move and they in front of his or her house, right?

Implicit in Shay's comments is the disjuncture between residents' ideas about ownership and the purposes of housing project hallways, on the one hand, and police officers' views of those same spaces, on the other. What Shay sees as a private domain—the hallway in front of her apartment—is still very much public property and subject to surveillance and control by police. As we learned in chapter 4, Shay actually takes comfort in the ubiquitous police presence outside her high school, but that may be because she has never had personal interactions with those officers. In her home environment, she and the other youth are subject to police interactions in the course of those same officers' efforts to serve and protect them, but the tone of these interactions can be such that she begins to resent them.

As Rina's and Shay's comments reveal, several students respond to my general questions about police by specifying "the White officer" or "the Black officer." These unsolicited racial descriptions of the police illuminate crucial elements of young people's racialized perceptions of criminal justice and how they understand police officers' behaviors. These perceptions should be central to our analyses of these reports of police-citizen interactions.[7] For instance, Shay uses race to "turn the tables" in the examples she gives of her interactions with police in her project hallways. She expresses doubt that the (implied White) officer ordering her and her playmates out of the hallway would want a "Black policeman to tell his child to move" from in front of his or her home. Hoping she will elaborate on these racialized distinctions, I ask, "Do you think White policemen are worse than Black policeman?" She replies:

> Yes, because a Black policeman really knows more about Black history than the Whites do. The Black polices will give you, like, warnings and stuff. If the kids playing in the hallway, they ain't gon' really say nothing. They'll just say, "Quiet it down a little bit," you know. They ain't go be so nasty with us, they'll be really nice with us sometimes. And then, the White police'll just get into it with us for no reason. We'll just be sittin' there talking, playing. "Do this, go over there." I say that's not right.

The difference in how the White and Black officers speak to her and the other kids is clear in her description, which resonates with the comments made by Boomer and other students about their racialized perceptions of police officers' behavior in schools.

Hunter, who lives in the same neighborhood as Harper High, holds a very negative perception of the police and echoes earlier comments on the policing practices of White and African American officers. Hunter volunteers his opinion on this issue before I can even complete my first question on the topic of the police.

AUTHOR: So, to talk about the police—

HUNTER: Oh Goddamn!

AUTHOR: What are your ideas or opinions on the police in general?

HUNTER: No disrespect, but fuck 'em.

AUTHOR: Why do you feel that way?

HUNTER: Man, I been messed with police a lot of times. I could just be walking to the store. Next thing you know, police look at me. They zoom off. Hit the block around. Bam! Right there. Next thing you know I'm stretched out on the car.

AUTHOR: Just for walking down the street?

HUNTER: Naw, just because I look like everybody else. You don't see too many Black police doing it, but you see White police doing it. Bang! "You got something on you? Let me check you. Get up on the car, don't say nothing. Why your heart beating so fast? What's this? What's that?"

AUTHOR: And how does that make you feel?

HUNTER: Man, that make me feel angry! 'Cuz I don't do nothing. I try to stay out of trouble. I ain't been arrested in a second. And every time they say, "Have you been arrested and what for?" And every time you gotta answer that question. Every time you gotta relive that. I'm getting tired of reliving it. I'm tryna put that behind me.

Hunter's frustration with the police is obvious. I can feel his anger in his voice and see it etched on his face at that point of the interview. He is forthright about having committed wrongs in the past, such as assault and breaking and entering, but he sees his avoidance of arrests "in a second" ("a long time," in street parlance, and more than a year for this study) as evidence of the illegitimacy of his recent contacts with the police: he has been searched multiple times, without arrest. Further diminishing Hunter's impression of White officers is his noteworthy observation that White police stop and check Black people more often than Black police officers do.

All of the youth with a highly racialized perception of criminal injustice give compelling details in recounting how police use stereotypes in stopping and searching people. These experiences inform their perceptions. (A few even speak of the likelihood that Muslims are being targeted even more often than Blacks and Hispanics in the "post-9/11 era.") Billy, a Hispanic student at Lincoln Park High who commutes nearly four miles each day from his diverse, mostly Hispanic Northwest Side neighborhood of Logan Square, has a highly racialized perception of injustice, as manifest in his belief that police are more likely to target Blacks and Hispanics. Although Billy has had contact with police, he believes that his low-level encounters (he's only been told to move on by the police) can be attributed to his light skin tone.

I think injustice is present in some of the cases. There's a lot of things that haven't happened to me. . . . I haven't had any issues with it profoundly because, like a lot of people mention, I don't look Hispanic, so I've never [been] racially profiled, I guess. . . . I think it is prevalent because a lot of people are attacked just by their race or, like, the way they dress or the way they act. And like, a lot of it's not justified. And like, this guy I know was talking about how the cops were attacking him, well, not attacking . . . they were pushing him around because they thought he had, like, pot on him or something and he didn't. And they were being really rude to him . . . obviously there are some cases where there is injustice.

Billy thinks he is able to "pass" because of his lighter skin complexion; he suspects that he does not "look Hispanic." His Mexican American ethnicity does not make Billy himself more likely to be profiled by the police in his community, but he has observed the plight of *other* Hispanics and Blacks, including his parents, in the southern adjacent neighborhood, Humboldt Park, where his parents own a store.

> AUTHOR: Do you think if you were darker in skin tone that things would be different?
>
> BILLY: I think it would, 'cuz like, well, like I said, my dad owns a store, and it's in Humboldt Park, and the main population around there is, like, Hispanic and Black. And the cops tend to go after the Hispanics and Blacks more than anything, even if they're not doing anything. I do notice it a lot.
>
> AUTHOR: You've observed that on your own?
>
> BILLY: Yeah, and like, even the cops actually went to my mom and dad's store and they're like, "Oh, aren't you guys supposed to be closed right now because of that health inspection." I was like, "No, we've never been caught. We've never had problems with that." It's kinda like the cops come up there attacking them for, like, no apparent reason.

Another Lincoln Park student, Gabrielle, is White and blends in racially with the majority of her neighbors in her Lincoln Park community. Gabrielle tells me that when her complexion is darker in the summer (at the time of the interview, she states that she is really pale), she is often stopped by mall security guards when she is with her "really pale White friends," and it makes her "feel awful." She recounts an incident where her friends were stealing in a mall. "I wasn't stealing anything," she says, "but I'm the only one they searched." Her father thought she might have been profiled because she had dyed her hair red, but Gabrielle counters, "Both my friends had bright red hair . . . and they looked far more strange than I do, and [the police] still only searched me." Gabrielle's explanation is that she was targeted by mall security because she is usually the darkest person in her White female peer group. She is not alone in this belief: all of the students in the study are firmly convinced that skin tone, combined with race, affects police behavior.

Vanessa, who is light-complexioned and identifies as Puerto Rican, disagrees with the statements "I respect the police" and "Police are fair" on the survey. Her elaboration on this view during the interview reveals her perceptions of police officers' racial and ethnic biases:

> VANESSA: [The police are] not fair to us, so why should we trust them or like them or whatever?

AUTHOR: So, do you think they're more likely to unfairly stop and question Hispanics . . .?

VANESSA: Mmm hmm. (*vigorously nods her head to say "yes"*)

AUTHOR: More than people who are White . . .?

VANESSA: Yeah.

AUTHOR: What about Asian . . .?

VANESSA: Super yeah!

AUTHOR: Or African American?

VANESSA: Oh, African American? They treat the Hispanics and African Americans just as equal, like bad. But if you're White or Asian, then you're fine. But like, if you're a White person who dresses like ghetto or whatever, with baggy jeans and stuff, then you're gonna get treated like, you know, Hispanic or whatever.

AUTHOR: Oh really, so just by their . . .

VANESSA: Appearance.

AUTHOR: Appearance can change the whole race privilege you think Whites have?

VANESSA: Yeah.

Vanessa perceives a very specific racial hierarchy, organized both by race and by outward appearance, that explains how the police treat different groups. She shares a perception with many of her peers that police treat Whites and Asians more favorably. Vanessa's assessment that Whites can be treated as badly as Hispanics by the police if they dress "ghetto" is rather intriguing and contradicts many of her peers' opinions. Several students believe that one's outward appearance, in clothing or style, can attract negative attention from police, but most of them believe that Whites, even if they are dressed in "baggy" or "ghetto" clothing, are still treated better than Blacks or Hispanics.

Carmen, a student at Payton who identifies as Puerto Rican, believes that Blacks and Hispanics are treated the same. She resides in Chicago's East Humboldt Park–West Town neighborhood, which underwent rapid gentrification in the 1990s, and she believes that the Puerto Ricans and Blacks in her community share a similar social experience in their treatment by the police. "I think, like, people joke about it, but Black people and Puerto Rican people, they're kinda close. Our community is Black and Puerto Rican, so I think they get treated equally. It doesn't mean it's good," Carmen explains. In her mind, the equal treatment of Blacks and Puerto Ricans by the police is still worse than their treatment of Whites and Asian Americans.

These young people have personally or vicariously experienced various kinds of biases that inevitably shape their perceptions of the police. They also have specific hierarchies in mind that help them make sense of why police may view them as criminal or suspicious. Race, skin tone, age, gender, appearance—all individual characteristics—in conjunction with place and the company they keep become important factors in adolescents' assessments and rationalizations of police behaviors. Their perceptions about their social realities are shaped not just by what they have seen in one place or during one encounter, but more importantly by the divergent or strangely similar social worlds revealed by the paths they routinely take between school and home.

Comparative Frames by Race and Place

Youth who travel farther along the racial-spatial divide have "expanded contexts," or wider frames of comparison, than their peers who travel shorter distances. They are much more sensitized to injustice, particularly if their school and neighborhood contexts are dissimilar on several measures of significance—racial composition, quality of resources, policing tactics, and so on. African American and Hispanic students from Lincoln Park and Payton Prep, for example, have very different perceptions of criminal injustice than do the students from the South Side schools, Tilden Career Community Academy and Harper High. The students who travel between social worlds have a much greater chance of witnessing or experiencing differential treatment by police because of their simultaneous insider (enrolled student) and outsider (racial minority) status in these spaces, while students in the more segregated schools are more "insulated" from opportunities to observe racially disparate treatment by police in their schools and around their neighborhoods.

Boomer, who commutes to Lincoln Park from his West Side home, notes that his perceptions of criminal injustice were directly influenced by observing police treat Black youth—especially those dressed in "baggy jeans and jerseys"—differently from White youth around the school. He explains:

BOOMER: Like, if we standing outside after school and we do have police officers that sit outside and make sure don't nothin' jump off, especially if it's a group of boys standing across the street and they have on, like, some baggy jeans and, like, jerseys and stuff like that, [the police] will be like, "You need to clear the corner." Well, on this side of the street, you have the White people standing there, and they're talking and communicating, so my thing is, why do they [Blacks] have to move and they [Whites] don't have to move? So, I've seen it before, I just seen it yesterday. They did it and told us that we have to clear off the corner, and we weren't doing anything but talking.

AUTHOR: Which corner was that?

BOOMER: Umm, our school's on this side. Across the street, it's the bus stop, and that's where we were standing. And on this side it's a cleaners and then it's a barbecue spot, and that's where the White people were standing. And we could [have] been standing there waiting on the bus, but yet and still, you sit and tell us to clear that side. That's not right. What about them? They actually on someone's property talking and you tell them to do nothing. You know, you just let them sit there. So, I don't feel that's right, but that's the way they go about doing stuff.

Boomer did not indicate on the survey that he had been told to "clear the corner" or to move on by the police in the past year. However, my further questioning on this topic during the interview provided the missing data as he gave me more detailed information on his perceptions of and contact with police. Boomer believes that "the way [the police] go about doing stuff" is quite commonplace around Lincoln Park High. It is plausible that he did not think to document this interaction on the survey because of its normalcy. The two other African American male students at Lincoln Park also recount issues they have had with police telling them to remove their belongings from the bus stop shelter (Andre) and telling them to leave the park by the school while "old ladies" were able to stay (Louie).

Amber, an African American student at Payton Prep who also lives on the West Side, discusses the differences she sees in how the police interact with businesses in her school's neighborhood versus businesses in her home neighborhood. Amber suggests that "there's a friendship bond between the [school] neighborhood and the police. . . . You see police at the shops down the street, but in my neighborhood you don't see them at our shops." Amber believes that the police are friendlier to residents of the Old Town neighborhood, where Payton Prep is located, than they are in her own poorer, predominantly African American West Side neighborhood.

The centrality of neighborhood to these analyses arises again when several of these same students mention the differences they see in police presence in their segregated residential communities. Amber's perceptions of injustice stem from seeing an extensive police presence in her neighborhood; she observes fewer police officers when visiting a friend from school who lives in the western suburb of Oak Park. She talks about police riding through her neighborhood five times per hour and stopping people, particularly Black males, if they drive through speeding. Amber reveals that her brother was once stopped for driving fast down the street, "but like, the next minute later a White man drove fast down our block, and they didn't even stop to go get him. They just kept looking after my brother, and that was kinda bogus." She finds it "bogus" or "messed up" that a White man can speed through her neighborhood while her brother is detained by police officers for the same offense.

Another African American student at Payton, Angela, indicates that her ideas about criminal injustice come from her observation of police and their ubiquity in her community, the South Shore neighborhood. She speaks of seeing people get "pulled over" by the police for walking down the street:

ANGELA: That comes from experience, not my experience, but visual, seeing that happen [to other people]. Because every day I go home and there is somebody getting pulled over. . . . They can just be walking and they'll pull them over. "Come here!" Then they get defensive, and they throw you in the car and take you off. I don't understand, I don't really understand. But okay, it can be a whole group of White kids walking down the street, the police will ride by, blow the horn, and say hello!

AUTHOR: Where? Around here [the school]?

ANGELA: Right! And then, my friends and me walk past; they slow down and look all suspicious. I'm like, I don't believe this. This is sumthin' off TV.

AUTHOR: So how does that make you feel about the police in general?

ANGELA: They need to go to hell. Some police are nice. Not nice, but are fair, and some police are not.

In contrast, David, Dre, and Terry, African American male students from Harper High and Tilden Prep, all of whom rank low on the racialized perceptions scale, are unable to make the same comparisons as the students from the North Side schools, which may explain why their perceptions of criminal injustice are much lower. David, a Harper High student who believes that Blacks encounter racial discrimination in hiring (see chapter 3), reports that the police frequently stop African Americans in his neighborhood. Still, he does not believe that racial discrimination is to blame. He explains, "Every time I walk, I see people getting checked. Black people going to jail every day." When asked during the interview about his racialized perceptions of injustice, David's answers correlate with his survey answers:

DAVID: They should just be doing their job, just watching and making sure the neighborhood and the environment is safe. Now, they can question people to help keep the environment in order. They can do that.

AUTHOR: So, do you think they do it more to Black people than people from other racial groups, or do you think it happens to everybody?

DAVID: It happens to everybody. I say that.

David believes that the police are fair and even says that he has respect for the officers who patrol his neighborhood and school. "I have respect for them," he explains, "because they putting they life on the line for us to keep the environment safe when we go outside and stuff. . . . 'Cuz if it wasn't never no police, it's no telling how the world would be right now." David would prefer the presence of police to quell possible violence committed by "some grimy kids out here picking fights with people" or by the gang members who control his neighborhood park, Murray Park—nicknamed "Murder Park," he says, because "a lot of people died up there."

Terry, a fellow South Side student, has a more extended viewpoint on why the police behave the way they do:

TERRY: It's a lot of Black gangbangers. I don't see no White gang-bangers. . . . So, when I look out my window and stuff, police be out there, see drugs on 'em or something, and they get stopped. . . . It's fair 'cuz they shouldn't be out there selling it anyway. So they know the police gon' come up on 'em to see what's going on if they see a crowd of people or someone going to a car, hand 'em something. They know something going on, that police gon' try to stop 'em, so they shouldn't do it.

AUTHOR: Do you think if people weren't doing anything wrong, like, if they didn't have drugs . . . if it was just a group of Black people standing on the corner and a group of White people standing on the corner, but neither of them had drugs or anything. Do you think the police would treat one group differently?

TERRY: As long as they ain't got nothing, no.

Terry lacks information about how police operate in more diverse or advantaged neighborhoods. He can only use what he sees "when I look out my window" to substantiate his perception that police are fair and do not discriminate by race. And precisely because his frame is limited, he does not realize that the police may behave differently in different neighborhoods. Similarly, Dre and Jackson from Tilden and David from Harper simply stick to their belief that everyone is treated the same because they do not have information that they would recognize as contradictory.

Keisha, a student at Harper High, has both a strong racialized perception of injustice and a high level of police contact (an arrest in the past year). In contrast to others who insist that the police treat everyone fairly based on what they see in their neighborhoods, Keisha recognizes the limited frame she has for assessing the fairness of police practices by race. She hypothesizes that other racial groups in different kinds of neighborhoods get differential treatment:

[Police officers] are racist, 'cuz like, a White officer will come around on the block or whatever and they'll get to talking trash. But I'll be saying to myself, *I wonder if they go over to a White neighborhood, to the suburbs, do they treat those people the way they treat the people out here?* I don't know. I think it's best for me to see than to just say. I need to go check out the suburbs and see how they treat them out there, and then maybe I can put two and two together to see what's going on.

Keisha sounds like a budding sociologist. She is aware that she cannot confirm that her race is treated unfairly because she lacks evidence either way.

In contrast, when confronted with evidence that any other person might construe as racially discriminatory, TB still insists that the police are fair. A ninth-grader at Harper High, TB recounts an incident in which he and his Black male cousins were asked to leave Naperville (coincidentally, the same White suburban neighborhood highlighted in the "school swap" described in chapter 1), while a group of White youth were allowed to hang out on the same street.

> TB: Like, me and my cousin [were] in the suburbs one time. . . . We used to hang by the pool, and they called the police on us. But when the White kids came, they had the skateboards and stuff talking. They didn't call the police on them.
>
> AUTHOR: So why do you think they treated you differently from the White kids if it wasn't about race?
>
> TB: They probably thought we was gang-related or something like that.
>
> AUTHOR: Do you think if you were out there with skateboards that it would have been different?
>
> TB: Yeah.
>
> AUTHOR: They would have been okay with you being out there?
>
> TB: Yeah.

TB believes that having a skateboard would have diminished any negative racial stigma and lessened his being marked as possibly "gang-related." He saw the skateboard as an objective indicator of innocence, or perhaps even legitimacy, that would have allowed him to remain in that space and not be negatively marked by his race, gender, or youthfulness. Although TB seems to be able to disaggregate presumptions about gang affiliation from other central identifying characteristics (young, Black, male) that might define outsiders' perceptions of him, others may not be willing or able to grant him the same courtesy.

Place indubitably shapes these young people's experiences and their perceptions of justice or injustice. From Terry's positive assessment of police fairness from the vantage point of "when I look out my window" to Angela's confidence in her cross-city assessment that Blacks on the South Side are treated differently by police than White students on the North Side, this study gives us only a glimpse into the range of perspectives these young people hold. What would happen if more young people like Keisha were required to cross the racial-spatial divide and thereby gained the information to fully assess their individual- and group-level advantage or disadvantage? More importantly, what would this experience do for a young person like TB who now, when treated with bias, seems not to discern it because of his restricted frame of comparison? He might retain the bliss of ignorance the first or second time police are "called on him" or stop to question or frisk him. But what if this begins to happen frequently? Adolescent development always requires seeing more, and experiencing more, than in childhood, but how might greater experience across the racial-spatial divide open adolescents' eyes to greater injustice and also subject them to increased suspicion?

"Coming of Age"

Adolescence is a distinct life stage during which youth, while undergoing numerous transitions in their personal and social development, are in flux with regard to society's expectations for them and their adherence to social norms. One of the major components of this developmental phase is the greater responsibility that young people are expected to assume for their behavior, which may subject them to more serious consequences if they deviate from the norms. The status shift from adolescent to adult may be prompted by age, experiences, role transitions, or some combination of these factors. A transitional life event such as marriage or parenthood can catapult an adolescent into adulthood, as can being arrested or searched by police.

Adolescence can be seen as a "protected role," while adulthood brings certain vulnerabilities, both legal and social.[8] Premature exits from adolescence and into adulthood have legal effects and life-course implications.[9] One of the reasons why adolescent experiences with the police are important is that negative experiences can derail normative life trajectories (such as moving from high school to college) and disrupt the timing of life transitions (such as school graduation).[10] Official police intervention in the lives of adolescents— particularly police contact that is unwarranted or discriminatory, as may be the case when youth are searched but released—can create an early exit from adolescence.

The life-stage principle holds that individual and social events can differentially affect life patterns, depending on the age at which events occur. "Cumulative criminal continuity" refers to a dynamic process in which delinquent behavior at one point in time has consequences that increase the likelihood of continued delinquent behavior at later points in time. Officially recorded criminal continuity leads eventually to "cumulative disadvantage"— a piling up of negative experiences and failures that make it difficult for a person to succeed.[11] Although this study does not have a longitudinal design, sociologists must consider the possibility that students are at an elevated risk of negative life trajectories as a result of their increased contact with police in their schools and neighborhoods.

This idea was one of the key motivators for this book. It is critical that we understand how adolescents' contacts with key authoritative figures, like police officers in their neighborhoods and teachers in their classrooms, can alter the course of their life trajectories. Police have a striking presence and impact on youths' formative experiences and their resultant attitudes about themselves and the world in which they live.

The remainder of this chapter pays particular attention to the social and contextual factors in students' perceptions of injustice. In particular, I discuss several students who have highly racialized perceptions of criminal injustice and whose opinions about police have progressed from positive or neutral to negative. (In contrast, no such progression has marked the experiences of the five female students from Lincoln Park High, profiled in chapter 4, who have not had personal contact with police and who hold a low racialized perception of injustice.) Not only has increased and intrusive police contact marked the "end of innocence" for these students, but it has also changed any basic notions they may have held about the police being a resource available to "serve and protect" them and their communities.

Amber's comments are representative of the answers given by many students regarding the shift in their perceptions of the police. Amber strongly believes that police see all young people as troublemakers: "They think young people is trouble, automatically. When you young, you get into trouble, but you should treat [us] equal. It's not much that a young person can do that is worse than an old person." She has no problem typing the police with the same default negative assessment now that she is older. Asked whether she ever thought of the police as good, Amber responds:

> AMBER: You know, when I was little, I used to look up to the police, but now I be, like, he just probably another crooked cop in the neighborhood or something.
>
> AUTHOR: When do you think that changed in your mind?
>
> AMBER: When you get older and you see more things. That's when I think, when it changed.

These comments come at the end of our thirty-five-minute interview, by which point in our conversation Amber seems quite subdued and reflective.

She notes that her thinking about the police changed during grammar school, prior to her enrollment at Payton Prep. It is noteworthy that all of the examples she gives regarding her negative impressions of the police are from her neighborhood, not her school.

Similarly, Michael from Harper High says that when he was growing up he had no reason to think about the police because he "wasn't thinkin' about doin' nothin' to get scared by the police." However, his conception of the police changed once he moved into his South Side neighborhood, which has a bad reputation for "silly kids out there fightin' or on the corner selling drugs." Michael then realized that if he was in the "wrong spot at the wrong time, they gon' stop me too."

Michael resides in his school's West Englewood community. He marked on his survey that he had been arrested once in the prior year, but his story changes a bit in our interview. When I ask him what happened, he explains:

Umm, well, it wasn't actually my fault. I was arrested. . . . Well, I wasn't arrested, I was just took down to the station. . . . One of my friend's female [girlfriend] was in a car. Me and my brother 'nem [and friends] had got in since they was going to the store. By the time we ended up back on the block [home], the police must've had followed us. They asked who was driving the car and stuff. And once they found out who was drivin', they took us all to the station and told us the car was stolen. And we ain't know that. They let us go after a while. They had us in there for a couple of hours, and they let us go 'cuz we was innocent. They just put us down for joyriding, which we wasn't, we was just goin' to the store.

It is possible that Michael received an informal "station adjustment," with some notation on his juvenile record that will matter if he is brought to the station or arrested in the future.[12] Unfortunately, I did not push Michael for more details about any "official directives" the police officer gave him about his behavior.

Michael spends a few more minutes talking about how upset he was with the "girl for lying" about the car and saying that it belonged to her sister. However, he says, he did learn one lesson directly from the experience: he tries hard to stay out of trouble and away from the police. He confides that his "arrest" is the reason he "[goes] nowhere now." Staying in the house is "more safer," he says, than walking around and "getting pulled over for no reason. . . . I ain't got time for that."

Perhaps because I have asked Michael to recall that one report of an arrest, he is more passionate, incensed even, when he describes one of the times he was stopped and searched. He believes that "proactive" policing—when police do not receive a call on a person but instead engage in what is now commonly referred to as "stop, question, and frisk"—is the most discriminatory and the most infuriating. Michael concludes that he is being searched simply because he is "walking while Black." He explains:

> MICHAEL: When they mess with me for no reason, then I feel like . . . I mean, what y'all messin' wit' me for? I ain't did nothin'. Y'all ain't got nothin', no call on me or nothin'. They just pull up and just start searchin' people, looking for drugs or guns, and then once they see that they ain't got nothin', they'll let us go.
>
> AUTHOR: So do they ever give an apology . . .?
>
> MICHAEL: No. They just get back in the car and ride off and go mess with somebody else.

Michael's final sentence speaks volumes about his perception of how often police officers harass and search youth for illegal guns and drugs. Michael strongly feels that his environment, combined with the actions of several "silly kids," puts him at the same risk of getting pulled over or stopped by police, even if he is doing nothing wrong. The police now scare him because he realizes that they have the power to group him in the same category with youthful wrongdoers.

Dewayne attends Harper High with Michael and has also been searched by the police multiple times. Dewayne recounts that he liked the police when he was younger, but that opinion has vastly changed since grammar school. "I had respect for the police a long time ago when I was little. I thought they would do nothin' wrong," Dewayne remembers. However, starting at around age fifteen, he says, "I got up to reality, they the most crooked people, [more so] than Black people killing each other. Police ain't nothing. They worser than a person without a badge."

Dewayne's current opinion of police as "worser than a person without a badge" is a long way from his earlier respect for them. As happened with Amber, this change did not occur until he "came of age," when it became more likely that police would stop and search him. When he describes one stop and search he endured, the experience of being criminalized for being a young Black male comes through clearly.

> Yeah, like, one day I was riding on a bike . . . and all of a sudden they just came around and almost ran me over. . . . And I'm like, "What you stop me for?" "You probably delivering a package on a bike." I'm like, "Man, I don't sell drugs. I ain't never sold drugs a day in my life." You know what I'm saying? "Oh, we gotta search you." They swear up and down I had drugs. I wasn't dressed like I had drugs on me. . . . We was 'bout to go to the movies. They got my ID number and stuff down. . . . And they like, "Well, we got your information now, just in case you do something."

Even in the rather small sample of this study there were two other males, both from Harper High, who reported that the police put their names and information into their computer after stopping, questioning, and searching them. All of these students were subsequently released.

This experience offers insight into young people's response to being subjects of police officers' "criminal gaze." The presumption that adolescents are criminally inclined instead of compliant informs the form and function of the carceral apparatus. When these young people report that they have seen police officers running checks on their names (most likely looking for outstanding warrants), they are suggesting that the police are precataloging them into their computer systems. This signals to young people that the police believe that they will inevitably encounter the same young people at some point in the future.

Some youth think of police contact as a routine component of adolescence—akin to growing pains—and their impassivity is telling. While Michael is very upset about the searches he has endured (two in the past year), other students are much more nonchalant about the experience of being stopped and frisked by the police. Vanessa and TB, both of whom have been searched multiple times in different areas of the city (but never arrested), have different scores on the perceptions of injustice measure. Vanessa, a student at Payton Prep who lives in the diverse neighborhood of Logan Square, ranks high on the racialized perceptions of injustice scale, while TB, who attends Harper High and resides only a mile away from the school, ranks low.

Vanessa reports that she has been stopped, asked questions, and searched more than five times in the past year. She nonchalantly recounts a couple of the situations in which police stopped her for curfew checks or searched her and other passengers in a car:

VANESSA: They'll just pull us over and if it's, like, really late, they'll ask how old we are. And if it's not late, then they'll just search us and be like, "Oh, where's the drugs." And then they'll just search us and ask us where we're going if they don't find nothing. And if they do, they'll take it or they'll arrest whoever. And sometimes they'll just arrest the person who had cases before or who's older than maybe the person who had it. Because they're gonna automatically choose the older person or the person who had cases before.

AUTHOR: Why?

VANESSA: I don't know. That's just the person they choose. And then they'd just let us go.

She gives a more specific example from the prior week.

VANESSA: Like, when was it? Friday. We were in a van. It was two of my guys and then two of my girls, and umm, we had pulled over or whatever, we were gonna go into the store. Then [the police] pull up behind us in the [narcotics] car. And then the guys come out [of the store] or whatever. [The police] were searching them just, you know, looking for drugs or whatever. So they were just looking for something to, you know, bring in so they can get paid more or you know, move on to higher levels I guess. You know, that's their job to find stuff.

AUTHOR: So, if there's an instance where they don't find anything, then they just move on . . .?

VANESSA: Then they'll just let us go. They'll be like, "All right, you can just go."

AUTHOR: So what do you think about that? Do you think that's enough?

VANESSA: Yeah, 'cuz if they don't find nothing, then they can't do nothing. So, yeah.

Vanessa's demeanor while describing her most recent contact with police is telling. She shrugs multiple times during this portion of the interview, and she seems resigned to the increased likelihood of police stopping and searching her when she is out with friends. And though her racial hierarchy of police stops is instructive, Vanessa also sees what she describes as "unfair" treatment by the police through an age- and gender-specific lens. Earlier, asked why she "strongly agrees" with the survey statement that "police treat young people worse than older people," Vanessa explains, "It's 'cuz the people I used to hang out with always used to chill on the streets and they look like gangs I guess. Obviously they're gonna pull us over, but they'd always pull us over for no reason." The word "obviously" is noteworthy: Vanessa makes the whole process seem inevitable and perhaps even rational, from the police perspective. She believes that the police have great incentives to perform their "jobs to find stuff" on youth, which is what she thinks leads to increased pay or perhaps a promotion for them.

Vanessa's perceptions of criminal injustice exemplify simultaneously her distrust of police and her belief that she has little power to avoid these interactions. Instead, she has adapted to this reality by "just let[ting] them search us or whatever, and don't say nothing to them unless they ask." Asked who taught her what to do in her interactions with police, Vanessa answers in a way that makes it clear that she does not see it as a learned response: "You just know to do it. 'Cuz if you say something back to them, then they'll probably, like, arrest you or something." Vanessa does not seem cognizant of how she has been socialized to respond during police contacts. In contrast to other interviewees I classified as "dispassionate," Vanessa's racial hierarchy regarding discriminatory police action, combined with her experience of multiple searches by the police, demonstrates that she has concrete ideas about how criminalization occurs and its many effects. For her, however, police interactions have become normal, an "experience of the expected," and do not alarm her.[13]

Similarly, TB, who attends Harper and lives only a few minutes away from the school, expects to be searched by the police. He gives me a few details about his most recent encounters with the police (being told to move on, stopped and asked questions, and searched for drugs):

TB: Well, we was walking down the street comin' from a funeral, and they asked us what we were doing, and we told them we was going home, we just came from a funeral. [Other times,] I'll be standing on the corner or something, looking for my little brother, and they'll pull over and start searching me and stuff, [asking] do I have drugs and stuff.

AUTHOR: And how does that make you feel when that happens?

TB: I don't even know.

AUTHOR: Do you say anything back to them?

TB: I'm calm.

AUTHOR: After they search you, and without finding anything, right, then what do you go back and tell your mom or your brothers and sisters?

TB: Uhh, the police had searched me. I bet they feel real mad that they didn't find nothin' on a Black kid.

AUTHOR: Does that make you feel upset?

TB: Makes me feel like, oh, that's what happens. (*shrugs*)

AUTHOR: Does that happen to a lot of people that you know?

TB: Uhh, most, kind of.

AUTHOR: Like who, boys or girls?

TB: Uhh, mainly boys.

AUTHOR: And do they get upset, or do they just feel like, oh well?

TB: They feel like, oh well, too.

AUTHOR: Why do you think they don't get upset?

TB: Because . . . I don't know. . . . It happens a lot of times, and they don't feel like they can get mad over that lil petty stuff.

TB believes that each time he is searched the police are "probably mad they didn't find anything"; moreover, he is clear that teens should not get mad about wrongful searches because they should not worry about "lil petty stuff." Having a blasé attitude is just one of many adaptive responses to police searches, which these youth view as inevitable and inefficient.

I was struck by TB's comment that an officer might be mad if he finds nothing on a *Black* kid, because TB's answers on the survey reflected low perceptions of race-, class-, and age-based injustice. During follow-up questions about his disagreement with the statement that "police unfairly stop and search members of his race," he replies, "Police [are] out here to help protect your community and stuff, and they gon' treat [Black] people the way they treat other people." TB also disagrees that officers treat young people worse than older people. He explains:

> TB: 'Cuz everybody the same people. They got the same feelings as other people. We all human beings.
>
> AUTHOR: And do you think rich people get treated better by the police than people that are poor?
>
> TB: No.
>
> AUTHOR: And you don't think the police treat Black people differently?
>
> TB: No.

I asked TB these questions about race, class, and age in multiple ways to ensure that his interview answers were consistent with his survey responses. He sincerely believes that police are fair and that they are just doing their job by searching him multiple times. In fact, TB states that he wants *more* police patrols around his home. He does feel, however, that there are enough police officers stationed outside Harper during arrivals and dismissals to make him feel "mostly safe." TB's respect for the police may be based on his appreciation of them for performing a dangerous job, but what will happen to his perceptions if he becomes better able to compare how police treat people across the dimensions of race, class, and place?

TB's characterization of the multiple searches he has endured as a ninth-grader as "lil petty stuff" deserves further elaboration. For some youth, these searches can escalate from being "petty" to something much more serious, especially in the minds of those who worry about police planting drugs on them during stops and searches. In contrast to TB's respect for police and his belief that all police are fair, Carmen, from Payton, is quite wary about police officers' motivations when stopping people and grants them respect according to how they treat her.

Well, 'cuz it depends on which police it is. Because if you know they're not gonna help you out, then you don't have to respect them because they're not giving you the respect that you would want in return. But if they're gonna help you and if they're the police, like, if you know them, and then you know they'll help you and you know that they're not gonna plant stuff on you, ask you questions when they know you're not doing anything, then you can respect them. Give them the respect they give you.

Similarly, Michael from Harper High is adamant about "watching my where-abouts" to make sure the police are not attempting to plant something on him. He says that it has never happened to him, but describes how it almost happened to his cousin outside his home:

MICHAEL: I don't trust the police. Some of them . . . they'll try to plant some drugs on you or somethin' just so they can take somebody in. That's why the last couple times they stopped us I always watch my whereabouts so I can see what's going on. Make sure they ain't tryna put it on the ground and pick it up and be like, "Oh, we found this," or sumthin' like that, 'cuz I done seen that happen once before.

AUTHOR: That happened to somebody else?

MICHAEL: To my cousin. He was comin' out my house, and they caught him by the alley. And they had him in [their] car, taking off his shoes and stuff. It was a good thing my grandmother came out . . . my cousin said they was tryna plant something on him. If my grandma wouldn't [have] come out, they probably woulda took him down to the station, by him being older than seventeen too, and by him being caught by the police, they coulda did anything.

That some young people believe that the police routinely plant drugs on people is disturbing, whether or not their perceptions are in alignment with social reality. For them, perception is reality. And none of this is petty stuff if we consider the implications of adolescent contacts with police along the continuum of severity (being told to move on, being stopped, being searched, and being arrested). These experiences, whether personal or vicarious, shape youth's assessments of themselves and the world in which they live.

Contact with police, then, becomes an important transition in the adolescent life course. It creates a loss of innocence and a concomitant burden that should be acknowledged, examined, and addressed. The following account by Chris, a student at Harper High, provides a lens into the physical and emotional impacts of police searches.

AUTHOR: So tell me about the times when you say the police have told you to move on or searched you. What were you doing, and where were you?

CHRIS: This happened on the West Side. When I used to live on the West Side, me and my friend were on the corner talking with some girls. And the police, you know, riding around, they riding around two times, and the third time they stopped and told us to come here. So we came to the car, they handcuffed us, check to see if we had some drugs on us, we didn't have no drugs on us, and they let us go. Put our name in the computer and they just drove off. That's happened to me like three times.

AUTHOR: So they actually searched you that time?

CHRIS: Yeah.

AUTHOR: So how did that make you feel?

CHRIS: It made me feel nervous. 'Cuz like, if they check one of my friends and they have something, like some drugs or something, we all gon' go to jail. They'll probably think we all was selling something. They'll take us to the police office, the police station, call our mamas, and tell her to come pick us up. So I think we'd all go to jail for that one person.

AUTHOR: So what was another instance? Anything ever on the South Side or around your neighborhood?

CHRIS: Naw, it all happened on the West Side.

AUTHOR: So how old were you about then?

CHRIS: I think I was fifteen . . . yeah, I was fifteen.

AUTHOR: So you've never been arrested. They never had to take you in or do anything like that?

CHRIS: No.

AUTHOR: How does that make you feel about the police and about the legal system?

CHRIS: (*pause*) I feel most policemen is nice, but most policemen try to do something to make it seem like we sell something. Like, they'll try, you know, go through our pockets, and then they'll come out with some drugs or something. But you know you ain't have nothing in your pocket. Then you be like, that [wasn't] in my pocket. So then they just put you in some handcuffs and take you in. I don't know what they'll do with the drugs. Probably put them in the back somewhere.

AUTHOR: Has that ever happened to you or to someone that you know?

CHRIS: Naw, that ain't ever happened to me, or I never seen nobody do it, but I heard that police be doing that sometimes.

AUTHOR: Planting stuff on people?

CHRIS: Yeah.

The young feel the asymmetry in power between police and citizens even more strongly than adults do. The prospect of police officers taking advantage of them through unlawful stops and searches (and maybe even planting drugs on their person to justify criminal charges) contributes to students' belief that police are not fulfilling their duties to "serve and protect" and may even be causing them undue harm. This is why Dewayne feels that he is safer around regular citizens he does not know, even drug dealers, than around the police.

> I'm more safe around people who I don't know, 'cuz I know they don't know me and I don't know nothin' about them. I feel safe around drug dealers more than I feel safe around the police. 'Cuz a drug dealer, it ain't no guarantee, [he] can get locked up for touching me, know what I'm saying. Police ain't gon' get locked up for touching me. All you gotta do is get uppity. All you gotta do is say one curse word, that's resisting arrest right there. All they gotta do is say you [were] resisting arrest or plant something on you. That's why I feel I'm more unsafe around the police than I am around people who I don't know.

The voices of these youth reveal the impact of personal and vicarious police encounters on their emotional, social, and physical being. More specifically, their assessments of whether police are effective and efficient and whether police treat people equally play a role in how these young people move around in the world and with whom. This is a form of socialization that leads to various adaptations. Some young people, like Keisha, stay close to home, while others, like Dewayne, seek to cross more boundaries. But seeing more of the world may have a negative impact on young people's assessments of how police operate within and across different social contexts.

Being socialized to think and act like a potential criminal is an important developmental marker. The loss of the protective cloak of childhood innocence to the generalized suspicion that may mark adults (Black and Hispanic males in particular) puts adolescents through the process of "adultification." Given that everyone is subject to the power of authoritative figures like the police, it is distressing to think that many people do not trust the individuals who should be serving them and protecting them from harm. This is especially true when the distrust is felt by adolescents, whose actual agency remains far behind that of adults.

Conclusion

Youth in Chicago come into contact with police throughout the city, but especially in school and in their neighborhoods. They recognize that police are supposed to be there to protect and serve them and their families, but they learn soon enough not to count on them—especially if they live in a neighborhood that is Black, Hispanic, or poor. Youth who do not trust the police are reluctant to call on them for help and are even less likely to aid the police in solving crimes in their neighborhoods. In their personal experiences, and in those of their family and friends, youth see evidence of race-, gender-, age-, and class-based bias that saps their trust in the police in particular, and in authority in general. They wish that the police would stop relying on stereotypes to harass them or potentially plant illegal evidence and go after the "real criminals" instead to make their communities safer.

Police encounters, whether warranted or unwarranted, mark a premature exit from adolescence. Such experiences as they come of age not only affect young people's perceptions but may also shape the lives they will lead and the people they will become. Moreover, there is a racial and ethnic variance in both perceptions of injustice and contact with police. Youth who are Black or Hispanic are more likely to have greater contact with police in their schools and in their neighborhoods. These same groups also hold higher perceptions of injustice. The belief that the police do not treat people who are Black or Hispanic as fairly as they treat Whites (and Asians) depends on identity, personal and vicarious experiences, and place.

Young people's perceptions are shaped by their observations of and interactions with police officers, and geography is a central force in determining what youth see and experience. The place-based nature of their assessments of police behavior, especially when the race of the officer is highlighted, shapes adolescents' expectations of what they can expect from police, both where they live and where they attend school. It even shapes their hypotheses about places they have never visited, as well as places they have visited but where they were made to feel that they did not belong. The continuity—or more powerfully, the discontinuity—in their observations within and across their residential and educational contexts influences their perceptions of injustice.

CHAPTER 6

Conclusion: Paradoxes of Progress

The social forces of race-ethnicity, crime, adolescence, and law converge daily, but their intersection is rarely given critical examination. In this book, I have investigated how both race and place shape youth perceptions of social and criminal injustice. The experiences and attitudes of the Chicago youth presented here offer a timely reminder that the concept of "justice" must be broadened. Researchers must broaden their exclusive focus on courts, jails, and police to link schools with these penalizing institutions because schools—and the daily journeys undertaken by students to get there—influence how the young learn about and experience equality and inequality.

This research has revealed the range of adolescents' actual contact with police in school, at home, and in the places in between. Just as important, it has analyzed adolescents' nuanced perceptions of social and criminal injustice and how their experiences and beliefs define and are shaped by their racially divergent social worlds. These perceptions, most often studied in adults, offer a great deal of insight into young people's perspectives at the formative stage when their decisions and resultant behaviors may drastically determine the trajectories of their lives. It is especially important to understand these interactions now when, under the guise of establishing safety, schools have increasingly become part of a universal carceral apparatus.

This study's use of mixed quantitative and qualitative data reveals that the individual voices of teenagers are just as important as the aggregate numbers of their survey responses. From the numbers and narratives alike, an innovative frame has emerged from which to view young people's ever more intertwined experience of education and criminal justice. The study, moreover, has combined a sociological perspective with a historical perspective on the current dilemma in the United States regarding racial-ethnic stratification, residential segregation and mobility, and educational policy. Combined, these varied perspectives offer crucial insight into how we arrived at this state.

My findings reveal how perceptions of both social and criminal injustice vary across the racial and spatial contexts of Chicago's ninth- and tenth-graders. The social injustice questions on the survey provide insight into young people's beliefs about their chances for upward mobility, while the criminal injustice measures capture their opinions about the variability of police treatment determined by race, gender, class, and age. African American and Hispanic students perceive greater social and criminal injustice than their Asian American and White counterparts. Black and Hispanic youth generally believe their race-ethnicity reduces their chances for upward mobility in occupation and education, restricts their pursuit of the American Dream of owning a nice home in a safe neighborhood, and usurps their ability to navigate their neighborhoods without worrying about the police stopping and searching them for weapons or drugs.

Students diverge in their opinions on the legitimacy of authority figures based on where they live and where they go to school; neighborhood and school contexts are central to their understanding of their interactions with police. The survey and interview data show that African Americans and Hispanics who attend more racially integrated (and better-resourced) schools have higher perceptions of social and criminal injustice than their racial counterparts who go to majority-Black or -Hispanic schools. This finding is especially true for youth whose school environment differs from their neighborhood environment. In contrast, I find that African American and Hispanic youth who live and attend school in the same highly securitized neighborhood have a restricted comparative frame from which to understand their position in society. The sociological literature has increasingly taken account of these and other contextual effects. It is time to make the combination of adolescents' school and neighborhood experiences—including the journey from one to the other—an integral unit of analysis in the examination of youth attitudes and experiences.

The "traditional" neighborhood public school, so often assigned credit or blame for shaping young people's lives, is nearly extinct. At the same time, the "long reach of the carceral state" extends farther than ever. Urban adolescents now experience the interaction of these two institutions in a remarkably different manner than did their counterparts even a decade ago. The confluence of declining budgets and wholesale educational reform with increased correctional spending has created an educational system that stratifies the paths taken by young people toward the next institution in their lives—whether the University of Chicago, a community college, or a correctional center—at ever earlier stages. The "restoration in apartheid schooling" in our nation's urban public schools, to use Jonathan Kozol's term, underscores the racial, spatial, and socioeconomic dimensions of the educational trajectories of our youth.[1]

This is particularly true for Chicago, where massive policy initiatives have transformed public schools and public housing, two of its central public institutions. In the early 2000s, the transformation and demolition of Chicago's immense stock of high-rise public housing converged with the "Renaissance 2010" educational reform that closed or combined over 100 public schools. Revamped school discipline policies in the 1990s and 2000s made even more substantial changes to the form and function of the city's public schools. In some schools, students now perceive the focus of the administration, teachers, and school-based police and security officers to be on surveillance and control instead of protection and education, and fewer of them feel safe and secure as they travel to and from school or even within their schools. More recently, Chicago public schools have incorporated the principles of procedural and restorative justice into their disciplinary policies and practices, but those changes may not always be felt on the ground.

These major spatial and social changes in the schools and neighborhoods of this "great American city" have required greater mobility from Chicago youth. The educational changes not only have provided a more extensive "portfolio of educational options" to students in the Chicago public school system but have also exposed them to the symbolic and actual dangers posed by navigating unfamiliar social and physical terrain. Nor does increased physical mobility necessarily create opportunities for greater social mobility. As the sociologist Patrick Sharkey demonstrates in his work on Chicago, many of these young people remain "stuck in place."[2]

The new model of urban education being pushed by Chicago Public Schools has resulted in a great number of lessons being learned outside of the schools' corridors and classrooms. Beyond traditional curricula, young people are tasked with learning the locations of boundaries of race, place, class, and more, and how to achieve safe passage within and across these boundaries. These "routines and rituals" force adolescents to recognize and be strategic in their responses to the myriad institutional, social, and physical controls that affect them.

Schools have become more powerful engines of social stratification than neighborhoods. This finding directly challenges the prevailing theories held by urban sociologists, such as Robert Sampson, who emphasize the "enduring neighborhood effect" on social inequality.[3] Still, paradoxes abound. Schools are one of the primary reasons young people traverse neighborhood boundaries, but they can also operate as the reason some adolescents remain cloistered within those boundaries. Schools present students with the risk of violence—either actual or symbolic—depending on the context. Students alternately see schools as safe havens and as staging areas for danger, an enigma that must be accounted for in any analysis that assesses neighborhood and school effects. Even as some administrators seem to see young people's presence in schools as threatening, some students see the adults who surveil and control them as a dangerous force. Finally, it is clear that the racial composition of a school's student body overwhelmingly shapes students' perceptions and experiences. The fact that increased school diversity may lead to higher perceptions of injustice among African American and Hispanic youth speaks to the "protective" properties of segregation and social isolation, which can prevent youth from confirming their individual- and group-level disadvantage.

The phenomena analyzed in this study might best be described as "rites of passage" for urban youth. Each of these adolescents has his or her own particular journey, but all of them are coming of age through experiences in their residential and educational domains. These experiences shape young people's larger understandings of fairness, equality, and justice, and their perceptions, in turn, reflect their demographic characteristics, their social circumstances as determined by their institutional contexts, and their relationships with different authority figures as they traverse these worlds. Most importantly, the particular ways in which adolescents navigate Chicago's physical and social geography have a significant influence on their beliefs about their individual and collective futures, as well as their prospects.

Of course, the situation in Chicago is not entirely unique. *Unequal City* stands as one of the few comparative studies that simultaneously captures the attitudes and experiences of White, African American, Hispanic, and Asian American respondents. While grounded in Chicago, the findings can be extrapolated to anyplace in the country where marginalized minors are likely to traverse neighborhood and school boundaries and develop a heightened sense of the injustice present in their own neighborhoods. These findings are critical because perceptions shape decisionmaking, behaviors, and outcomes; thus, the social-psychological, educational policy, and urban policy dimensions of this work should be crystal clear. When young people think that the authority figures in their lives extend fair treatment to them, they are likely to accept even a negative outcome from their interactions with those authorities (such as arrest). When youth whose lives are governed by unjust institutions fail to perceive injustice, but also fail to succeed, they understand their failure to be personal instead of perceiving race, class, or other social factors as key contributors to social inequality.

My research suggests that transmitting a sense of fair treatment and procedural justice should be central to the organization of authoritative institutions. Moreover, a commitment to fairness and procedural justice must be duly executed by authority figures, including not only judges in the courts but also teachers in the schools and police officers in the streets, since young people are often introduced to the criminal justice system without setting foot in a jail or courtroom. For too long, such a commitment to fairness and procedural justice has been inconsistent or lacking in the urban institutions that so profoundly affect the lives of urban youth, and now is the time to take stock of the potentially devastating consequences for urban communities and our society at large.

* * *

They don't even realize the paradigm of violence they exist in. A fish doesn't realize it's swimming in water. It just swims.

—Carolyn Elaine

Carolyn Elaine, an artist and Fenger High alumna (class of 1980), worked with students several months after Derrion Albert's death in 2009 to create something positive out of yet another American tragedy.[4] Their collaborative mural, entitled *Choose Your Own Legacy,* memorializes Albert and other students lost to violence. It chronicles Albert's accomplishments in his short life and recounts other positive characteristics associated with the school and its history. Instead of fixating on Albert's heartbreaking demise, Elaine wanted this mural and the students' communal efforts in producing it to be Derrion Albert's legacy.

The idea that adolescents navigating through Chicago's neighborhoods and schools could be akin to fish who swim without realizing they are in water is visually and conceptually arresting. The image also succinctly captures the central argument of this research. Perceiving injustice—that is, recognizing that there is an unequal distribution of justice—requires that an individual both *expect* that equitable treatment is possible for others, even if not for himself or herself, and be able to *confirm* that others have received better treatment. Individuals who perceive low levels of injustice may believe that members of their group are treated as fairly as other groups, or even better, because they truly are (the case with the White and Asian American or Filipino students in the sample), or because they have a "restricted comparative frame" or reduced expectations (the experience of youth who live and learn in the same neighborhood, in a low-resource environment). The ninth-grader attending Harper who has been searched but not arrested multiple times in one year may simply assume that this happens to everyone. What will happen to him when he realizes that this is not in fact the case?

The consequences of this dawning realization must be addressed, especially since police contacts are the most direct link between law enforcement and the public. Adolescents begin to have contacts with police during a formative period that simultaneously shapes their lifelong attitudes and their life trajectories. "Stop and frisk" is only the first of what may be repeated contacts with the justice system at deeper and more severe levels for the young men and women involved in these searches.

Even so, it is necessary to move beyond the micro-level analyses of police contacts to better understand the larger nexus of state-based interventions in the lives of urban adolescents. Simply put, we must examine the fundamental relationship that citizens of every racial and ethnic designation have with the state. This is particularly true for urban citizens, who receive state support and for whom pervasive and invasive interactions with legal and social authorities are all but inevitable.

It is time to fully interrogate the meaning of "public." For instance, the home is considered a private domain—unless one resides in public housing, in which case "home" is the property of the state. Who remains in the public schools in Chicago? Unless you count the surging population of White students returning to the city's top public selective enrollment schools, African American and Hispanic youth are the children who have been "left behind."[5] And both of these public institutions, housing and education, fully embed the police within their authority and governance structures (to positive and negative effects).

Just as schools are beginning to resemble prisons, the youth contained in these spaces are in danger of fulfilling the expectations that authorities project onto them via negative racial, gender, class, and neighborhood stereotypes. *Unequal City* has tracked adolescents' experiences within and navigation through ostensibly free yet potentially penalizing places. In the name of justice, and often in the name of protecting our youth, America's school and criminal justice systems are veering toward a curious alliance that I have called the universal carceral apparatus, with dangerous repercussions for the children in their grasp. America's teenagers, who daily seek safe passage as they journey from home to school, are the guinea pigs for an enormous experiment in the ways we create (or fail to create) a citizenry that feels safe and has faith in the country's institutions. We must reckon with the attitudes and experiences of youth today because they, in turn, will have the greatest effect on the state of America tomorrow.

ACKNOWLEDGMENTS

There are many individuals and institutions that have provided tremendous support throughout my journey from the southern roads of Piney Woods, Mississippi, to my current home, Harlem, New York. Without them this book would not have been possible.

I am greatly indebted to the members of my dissertation committee at Northwestern University not only for shaping this research, but for shaping me as a lifelong student and scholar. Bob Nelson's commitment to deeply analyzing the intersections between sociology and law has greatly influenced my current scholarship and will continue to shape my future research endeavors. I am grateful to my committee chair, John Hagan, for his insightful, patient, and gentle guidance through the graduate school process and for the many invaluable lessons he continues to teach me as I navigate this next phase of my academic career. Working with Mary Pattillo has been one of the highlights of my academic experience. Mary makes balancing academia with a "regular life" look effortless. She is an amazing mentor and advisor, and I am also honored to have her as a friend. Thanks too to Aldon Morris, Wendy Espeland, Penny Warren, Julia Harris, and many other faculty and staff at Northwestern University for their support and encouragement through my graduate school career.

The National Consortium on Violence Research under Alfred Blumstein funded the research assistantship that allowed me to begin working with the data used for the quantitative portion of the research that informed this book. I would like to thank Dr. Holly Hart at the Consortium on Chicago School Research (CCSR) and Dr. John Q. Easton. John Weinberger (formerly) of the Chicago Public School Law Department was quite instrumental in facilitating the research approval process. Ruth Diane Wallace was an incomparable resource helping facilitate my entry to the four Chicago Public High Schools that I studied for this project, as were the principals, teachers, police/security personnel, research department personnel, and many other CPS staff members.

Several fellowships allowed me to concentrate on this work at different stages of my career. Roz Caldwell, Lucinda Underwood, and the rest of the staff of the American Bar Foundation in Chicago were immensely helpful during my time as a Law and Social Science Certificate Fellow. A summer fellowship in the Department of Criminology at the University of Maryland College Park gave me the time and space to transcribe and code my interviews. The Department of Sociology at Bryn Mawr College was a stimulating and nurturing environment during my tenure as an Andrew Mellon Pre-doctoral/Post-Doctoral Fellow where I wrote the first draft of this research (the dissertation). David Karen, Mary Osirim, Bob Washington, and Nathan Wright were especially supportive. The Ford Foundation Post-Doctoral Diversity Fellowship and the Russell Sage Foundation Fellowship provided additional support to allow me to focus on revising and rewriting this project. My fellow visitors at Russell Sage provided sage comments that sharpened the material and the arguments presented herein, especially Robert Sampson, Dorothy Sue Cobble, James House, Judy Seltzer, Miguel Urquiola, and the late Suzanne Bianchi.

I am grateful for the many colleagues and friends who read this work at different stages and provided invaluable feedback and encouragement. Thank you Charmaine Mangram, Keesha Middlemass, R. L'Heureux Lewis-McCoy, Natasha Lightfoot, Jenny Korn, Tennille Allen, Shamus Khan, Stacey Sutton, Christina Greer, Premilla Nadasen, Leith Mullings, Leslie Paik, Diane Vaughan, Priscilla Ferguson, Thomas DiPrete, Gil Eyal, Alondra Nelson, Karen Barkey, Samuel K. Roberts, Marcellus Blount, Farah J. Griffin, Carl Hart, Josef Sorett, Dorian T. Warren, Mabel O. Wilson, Steven Gregory, Priscilla Ferguson, Debra Minkoff, Sudhir Venkatesh, Peter Bearman, Susan Sturm, Jeff Fagan, Marcia Sells, the late Manning Marable, (remaining) colleagues in Sociology, the Institute for African American Studies, and the Center for Justice, members of the Racial Democracy, Crime, and Justice Network, and my writing and support group—Sister Scholars.

I must also extend my appreciation to students who provided research assistance for this book including Brittany Fox, Essane Diedro, Nereira Greene, Kathryn Benjamin, Danielle Gonzalez, and Andrew Avorn. James Quinn created the maps, and Galo Falchettore provided technical assistance for several of the figures. I am grateful for administrative support from Anne Born, Nusaiba Jackson, Afton Battle, Dora Arenas, Kiamesha Wilson, Jacqueline Pineda-Vega, Sharon Harris, and Shawn Mendoza. Thank you to the hardworking staff at the Russell Sage Foundation (RSF) including Suzanne Nichols, David Haproff, Aixa Cintrón-Vélez, Jacqueline Cholmondeley, and the RSF editing and publication team.

I am extremely grateful to my incredible network of family and friends, some of whom are already mentioned above. Thank you Dania Francis, Nesheba Kittling, Dana Powell, Brandye Lee, Lamaretta Simmons-Kelderman, Keesha Green, Jade Moore-Spradley, Leslie Wingard, Laverne Horton, Terry Wynn, Kamilah Allen, and Adam Theoharis. After the birth of my son, Benjamin, I joined a supportive circle of NYC moms and dads who have provided a lifeline in myriad ways. I also had the good fortune to have wonderful caregivers who looked after Benjamin affording me the necessary time and peace of mind to work on this book: Dora, Cornelia, Veronica (Soto), Vicki, Glenda, Iris, Gail, and Rita.

To my dear aunts, uncles, godparents, and cousins who are too numerous to name, you have been amazing models of accomplishment, strength, and spirit, especially after I lost both of my parents at age thirteen. I could not have made it this far without your love and support. To my nephew and niece, Javae and Sydney, thank you for being a constant source of inspiration and love. To Vikki and Carmen, my dear sisters, thank you for championing all of my endeavors and keeping me rooted no matter how far I am away from home. And to Joshua, my friend, husband, and co-parent, you have been an amazing partner in our shared journey in both academia and life. Thank you for your love, patience, support, and for always pushing me to be my best self. Benjamin, you amaze and inspire me every day with your wit, beauty, and curiosity. I truly hope this world we've brought you into will allow you to realize your full potential. I dedicate this book to the spirits of your future sibling, your late step-grandfather, Cordell "Doc" Jackson, and your late grandparents, Charles Clifton Shedd, Jr., and Virgia Brocks-Shedd.

Most importantly, I thank the students who participated in this study (all names are pseudonyms they chose themselves). I appreciate you letting me into your lives and sharing your perspectives and experiences with the world. Without your voice, I would not be able to have my own.

APPENDICES

Appendix A: Methods

Every other year, the Chicago Consortium on School Research (CCSR), based out of the University of Chicago, conducts surveys of principals, teachers, and students in the majority of Chicago public schools to gather information on their experiences and use their answers to improve the school system. The 2001 iteration of the high school survey included several questions about perceptions of social and criminal injustice and contact with police, thereby allowing access to the backgrounds, thoughts, and experiences of over 20,000 ninth- and tenth-grade students enrolled in public schools. As a baseline assessment, the timing of this survey was fortuitous: Chicago underwent monumental transformations in schooling and public housing that would reshape its physical and social landscape in the first decade of the twenty-first century under the mayoral administration of Richard M. Daley II.

The survey yielded almost 200 measures, ranging in topic from students' attachment to teachers, their plans for the future, and safety and order in their schools to their assessments of their home neighborhoods, in addition to the questions on equality and justice that are central to this study. The sample is representative of the population of Chicago public high schools, in that it includes sixty-eight high schools with more than 50 percent of students responding, out of the eighty-five eligible schools that were sent the surveys. The survey's focus on ninth- and tenth-grade students is also significant. These first two years of high school are considered crucial, both developmentally and socially, since freshman year is the grade during which the largest number of students leave Chicago public high schools.[1] These survey data therefore allow me to access the attitudes and experiences of Chicago youth just before a substantial number of them drop out.

The survey gauges multiple facets of these teenagers' thinking about their lives and the lives of those who go to school with them, teach them, police them, parent them, and reside with them in their neighborhoods. My use of the survey concentrates mostly on the questions concerning issues that young people think about but are usually never asked about, especially two scales that were created to assess students' perceptions of injustice. The first of these is the *perceptions of social injustice scale,* which charts the range of attitudes that students hold about life's equality. Each student was asked whether racial discrimination makes it difficult for members of his or her race to "find a good job" and "find a place to live." These measures of general injustice are important because students' beliefs about employment outcomes and housing opportunities for themselves and their racial counterparts aid in gauging their thoughts about mobility and life chances more generally.

A second measure, the *perceptions of criminal injustice scale,* assesses various forms of discrimination and measures perceptions of whether or not police engage in racial, gender, age, and class discrimination. Specifically, students were asked to indicate their level of agreement with five statements concerning whether people from their racial group are more likely to be unfairly stopped and questioned by the police or treated worse by police than people from other racial groups; and whether police treat young people worse than old people, males worse than females, and the rich better than the poor.

To gain a bit more information about the kids and their experiences, as well as eliminate any potentially confounding issues in their responses to these questions, the survey asked a variety of other questions. Information on demographics and family background measures (including race-ethnicity and parental educational attainment); school achievement, self-efficacy, collective efficacy, school attachment, perceptions of safety at home and school, adult support, adult supervision, trouble in school, police contact, and relevant school and neighborhood measures (for example, the percentage of low-income students in their school and their neighborhood's socioeconomic status) all served as controls that allowed me to separate these important social indicators from the questions that gauged students' perceptions of social and criminal injustice.

As I worked with these data, I became increasingly aware that numbers alone were not enough. Like all of us, teenagers can be both shockingly profound and amazingly hard to read. The sheets of tables, charts, and graphs generated from the quantitative survey analyses provided a rich portrait of a few particular lines of thinking, but could not represent the richness and variety—and yes, the frustration, surprise, and bewilderment—of actually interacting with the students themselves. As a result, in 2005 I surveyed and interviewed forty teenagers from four schools across Chicago to supplement the 2001 quantitative data. The four schools were selected primarily on the basis of the racial composition of their student body, their selective enrollment status (two were selective, two were regular), and their surrounding neighborhoods. Principals in each school gave me a typical homeroom from which to draw a sample of students. From the pool of students who returned parental consent forms, I selected a group of ten students who allowed me to maximize the variation of respondents by racial composition, perceptions of social and criminal injustice, and police contact.[2] After completing a replication of the 2001 survey, the forty students (ten from each school) participated in a semistructured, open-ended interview. These sessions, conducted in unoccupied classrooms in two schools and in semiprivate rooms in the libraries of the remaining two, were each approximately forty-five minutes long. Getting students to answer the questions was like pulling teeth with only a few of them; the vast majority had so much to say that we could have talked for hours. We talked about everything from how they traveled to school to which class they enjoyed best, how much their parents supervised their free time, and even their ideas about the rules and laws they had to follow inside and outside the schoolhouse doors.[3]

In 2010 I tracked and reinterviewed four students from two schools, Payton Prep and Tilden Career Academy, after a very extensive process navigating the Institutional Review Boards (IRBs) for both Columbia University and the Chicago Public Schools. Since I received IRB approval to do the original research for my dissertation in 2005, CPS had revised the process to be more rigorous than that of university IRBs. For example, I had a pending acceptance from Columbia's IRB for a more ambitious study plan to survey and interview twenty students from each of the same four schools in 2009 to collect their assessments of opportunity and perceptions of injustice after former Illinois senator Barack Obama became President Barack Obama. I applied through the revamped IRB process for permission through the CPS system at the same time and received a pending acceptance. Both IRB applications required the other institution's acceptance before granting their own. I was at an impasse. So I modified the plan by attempting to contact the original thirty-six students I surveyed and interviewed to get a purposive sample of students by school with varying perceptions on social and criminal injustice and divergent outcomes with regard to educational attainment and police contact. This was allowed under the original IRB proposal with a "consent to recontact" provision, and all research participants were older than eighteen.

I corresponded with all thirty-six individuals by mail, email, and social media (I created a dedicated Facebook page) and/or called and left messages by phone. As one can imagine, the population I studied was extremely mobile owing to relocation because of housing, schooling, or personal reasons. Six mailed envelopes came back to me as undeliverable because the recipient was unknown or had moved. Eight email addresses no longer worked. I was able to reach eleven individuals by email or Facebook. Six of them responded and were excited to get an update on the project and expressed an interest in participating in a second phase of the study. I ultimately decided to survey and interview four of them: Jackson and Jasmine from Tilden and Vanessa and Gabrielle from Payton. I reinterviewed Jackson and Jasmine at their residences in August 2010. Vanessa was in New York in August 2010, so she completed the interview and survey in a seminar room in Columbia's Sociology Department. Gabrielle was unable to make our scheduled appointment in Chicago in August 2010, so she submitted her survey via email, and I conducted her interview by phone in September 2010.

The blend of the quantitative data from 2001 and the qualitative data from 2005 and 2010 creates a potent mix of information. By blending quantitative and qualitative data, I am trying to do justice to the complexity of my subject, allowing greater depth than either method could provide alone.[4] Also, in the time that passed as I tried to secure permissions to follow up with these youth, I got a better grasp of the long-range and wide-angle view of this work. I realized that this study was more than just an examination of how schools have become more "prisonized" and how kids are being "criminalized." The revision process made it clear that this work would be a force that could shift the debates from studying neighborhood effects, especially in Chicago, to analyzing schools as sites of social mobility and determinants of adolescents' physical mobility.

In changing to a focus on schools and how young people navigate Chicago's social and physical terrain en route to and from those institutions, I realized that I would have to reveal the schools I studied in order to be transparent in my arguments and truly open the debate, especially in light of the monumental transformations in the formation and dynamics of Chicago's schools and neighborhoods since 2005. Doing so required that I return to the CPS legal department and demonstrate that I was not revealing students' identities even though I did plan to name the schools. Since 2010, there have been significant changes in all schools, but I went back to each of the four and touched base with the administration, took pictures, and let them know the book was in preparation. It was important for them to know that the schools would be named, but that naming them would provide an opening for validation and recommendations suited for their specific contexts toward improving students' experiences and educational outcomes. Identifying the four schools also fully allows readers to ground the research findings across the various neighborhood and school settings discussed here. This would not have been so powerfully true if I had only been able to use school and neighborhood pseudonyms for a book about adolescent journeys within and across Chicago's neighborhoods and schools.

Appendix B: Survey Questionnaire: Perceptions of Social Injustice and the Legitimacy of the Law and Compliance with the Law

INTRODUCTION AND PURPOSE

You are being asked to participate in a research study on youths' experiences with discrimination, perceptions of injustice, and the law. You are being asked to participate in this study because your feelings about social justice and the law are important for understanding how you process these feelings and how they may influence past, present, and future behavior. Your answers will be combined with those of other students to tell people who work to improve schools what students at CPS think, do, and experience. Your answers are CONFIDENTIAL and will not be identified as yours.

This survey is voluntary. We hope you will answer as many questions as you can but *you do NOT have to answer any question you do not wish to answer.* Thank you very much for your help!

School Number _____

Student ID _____

Survey Instructions

This is not a test; there are no right or wrong answers. Please feel free to give your honest opinions.

This study is voluntary. If there is a question you do not wish to answer, you may skip it. But we hope you will answer as many questions as possible.

If there is something you do not understand, just raise your hand.

Please use a No. 2 pencil to mark your answers.

Please mark one answer for each question, unless the question asks you to do something else. Choose the answer that is most true for you.

Your Background

1. Were you born in the United States?	Mark (X) one
YES (then skip to question 3)	
NO (then continue to question 2)	

2. How old were you when you first moved to the United States?	Mark (X) one
Less than six years	
More than six years	
Nine to twelve years	
More than twelve years	

3. Do you speak any language other than English?	Mark (X) one
YES (then continue to question 4)	
NO (then skip to question 6)	

4. How often do you use this language when talking to your parents?	Mark (X) one
Never	
Once in a while	
Most of the time	
All of the time	

5. How often do you use this language when talking to your school friends?	Mark (X) one
Never	
Once in a while	
Most of the time	
All of the time	

6. Where was your *mother* born? Please write the city, state, and country below.

7. How do you identify your race? (for example, Asian, Black/African American, Hispanic/Latino, White, etc.)

8. How do identify your ethnicity? (for example, African American, Chinese, Mexican, Puerto Rican, etc.)

9. Gender?	Mark (X) one
Male	
Female	

10. How do you identify your skin complexion *in relation to others in your racial-ethnic group?*	Mark (X) one
Very light	
Light	
Medium	
Dark	
Very dark	

11. How do you identify your skin complexion *in relation to others in your family?*	Mother	Father	Sister	Brother
Lighter than me				
Same/nearly the same complexion				
Darker than me				

12. Which of the following adults live in your home?	Mark (X) all that apply
Mother	
Father	
Stepmother	
Stepfather	
Grandmother	
Grandfather	
Other relatives	
Other male adult (not related to you)	
Other female adult (not related to you)	

13. What is the highest level of schooling your mother or other adult female living in your house has completed?	Mark (X) one
Some grade school or high school	
Completed high school	
Vocational or trade school	
Some college	
Completed college	
Completed advanced degree after college	
Don't know	

14. Which of the following does your family have in your home?	Mark (X) all that apply
A quiet place for you to study and do your homework	
A dictionary	
A computer	
Internet access	
A daily newspaper	
An encyclopedia	
More than fifty books	
An atlas	
A room of your own	

Your Perceptions of Injustice

15. How much do you agree with the following?	Strongly disagree	Disagree	Agree	Strongly agree
People from my racial group are more likely to be unfairly stopped and questioned by the police than people from other racial groups.				
Discrimination makes it harder for people from my racial group to find a good job.				
Discrimination makes it harder for people from my racial group to find good places to live.				
Discrimination makes it harder for people from my racial group to get good grades in school.				

16. How much do you agree with the following?	Strongly disagree	Disagree	Agree	Strongly agree
The police treat young people worse than old people.				
The police treat rich people better than poor people.				
The police treat people from my racial group worse than people from other racial groups.				
The police treat males worse than females.				

17. How many times *in the past year* have the following happened to you?	Never	One to two times	Three to five times	More than five times
Been told to move on by the police				
Been stopped and asked questions by the police				
Been searched by the police				
Been arrested by the police				

18. How much do you agree with the following?	Strongly disagree	Disagree	Agree	Strongly agree
I respect the police.				
Police are fair.				
I trust the police.				
I am willing to help the police.				
Police think youth are bad.				
Police hassle youth.				
Police care about the neighborhood I live in.				
Police care about the neighborhood I go to school in.				
Police make me feel afraid.				

19. How much do you agree with the following?	Strongly disagree	Disagree	Agree	Strongly agree
Laws are made to be broken.				
It's okay to do anything you want as long as you don't hurt anyone.				
To make money, there are no right and wrong ways anymore, only easy ways and hard ways.				
Fighting between friends or within families is nobody else's business.				
Nowadays a person has to live pretty much for today and let tomorrow take care of itself.				

Safety and Order in Your School

20. How safe do you feel . . .	Not safe	Somewhat safe	Mostly safe	Very safe
Outside around school?				
Traveling between home and school?				
In the hallways and bathrooms of the school?				
In your classes?				

21. How many students at your school are in a gang?	Mark (X) one
Almost none	
About one-quarter	
About half	
More than half	

22. How many times *this school year* have you . . .	Never	One to two times	Three to five times	More than five times
Gotten in trouble at school?				
Gotten into a physical fight with another student at school?				
Been put on in-school suspension?				
Been suspended from school?				

23. How many times *this school year* have . . .	Never	One to two times	Three to five times	More than five times
Your parents been contacted because you got into trouble?				
Your parents had to come to school because you got into trouble?				

Your Parents and Other Adults You Live With

24. During this school year, how often have you discussed the following with your parents and other adults living with you?	Never	One to two times	Three to five times	More than five times
Selected courses or programs at school				
School activities or events of interest to you				
Things you have studied in class				
Homework				
Going to college				
Your grades				

25. How often does a parent or other adult living with you . . .	Never	Once in a while	Most of the time	All of the time
Help you with your homework?				
Check to see if you have done your homework?				
Praise you for doing well in school?				
Encourage you to take responsibility for things you have done?				
Encourage you to work hard at school?				
Make sure you get to school on time?				
Know where you are after school?				
Is somewhere that you can get in touch with anytime you need to?				
Wait for you at home after school?				

Your Plans for the Future

26. What is the highest level of education you expect to complete?	Mark (X) one
Complete tenth grade	
Graduate high school/get a GED	
Trade/vocational school	
Graduate from a two-year community college	
Graduate from a four-year college or university	
Get a degree beyond college (law, medical, master's, or doctorate)	

27. Think about the teacher, coach, counselor, or other adult at your school who is closest to you. Does that person . . .	Yes	No
Encourage you to continue your education after high school?		
Talk to your parents/guardian about your plans after high school?		
Help you think about what job or occupation you want as an adult?		
Help you to prepare for your plans after high school?		

28. Do you think your parents/guardian . . .	Yes	No
Expect you to graduate from high school?		
Expect you to continue your education after high school?		
Expect you to work full-time after you graduate from high school?		
Are helping you prepare for your plans after high school?		

29. Do you have an idea of what job or occupation you would like to have as an adult?	Mark (X) one
Yes	
No	
If yes, please write that job or occupation in the space below.	

You and Your School Experiences

30. How much do you agree with the following?	Strongly disagree	Disagree	Agree	Strongly agree
I usually look forward to school.				
I wish I didn't have to go to school.				
I wish I could go to a different school.				
I'm bored in school.				
I'm glad to get back to school after summer vacation.				

31. How much do you agree with the following?	Strongly disagree	Disagree	Agree	Strongly agree
I can always find a way to help people end arguments.				
I listen carefully to what other people say to me.				
I'm good at taking turns and sharing things with others.				

	Strongly disagree	Disagree	Agree	Strongly agree
It's very easy for me to make suggestions without being bossy.				
I'm very good at working with other students.				
I'm good at helping people.				
I should just take care of myself and let others take care of themselves.				
It is important to help others in my community.				
It is important to solve the problems of poor people.				

32. During the typical week, how many hours do you spend studying or doing work outside of school?	Mark (X) one
Less than one hour	
One to three hours	
Three to five hours	
Five to ten hours	

33. This year, how often have you . . .	Never	Once in a while	Once a week	Almost every day
Attended after-school programs for help with schoolwork (like tutoring, discussions, or Saturday school)?				
Participated in *school* clubs and organizations (like a sports team, student council, drama club, school newspaper, etc.)?				
Participated in other groups *outside of school* (like boys and girls club, parks program, Boy/Girl Scouts, or church group)?				
Hung out with friends after school without an adult there?				
Worked at a job?				

Your Teachers

34. How much do you agree with the following?	Strongly disagree	Disagree	Agree	Strongly agree
My teachers really care about me.				
My teachers always keep their promises.				
My teachers don't care what I think.				
My teachers always try to be fair.				
My teachers punish kids without even knowing what happened.				
I feel safe and comfortable with my teachers in this school.				
My teachers get mad whenever I make a mistake.				
When my teachers tell me not to do something, I know they have good reason.				
My teachers will always listen to students' ideas.				

35. About how many teachers at this school know you by name?	Mark (X) one
None	
A few	
About half	
Most	
All	

36. In the past year, about how often have you attended religious services?	Mark (X) one
More than once a week	
About once a week	
Two to three times a month	
Once a month	
Several times a year	
Not at all	

37. Do you think of yourself as a religious person?	Mark (X) one
Yes, very.	
Yes, somewhat.	
No, not at all.	

Your Community

38. How much do you agree with the following statements about the community *in which you live?*	Strongly disagree	Disagree	Agree	Strongly agree
If there is a problem in the community, neighbors get together to deal with it.				
No one in this neighborhood cares much about what happens here.				
There are adults in this neighborhood that children can look up to.				
You can count on adults in this neighborhood to see that children are safe and do not get into trouble.				
During the day, it is safe for children to play in the local park or playground.				
People in this neighborhood can be trusted.				
The equipment and buildings in the neighborhood park or playground are well kept.				

Appendix C: General Interview Protocol

Note: I will have the respondents' answers from the previously administered questionnaire to most efficiently guide my questions and probes.

1. Background
   a. Name
   b. Grade
   c. Extracurricular activities/hobbies
   d. Aspirations for education and occupation

    e. Neighborhood
    f. Parents/siblings

2. School
    a. Happiness with school
    b. Best/worst attributes of school
    c. Reasons they look forward to (or don't look forward to) school
    d. Perceptions of safety around the school
    e. Issues with gangs
    f. Transportation to/from school

3. Neighborhood
    a. Proximity of neighborhood to school
    b. Happiness with neighborhood
    c. Best/worst attributes of neighborhood
    d. Perceptions of neighbors (both youth and adults)
    e. Happiness with neighborhood facilities (parks, etc.)
    f. Issues with gangs/safety

4. Peers
    a. Distribution of friends inside and outside of the neighborhood
    b. Distribution of friends from school
    c. Places where they hang out with friends (supervised or unsupervised)
    d. Activities they engage in with friends
    e. Aspirations of friends
    f. Their placement of leadership within peer group (leader or follower)

5. Family
    a. Intact or "disrupted" family
    b. Role respondent plays within household (just a child or expected to help out financially, etc.)
    c. Nature of relationship with parents, other adults in household, siblings (close or distant)
    d. Parental involvement in their education
    e. Parental accessibility
    f. Parental supervision/strictness

6. General feelings about authority figures/legitimacy *(does respondent believe these individuals have the right to tell them what to do?)*
    a. Parents
    b. Neighborhood adults
    c. Teachers
    d. Principals
    e. Police

7. Ever in "trouble" with authority figures
   a. Parent/guardian punishments
   b. Neighborhood adults
   c. Teachers
   d. Principals
   e. Police

8. Ever had contact with police
   a. Nature of contact
      1. voluntary or involuntary
   b. Extent of contact
      1. Told to move off or move on
      2. Stopped
      3. Searched
      4. Arrested
   c. Outcome of contact
      1. Disposition of contact (warning, citation, detention, etc.)
   d. Feelings on fairness of contact and outcome

9. Perceptions of injustice *(probe questions according to above answers on trouble with authority figures)*

10. Potential role played by perceptions of injustice in past behavior

11. Potential role that perceptions of injustice may play in future behavior

12. Open discussion/necessary follow-up questions

Appendix D: Chicago Community Areas

Community Area	Community	Community Area	Community
1	Rogers Park	6	Lake View
2	West Ridge	7	Lincoln Park
3	Uptown	8	Near North Side
4	Lincoln Square	9	Edison Park
5	North Center	10	Norwood Park

Community Area	Community	Community Area	Community
11	Jefferson Park	45	Avalon Park
12	Forest Glen	46	South Chicago
13	North Park	47	Burnside
14	Albany Park	48	Calumet Heights
15	Portage Park	49	Roseland
16	Irving Park	50	Pullman
17	Dunning	51	South Deering
18	Montclare	52	East Side
19	Belmont Cragin	53	West Pullman
20	Hermosa	54	Riverdale
21	Avondale	55	Hegewisch
22	Logan Square	56	Garfield Ridge
23	Humboldt Park	57	Archer Heights
24	West Town	58	Brighton Park
25	Austin	59	McKinley Park
26	West Garfield Park	60	Bridgeport
27	East Garfield Park	61	New City
28	Near West Side	62	West Elsdon
29	North Lawndale	63	Gage Park
30	South Lawndale	64	Clearing
31	Lower West Side	65	West Lawn
32	Loop	66	Chicago Lawn
33	Near South Side	67	West Englewood
34	Armour Square	68	Englewood
35	Douglas	69	Greater Grand Crossing
36	Oakland		
37	Fuller Park	70	Ashburn
38	Grand Boulevard	71	Auburn Gresham
39	Kenwood	72	Beverly
40	Washington Park	73	Washington Heights
41	Hyde Park	74	Mount Greenwood
42	Woodlawn	75	Morgan Park
43	South Shore	76	O'Hare
44	Chatham	77	Edgewater

NOTES

Preface

1. Common designations of ethnic groups by color, such as Black and White, are capitalized in this work. Study participants may also use Black and African American interchangeably. When possible, specific ethnic designations are used, including Filipino, Mexican American, and Puerto Rican.
2. NRC and IOM (2003). Northwestern's John D. MacArthur Professor of Sociology and Law, John Hagan, was the principal investigator. Paul Hirschfield and I were his graduate research assistants. See Hagan, Hirschfield, and Shedd (2003a, 2003b) for further information on this project.
3. Eric Harrison and Tracy Shryer, "Chicago Police Brutality, Racism Alleged: Blacks Say Officers Have Declared 'Open Season' Under Daley," *Los Angeles Times,* September 30, 1989, 18; William Recktenwald, "2 Blacks Dropped Off in White Area Sue City," *Chicago Tribune,* December 15, 1989, 18.
4. Matt O'Connor, "Cops Cleared in Racial Beating Case," *Chicago Tribune,* April 3, 1991, 1.
5. "Police Fire Two Police Officers over Incident with Teens," *Chicago Sun-Times,* March 21, 1992, 4.

Chapter 1: Introduction: Crossing Boundaries of Race, Class, and Neighborhood

1. "Failing Grade," *Oprah,* April 11, 2006, available at: http://www.oprah.com /slideshow/oprahshow/oprahshow1_ss_20060411/3.
2. "Trading Schools," uploaded September 11, 2008, available at: http://www.you tube.com/watch?v=MXBUdwKk4Fw.
3. See Briggs (2005) for a place-centered analysis of opportunity that focuses on urban housing policies.
4. This book draws on sociologists Ruth Peterson and Lauren Krivo's (2010), 45,

definition of "divergent social worlds," a term they use for the residential separation of Whites, African Americans, and Latinos as it connects to the "dramatic differentiation in the social and economic character of neighborhoods."

5. There are some notable exceptions. Prudence Carter's (2006) ethnographic research reveals how race, ethnicity, and culture influence African American and Latino students' approaches to school. John Hagan and Bill McCarthy (1998) broadly present the lives, experiences, and criminalization of homeless Canadian youth in their own voices, and Mary Pattillo (1999/2013) explores the plight of youthful residents of a Black middle-class Chicago neighborhood.

6. Mortimer and Larson (2002), 15. Victor Rios (2011) ethnographically investigates Black and Latino youths' interactions with police in their neighborhoods, while Kathleen Nolan (2011), and Aaron Kupchik (2010), do the same for school-based police interactions.

7. Collins (2009), 63. See also Kupchik (2010) and Devine (1996).

8. My work draws on Robert Sampson and John Laub's (1993) age-graded theory of social control.

9. Lawrence Bobo and Devon Johnson (2004), 155, argue that "political and social values emerge early in life and are persistent."

10. In general, "youth" is defined as the period between puberty and adulthood (ages fifteen to twenty-four), but this terminology is relatively recent. The term replaced "adolescence," which, according to the psychologist Philip Graham, had been used "in classical times and in the Middle Ages to describe young people who had not achieved full adult social rights." English-speaking countries began replacing the term with "youth" in the early modern period, but the new term retained some of the ambiguity of "adolescence," in that a youth's status often changed once he or she experienced a transitional life event, such as marriage or employment. See Graham (2004), 25.

11. Jacob (1971).

12. Ibid., 79.

13. Davis (1959) and Runciman (1966), 9.

14. Runciman (1966), 9.

15. "As the dominant group in American society, Whites are at the top of the economic and social hierarchies; Blacks, conversely are at the bottom"; see Charles (2000), 205; see also Zubrinsky and Bobo (1996), Jaynes and Williams (1989), Massey and Denton (1993), Peterson and Krivo (2010), and Sugrue (2010).

16. Several social science studies demonstrate significant racial differences in Americans' perceptions of inequality, including discrimination in education, employment, health care, and housing; see Dawson (1994), Feagin and Sikes (1994), Hochschild (1995), and Schuman et al. (1997).

17. Harris (2011), Tyson (2011), and Carter (2005).

18. Kluegel (1995) and Kluegel and Smith (1986).

19. Hagan and Albonetti (1982) and Brooks and Jeon-Slaughter (2001). The sociologists John Hagan and Celesta Albonetti, for example, use data from a national survey of adults to show that Black Americans are considerably more

likely to perceive discrimination and bias within the criminal justice system than White Americans, even after controlling for class, education, income, and age. Their measure of perceived injustice includes questions on law enforcement officials and the police, the courts, juries, lawyers, and judges. In sum, as they move up the class structure to the working class and then into the professional and managerial classes, Blacks and Whites become increasingly divided in their perceptions of criminal injustice. Other studies have similarly found that, as Black people's incomes increase, they perceive less and less fairness in institutional control structures, such as the courts and the police (Brooks 2000; Brooks and Jeon-Slaughter 2001). The most intriguing of Hagan and Albonetti's findings, however, is that the influence of race on perceptions decreases with each step down their three class categories (the professional and managerial class, the working class, and the unemployed "surplus" population). The authors suggest that these scores indicate a class-consciousness among the unemployed vis-à-vis the criminal justice system that largely overcomes the factor of race (Hagan and Albonetti 1982), 343.

20. Tyler (1990). In a telephone survey of nearly 2,500 randomly selected residents of Chicago, Tyler queried respondents on their perceptions of the police; the fairness of the procedures and outcomes when they came into direct contact with the police; the fairness and effectiveness of courts and judges; and their perceptions of punishment, that is, how likely they were to be sentenced for committing a range of minor and major legal infractions.

21. Brunson (2002), La Vigne et al. (2014), Meares et al. (2009), Skogan (2005), Sunshine and Tyler (2003), Tyler and Fagan (2008), Tyler and Huo (2002), and Tyler and Wakslak (2004).

22. Jacob (1971), 87–88.

23. Gieryn (2000).

24. Ibid., 474 and 476.

25. Sibley (1995), xii–xiii.

26. Sibley defines areas where difference is less likely to be noticed and to be felt as a source of threat as "weakly classified environments," in contrast to "strongly classified, purified space" (ibid.), 90.

27. Ibid., 32.

28. Gieryn (2000), 479.

29. Sampson and Bartusch (1998), 800.

30. Anderson (1999), O'Connor (1999), and Young (2004).

31. See also Hagan and McCarthy (1998), 205.

32. Pattillo (1999/2013), Sampson (2012), Sharkey (2013), Venkatesh (2000), Wilson (1987), and Young (2004).

33. See Briggs (2005) for a place-centered analysis of opportunity focusing on urban housing policies.

34. For an overview of the connection between concentrated poverty and educational disadvantage in Chicago, see Massey and Denton (1993), 141; and Sharkey (2013), 14.

35. Illinois General Assembly, "Illinois Compiled Statutes," Schools (105 ILCS 5/) School Code, article 27A, Charter Schools, section 27A-2.b.8, available at: http://www.ilga.gov/legislation/ilcs/ilcs4.asp?ActID=1005&ChapterID=17 &SeqStart=164500000&SeqEnd=166400000 (accessed September 17, 2014).

36. "A Push for Charter Schools, But Little Difference in Test Scores," *Chicago Sun-Times*, April 15, 2014, available at: http://chicago.suntimes.com/chicago -politics/7/71/167471/a-push-for-charter-schools-but-little-difference-in-test- scores.

37. Becky Vevea, "Neighborhood High Schools Again Take Hit in New CPS Bud- get," WBEZ91.5, July 3, 2014, available at: http://www.wbez.org/news/neigh borhood-high-schools-again-take-hit-new-cps-budget-110444.

38. Linda Lutton and Becky Vevea, "Chicago Proposes Closing 53 Elementary Schools, Firing Staff at Another 6," WBEZ91.5, March 21, 2013, available at: http://www.wbez.org/news/chicago-proposes-closing-53-elementary-schools -firing-staff-another-6-106202; Steven Yaccino, "Protests Fail to Deter Chi- cago from Shutting 49 Schools," *New York Times,* May 22, 2013.

39. Lorraine Forte, "School Choice No Guarantee of Equal Education for Kids," *CatalystChicago,* November 7, 2008, available at: http://catalyst-chicago.org /2008/11/school-choice-no-guarantee-equal-education-kids/; see also Becky Vevea, "Neighborhood High Schools Again Take Hit in New CPS Budget."

40. Buckler, Unnever, and Cullen (2008), Hagan and McCarthy (1998), Hender- son et al. (1997), Matza (1964), Piquero (2008), Rice and Piquero (2005), and Tyler (1990).

41. When I was conducting this research, the area had been undergoing gentrifica- tion for several years. From 1995 to 2005, the residents of Cabrini-Green saw the construction of a new public library, a new grocery store (Dominick's), a Starbucks outlet, and other essential and non-essential amenities before the high-rises in the project were razed in 2011.

42. "Selected Economic Characteristics" for zip code 60614, Census 2008–2012, American Community Survey.

43. As of August 2014, there were nine selective enrollment schools in the CPS system.

44. Walter Payton College Prep, "Payton Profile," http://www.wpcp.org/About /AboutWPCP.aspx.

45. "Selected Economic Characteristics" for zip code 60610, Census 2008–2012, American Community Survey.

46. Walter Payton College Prep, "Payton Profile"; see also Chicago Public Schools (CPS) report on Payton College Prep, http://www.cps.edu/Schools/Pages /school.aspx?unit=1090.

47. "Selected Economic Characteristics" for zip code 60609. Census 2008–2012. American Community Survey.

48. Linda Lutton, "Future Uncertain for Chicago's Neighborhood High Schools," WBEZ91.5, October 3, 2013, available at: http://www.wbez.org/news/future

-uncertain-chicagos-neighborhood-high-schools-108834 (accessed July 14, 2014); see also WBEZ's compilation of Chicago ninth-graders' residence by high school attendance area at: http://llnw.wbez.org/FOIA%20response_WBEZ _09-22-2013_law%20review%20%283%29.pdf.

49. Tilden Career Community Academy, "In the Beginning," available at: http:// tilden.cps.edu/our-history.html.

50. For more history on Tilden, see Hagan et al. (2003a, 2003b) and Patterson (2013).

51. Tilden Career Community Academy, "In the Beginning."

52. "Selected Economic Characteristics" for zip code 60636, Census 2008–2012, American Community Survey.

53. William R. Harper High School, "School Profile," available at: http://www .harperhighschool.org/about/profile.jsp.

54. "487: Harper High School, Part One," *This American Life*, February 15, 2013, available at: http://www.thisamericanlife.org/radio-archives/episode/487/harper -high-school-part-one.

55. Peterson and Krivo (2010), 132.

56. Cullen and Wright (2002), 90.

Chapter 2: "And We Are Not Saved": Safe Passage Through a Changing Educational Landscape

1. Hagan et al. (2003a, 2003b); see also Devine (1996) and Kupchik (2010).

2. The title of this chapter refers to the book of the same title by the distinguished legal scholar Derrick Bell (1987). Bell uses ten metaphorical tales to examine the persistence of racial inequality in the aftermath of legal affirmations of equality, starting with the 1954 Brown v. Board of Education Supreme Court decision on school desegregation.

3. City of Chicago, "Mayor Daley Appoints Ronald Holt as New Director of CAPS Program," June 8, 2010, available at: http://www.cityofchicago.org/city /en/depts/mayor/press_room/press_releases/2010/june_2010/0608_caps_appt .html; see also Susan Saulny, "After Killings, Escorts for Chicago Students," *New York Times*, April 27, 2008; and Illinois Senate, "Senate Resolution" (on the death of Deverra Beverly), available at: http://www.ilga.gov/legislation/fulltext. asp?DocName=09800SR0788lv&SessionID=85&GA=98&DocTypeID=SR &DocNum=0788&print=true.

4. Emma Graves Fitzsimmons, "4 Teenagers Charged in Youth's Beating Death," *New York Times*, September 28, 2009.

5. Justice Maureen Connors, "Appeal from the Circuit Court of Cook County No. 09 CR 19310: The People of the State of Illinois v. Silvonus Shannon," Appellate Court of Illinois, First Judicial District, 2012, 2–3.

6.   Mallory Simon, "Official: Suspect Admits Role in Beating Death of Chicago Teen," CNN, September 29, 2009, available at: http://www.cnn.com/2009 /CRIME/09/28/chicago.teen.beating/index.html; see also Connors, "Appeal from the Circuit Court of Cook County No. 09 CR 19310," 2.

7.   Fitzsimmons, "4 Teenagers Charged in Youth's Beating Death"; Simon, "Official: Suspect Admits Role. . . ."

8.   For an in-depth exploration of the "Black Mobsters" in the "Groveland" neighborhood on the South Side of Chicago, see Pattillo-McCoy (1999/2013).

9.   Hagedorn (n.d.).

10. For more on schools and neighborhoods as staging areas, see Anderson (1999).

11. Anonymous, "Last Year, the Police Maced the Whole Hallway," *Salon,* October 19, 2009, available at: www.salon.com/opinion/feature/2009/10/19/chicago _fenger.

12. Their punishments ranged from seven years in a juvenile detention facility for the fourteen-year-old defendant to twenty-six years for one defendant who pled guilty and thirty-two years for the three others who went to trial. See Fitzsimmons, "4 Teenagers Charged in Youth's Beating Death"; B. J. Lutz and Jeff Goldblatt, "Juvenile Convicted in First Fenger Beating Death Trial," *NBC-Chicago,* December 8, 2010, available at: http://www.nbcchicago.com/news /local/juvenile-trial-derrion-albert-fenger-high-beating-death-111546674 .html; Connors, "Appeal from the Circuit Court of Cook County No. 09 CR 19310," 5; Jason Meisner, "4th Defendant Gets 32 Years in Teen's Beating Death," *Chicago Tribune,* July 20, 2011; Justice Maureen Connors, "Appeal: People v. Eugene Riley," 23; Jason Meisner, "Guilty Verdict in Final Trial of Videotaped Fenger Beating Death," *Chicago Tribune,* June 1, 2011; Sarah Schulte and Jessica D'Onofrio, "32-Year Sentence in Derrion Albert Beating Death," *ABC News,* August 29, 2011, available at: http://abclocal.go.com /ktrk/story?section=news/local&id=8332848.

13. Drawing on the work of other cultural sociologists, Prudence Carter (2005), 56, argues that the drawing of symbolic cultural boundaries allows for the creation of groups that "potentially produce inequality because they enable individuals to acquire status, monopolize resources, or ward off threats"; see also Lamont (1992) and Lamont and Molnár (2002).

14. Neckerman (2007).

15. Ibid., 178.

16. Ibid., 8.

17. Brown v. Board of Education, 347 U.S. 483 (1954).

18. Southern Poverty Law Center (2004).

19. Swan v. Charlotte-Mecklenburg Board of Education, 402 U.S. 1 (1971).

20. United States of America v. Board of Education of the City of Chicago, 80 C 5124 (2009), U.S. District Court, Northern District of Illinois, Eastern Division.

21. Ibid.

22. "U.S., Chicago Reach Pact on Desegregation," *Washington Post,* September 25, 1980, A1.

23. United States of America v. Board of Education of the City of Chicago, 1–3.

24. Ibid., 2–3.

25. Ibid., 1–2.

26. United States of America v. Board of Education of the City of Chicago, 1–3.

27. "Whites Getting More Spots at Top Chicago Public High Schools," *Chicago Sun-Times,* April 28, 2014, available at. http://chicago.suntimes.com/?p=166698.

28. Cassidy et al. (2009), part 3 of this five-part report; see also part 1, Humphrey and Shields (2009).

29. Humphrey and Shields (2009).

30. Popkin (2013).

31. Hailey and Gallagher (2013) and Sampson (2012).

32. For an overview, see Popkin (2013); for details on the impact on youth, see Hailey and Gallagher (2013).

33. Hailey and Gallagher (2013).

34. This assertion is not easily reconciled with Robert Sampson's (2012) claims about the enduring effects of the neighborhood on social life in Chicago.

35. Papachristos (2011, 2013).

36. For a description of a walk along Michigan Avenue, see Sampson (2012), 3–13.

37. See the methodological appendix for more details on the CCSR data; see also CCSR (2004).

38. Uptown has historically had more social service organizations and more transient populations, and its housing stock includes a relatively high percentage of single-room occupancy units (SROs) and nursing home facilities for the mentally ill and for criminally involved persons; see Gary Marx and David Jackson, "Chicago Nursing Homes: Slaying of Nursing-Home Resident in Nearby Motel Shows How Violence Can Spill into Neighborhoods," *Chicago Tribune,* December 1, 2009.

39. Looking at the community by census tract also reveals a great deal of variation in levels of poverty within the Uptown neighborhood.

40. Steve Bogira and Mick Dumke, "The Most Important Issue No One's Talking About in the Mayoral Race," *Chicago Reader,* February 4, 2015.

41. Ibid.

42. For more on race, poverty, and mobility patterns within and across Chicago neighborhoods, see Pattillo-McCoy (1999/2013), Sampson (2012), and Sharkey (2013).

43. For neighborhood crime studies that use Chicago neighborhood-level data, see Kirk and Papachristos (2011), Sampson (2012), and Sharkey (2013).

44. For more on the allocation of police resources and the higher officer-to-call ratio in higher-crime police districts, see Klinger (1997).

45. Peterson and Krivo (2010).
46. Booher-Jennings (2008).
47. In 1852, Massachusetts initiated compulsory school attendance for all children age eight to fourteen; all other states had followed by 1918; see National Conference of State Legislatures, "Compulsory Education Overview," available to subscribers at: http://www.ncsl.org/IssuesResearch/Education/Compulsory EducationOverview/tabid/12943/Default.aspx; see also Massachusetts Home Learning Association, "Massachusetts Compulsory Attendance Statutes from 1852–1913" (compiled in 2003), available at: http://www.mhla.org/infor mation/massdocuments/mglhistory.htm.
48. Illinois General Assembly, "Illinois Compiled Statutes," Schools (105 ILCS 5/) School Code, article 26, Pupils and Compulsory Attendance, available at: http://www.ilga.gov/legislation/ilcs/ilcs4.asp?DocName=010500050HArt.+26 &ActID=1005&ChapterID=17&SeqStart=147300000&SeqEnd=14970 0000.
49. U.S. Department of Education (2014).
50. Bowles and Gintis (1976, 2002) and Willis (1977).
51. Carter (2005), 9.
52. Bowles and Gintis (1976, 2002) and Willis (1977).
53. For more on boundary objects, see Star and Griesemer (1989), 393.
54. For more on approaches to studying "boundary-making," see Lamont and Molnár (2002), 187.
55. Two other girls mentioned not wanting to make friends at all in order to avoid trouble. However, they were mostly referring to the conflicts that arise between girls. See also Jones (2009).
56. Lamont and Molnár (2002), 186.

Chapter 3: Of the Meaning of Progress

1. The neighborhood around Tilden Career Community Academy has long been a prime example of a defended neighborhood. In October 1968, the Chicago Tribune reported that police were sent to Tilden "following a series of clashes between White and Negro students. The policemen were assigned at the request of parents of children attending a nearby parochial elementary school." See "2 Schools Get Extra Cops to Halt Violence," *Chicago Tribune*, October 7, 1968, B11.
2. For further analysis and discussion of clustering by race and ethnicity in high school and college, see Tatum (1997/2003).
3. For more on this phenomenon of "integrated segregation" in public space—the idea that diverse groups can be physically close to one another yet never have meaningful interactions—see May (2014).
4. For more analysis of racial-ethnic identification and changing racial-ethnic self-identification and externally ascribed racial-ethnic categories for Whites, Asians,

and, in particular, Latinos/Hispanics, see Frazier, Margai, and Tettey-Fio (2003), ch. 1; and Lee and Bean (2010).

5. Recent research on this topic reveals that Asians and Hispanics/Latinos with mixed ancestry are not as constrained by strict racial categories as individuals with African American ancestry. In fact, the former two groups exercise privilege, achieve social gains, and are able to choose their racial-ethnic category according to the situation, with little questioning from outsiders and institutions regarding their exercise of their "ethnic options." See Lee and Bean (2010), Waters (1990), and Bonilla-Silva (2006).

6. According to the CPS eligibility requirements, foster children, children from families already receiving government assistance for food, and/or children meeting specified income ceilings (for example, residing in a household of four with an annual income of less than $41,000) qualify for free or reduced-price lunch; see Illinois State Board of Education, "Nutrition and Wellness Programs: Household Eligibility Applications (HEAs)," available at: http://www .isbe.net/nutrition/htmls/household_eligibility.htm (accessed July 24, 2014).

7. Census tract 718, across from Lincoln Park High School, had a median household income of $120,625 according to the U.S. Census Bureau's 2006–2010 American Community Survey (ACS). The neighborhood median income was $88,763 according to the Census Bureau's 2008–2012 ACS estimates for the 60614 zip code. See http://factfinder2.census.gov/faces/nav/jsf/pages/community _facts.xhtml (accessed July 24, 2012). See also Zoe Galland, "How Rich Is Your Neighborhood?" *Crain's Chicago Business,* January 8, 2013, available at: http://www.chicagobusiness.com/article/20130108/BLOGS08/130109821 /how-rich-is-your-neighborhood# (accessed July 24, 2014).

8. Matt Woolsey, "In Pictures: The Most Expensive Blocks in the U.S." *Forbes,* August 31, 2007, available at: http://www.forbes.com/2007/08/30/most-ex pensive-blocks-forbeslife-cx_mw_0831blocks_slide_3.html (accessed July 24, 2014).

9. For an analysis and typology of how African American and Latino youth negotiate the boundaries between school and peer group contexts, see Carter (2006).

10. Michael responded "strongly agree" to the statement: "I wish I could go to a different school."

11. "Dr. King Is Felled by Rock," *Chicago Tribune,* August 6, 1966.

12. Arguing that there is a racial-spatial divide in the United States at the neighborhood level, especially in the realm of crime and inequality, Peterson and Krivo (2010), 32, define that divide as "a social arrangement in which substantial ethno-racial inequality in social and economic circumstances and power in society is combined with segregated and unequal residential locations across major racial and ethnic groups."

13. For more work that builds on Charles Tilly's (1998) idea of "opportunity hoarding," but with respect to educational resources, see Lewis-McCoy (2014).

14. Stinchcombe (1964).

15. Young (2004), 118.
16. Ibid., 129.
17. On the increase in the last decade in the number of neighborhood youth choosing not to attend Tilden, see Becky Vevea, "Neighborhood High Schools Again Take Hit in New CPS Budget," WBEZ91.5, July 3, 2014, available at: http://www.wbez.org/news/neighborhood-high-schools-again-take-hit-new-cps-budget-110444.
18. For more on post–Brown v. Board diversity and school tracking, see Tyson (2011).
19. Walter Payton College Prep, "About WPCP," available at: http://www.wpcp.org/About/AboutWPCP.aspx.
20. "Selected Economic Characteristics" for zip code 60636, Census 2008–2012, American Community Survey.
21. Anderson (1999), Sampson (2012), Sharkey (2013), Wilson (1987), and Wilson (1996).
22. Pattillo (1999/2013), 103–4.
23. See Pattillo (2005).
24. Pattillo (1999/2013, 103–4) gives several examples of the human capital gains (education, skills, and so on) of the Black middle class; however, these individuals are usually not afforded great social or spatial distance from their less-advantaged racial counterparts. See also Lacy (2007).
25. Young (2004), 118.
26. Ibid.
27. Peterson and Krivo (2010), 32.
28. Hagan and Albonetti (1982).
29. Kirschenman and Neckerman (1991), Anderson (1999), and Newman (1999).
30. When David was interviewed in 2005, Barack Obama had been elected as a U.S. senator for Illinois the previous November.
31. Kirschenman and Neckerman (1991) and Pager and Quillian (2005).
32. Economists Roland Fryer and Steven Levitt (2004) review this literature in which some studies, including audit studies that use matched résumés with the same information and qualifications except for the name at the top, suggest that individuals with a "unique" Black name do not do as well as individuals with a more traditionally White name. However, they find no name effect from testing their own data. In fact, their results align with the racial-spatial divide discussion in showing that individuals' unique Black names are primarily seen as "a *consequence* rather than a cause of poverty and segregation" (Fryer and Levitt 2004), 801.
33. Young (2004).
34. See Sampson (2012) and Sharkey (2013).
35. Pattillo (1999/2013), Sharkey (2013), and Peterson and Krivo (2010).
36. See Massey and Denton (1993), Pattillo (1999/2013), Hirsch (1983/1998), Wilson (1987), and Venkatesh (2000).

37.   Anderson (1999), Kluegel and Bobo (2001), Oliver and Shapiro (1995), and Coates (2014).
38.   See Khan (2011).
39.   See the discussion of Blacks' reliance on government jobs in Pattillo-McCoy (1999/2013), 210.
40.   Pager (2003), 960. Pager later included Latino/Hispanic testers in her study and found that this group fared better than Blacks but were still at an employment disadvantage compared to Whites with a criminal record; see Pager (2007).
41.   Pager (2003), 961.
42.   Ibid.

Chapter 4: The Universal Carceral Apparatus

1.   Collins (2009), 63; Simon (2007), 9. Two noteworthy examples of sociological research that explore the "prisonization of schools" are Kupchik (2010) and Nolan (2011).
2.   Tyler and Huo (2002), xiii.
3.   Devine (1996).
4.   Simon (2007), 209.
5.   Cullen and Wright (2002), 89.
6.   Ibid., 90.
7.   Puzzanchera (2013). As of 2014, these data are the most recently published nationwide figures on youth arrests. Official determinations of juvenile status may vary by state. There are eleven states where seventeen-year-olds are considered adults and two states that consider both sixteen- and seventeen-year-olds to be adults. Arrest statistics represent neither the number of crimes committed by individuals nor the number of individuals committing crimes. One individual can commit multiple crimes and/or be arrested multiple times. Also, more than one person can be arrested for a single crime, a situation that is relatively common among juveniles since they are more likely than adults to commit crimes in groups. See also Puzzanchera (2009).
8.   Violent Crime Index offenses increased from 2004 to 2006 and then declined each year through 2011. The decline in juvenile Property Crime Index arrests was also briefly interrupted between 2007 and 2008. By 2011, both juvenile Violent Crime Index and Property Crime Index arrests had reached their lowest levels since 1980. See Puzzanchera (2013), 4.
9.   Chicago Police Department (2009), 44.
10.   Chicago Police Department (2008). Individuals age sixteen or younger are officially considered "youths" in Chicago. See also Patterson and Kaba (2011), 4.
11.   Chicago Police Department (2009), 44 and Chicago Police Department (2008), 1.

12. Alderden (2005), 1. The location of the remaining 11 percent of juvenile arrests was not specified in the report.

13. Kaba (2014), 12.

14. According to figures reported by the *Chicago Sun-Times,* from 2009 to 2011 CPS paid the Chicago Police Department $8 million annually to station two police officers at every high school, at a cost of approximately $80,000 per school. The actual cost of those services was $25 million, or $250,000 per high school.

15. Advancement Project (2005).

16. Skiba and Rausch (2006); see also Nolan (2011), ch. 1.

17. Advancement Project (2005), 7.

18. Skiba and Rausch (2006).

19. Tracy Dell'Angela, "Schools Hit on Student Arrests," *Chicago Tribune,* December 13, 2005.

20. Teske (2011).

21. Hirschfield (2003), as cited in Hagan, Shedd, and Payne (2005).

22. On the history and process of the Chicago Student Safety Act, see Chicago Student Safety Act, Accountability: Transparency, Safety, "About," available at: http://chistudentsafetyact.com/; for an update, see Sarah Karp, "More Transparency on Suspensions and Expulsions, but Racial Disparity Lingers," CatalystChicago, January 8, 2014, available at: http://www.catalyst-chicago.org /notebook/2014/01/08/65160/more-transparency-suspensions-and-expul sions-racial-disparity-lingers.

23. Advancement Project (2005), 8.

24. See Hirschfield (2009), Kirk and Sampson (2011), and Advancement Project (2005), 8.

25. Advancement Project (2005), 33.

26. Chicago Youth Justice Data Project, "Arrests at Public School Locations" and "Total Reported Incidents by Offense Type, 2008 and 2009," available at: http://www.chicagoyouthjustice.com/downloads/Arrests%20at%20Public %20School%20Locations%202008%20and%202009.pdf (accessed July 29, 2014).

27. Kirk and Sampson (2011), 412.

28. Chicago Public Schools (CPS), "Chicago Public Schools Policy Manual: Student Code of Conduct for Chicago Public Schools (Effective September 2, 2014)," section 705.5, board report 14-0625-P01, adopted June 25, 2014, available at: http://policy.cps.k12.il.us/download.aspx?ID=263 (accessed August 10, 2014).

29. Becky Schlikerman, Fran Spielman, and Art Golab, "Charter School Students 11 Times More Likely to Be Expelled: CPS," *Chicago Sun-Times,* February 26, 2014; see also "Why Do Charter Schools Expel More Students?" (editorial), *Chicago Sun-Times,* February 26, 2014; Chicago Student Safety Act: Account-

ability: Transparency, Safety, "About"; and Karp, "More Transparency on Suspensions and Expulsions. . . ."

30. On a four-point scale for police contact ranging from "never" to "more than five times," African American youth scored significantly ($p < 0.001$) higher (6.6) than Latino (6.27, $t = 7.63$) and White (6.22, $t = 6.01$) students. (Asian adolescents scored 4.9). For more information on this measure, see Hagan et al. (2005), 390–91.

31. The most severe sanction determined where I placed the respondent in the police contact distribution table. I counted only the most severe sanction for each respondent. In other words, a respondent who had been searched could have also been stopped and asked questions, but I tallied him or her only in the "searched" category.

32. For more on the limitations of the CCSR self-report data, see Hagan, Shedd, and Payne (2005). It is also possible that non-reporting due to stigma or shame may not be an issue among those who are often targeted by or who interact with police in their schools and neighborhoods; see Hirschfield (2008).

33. Students who have contact with the justice system are more likely to miss classes owing to court appearances and/or detention, and they are also more likely to eventually drop out of school. Those students are unlikely to have been included in the CCSR survey or in my own study. See Hirschfield (2009) and Kirk and Sampson (2011).

34. Friedman and Hott (1995).

35. Lurigio, Greenleaf, and Flexon (2009).

36. "Hassled" was defined as being "stopped or watched closely by a police officer, even when you had done nothing wrong." "Vicarious hassling" is the experience of not being personally harassed but feeling that members of one's racial group are subject to police harassment; see Browning et al. (1994).

37. See Hagan et al. (2005), Brunson (2007), and Brunson and Miller (2006a).

38. Browning et al. (1994), 4.

39. Brunson and Miller (2006a), 622.

40. For a good outline of the CPS mission and its major programs, Chicago Public Schools, "2015 Fiscal Year Budget: Department Narratives Overview," available at: http://www.cps.edu/FY15Budget/Documents/Departments.pdf (accessed August 4, 2014).

41. Chicago Public Schools, "About CPS," available at: http://www.cps.edu/Pages/AboutCPS.aspx.

42. No previous study has considered this range of factors and levels of analysis with a large survey representative of a major American city such as Chicago. To assess the micro- as well as macro-level influences of the racial-ethnic and socioeconomic group memberships, non-normative behaviors and police contacts, and school contexts identified earlier, I undertook a multilevel and multivariate analysis, assigning mean school scores of police contact to capture the contextual effects of these encounters with the police.

43.   Elaine Allensworth, director of the University of Chicago Consortium on Chicago School Research, quoted in Jamie Bumbrecht, "Chicago's $8 Million Push to Protect Students from Gangs," CNN, April 10, 2014, available at: http://www.cnn.com/2014/04/10/us/chicagoland-safe-passage/; see also Steinberg, Allensworth, and Johnson (2011).

44.   See the report from Voices of Youth in Chicago Education (VOYCE), a student-led education advocacy group that conducted research in schools across the country on the impact of school discipline on students' perceptions and experiences (VOYCE 2011). See also Hagan et al. (2003a, 2003b).

45.   Kirk and Sampson (2011, 2013), American Psychological Association (2008), and Burdick-Will (2013).

46.   See David Mendell, "Schools, Cops Aim to Curtail Arrests," *Chicago Tribune,* February 6, 2006; Noreen S. Ahmed-Ullah, "More Tolerance in New CPS Code of Conduct," *Chicago Tribune,* July 28, 2011; Chicago Newstips, "CPS Discipline Code Revised—Slightly," Community Media Workshop, August 24, 2005, available at: http://www.newstips.org/2005/08/cps-discipline-code-revised-slightly/.

47.   Chicago Board of Education, "Adopt Student Code of Conduct (Formerly the Uniform Discipline Code) for Chicago Public Schools for 2006–2007 School Year," July 26, 2006, available at: http://www.cpsboe.org/content/actions/2006_07/06-0726-PO8.pdf; Chicago Board of Education, "Adopt Uniform Discipline Code: The Student Code of Conduct for All Chicago Public Schools Students for the 2005–2006 School Year," July 27, 2005, available at: http://chicagoschoolboard.com/content/actions/2005_07/05-0727-PO1.pdf (accessed August 10, 2014).

48.   Policing Chicago Public Schools, "Announcing the Release of [Project NIA's] 'Policing Chicago Public Schools 2': A New Report About School-Based Youth Arrests in Chicago 2011 and 2012," May 29, 2013, available at: http://policeinschools.wordpress.com/; see also Voices of Youth in Chicago Education, "Research Findings and Solutions," available at: http://voyceproject.org/research-findings-solutions/.

49.   Skiba et al. (2006), 91–93.

50.   Illinois Criminal Justice Information Authority (n.d.).

51.   Ibid.

52.   Ibid., 6.

53.   Chicago Public Schools, "2014 Student Code of Conduct" (effective September 2, 2014), 6.

54.   Ibid., 20–21.

55.   Ibid., 6; Illinois Criminal Justice Information Authority (n.d.), 6.

56.   Chicago Public Schools, "Chicago Public Schools Policy Manual: 2014 Student Code of Conduct for Chicago Public Schools," 11–13.

57.   Chicago Public Schools, "2014 Student Code of Conduct," 5.

58.   VOYCE (2011).

59. Rosalind Rossi, "High Schools to Beef Up Security," *Chicago Sun-Times,* April 17, 2006.

60. Originally, the exact numbers were not reported to keep the identity of the sampled high schools confidential, but they can now be changed to specific numbers with the time lag; see Rossi, "High Schools to Beef Up Security."

61. Devine (1995), 1996.

62. Devine (1995), 188.

63. Devine (1995), 188, further states that the "quasi-anarchy of the inner-city high school corridor presents a formidable challenge to the central thesis of *Discipline and Punish.*"

64. Devine (1995) continually reiterates this point. See also Nolan (2011) and Kupchik (2010).

65. In his study of New York schools, Devine (1995) reports on both guards who positively influence youth by asking them about their grades or ensuring that they stay out of trouble and guards who inappropriately "fraternize" with students, having sex with them or dealing illegal substances to them. The positive and negative consequences of student-guard interactions are also highlighted in this study's sample of respondents.

66. Seven African American students independently used the term "polices": Shay, Andrea, Mike, and Jasmine at Tilden; David and Dewayne at Harper; and Darrell at Payton. I mentioned this usage to the sociologist Mary Pattillo when I first started analyzing the data, and it was she who suggested that I highlight it and think deeply about what it means.

67. Part-time Chicago Police Department officers can be contracted to work four-hour shifts at schools. The schools see their arrest authority as a bonus. See Chicago Public Schools, *Proposed Budget 2013–2014,* 116, available at: http://cps.edu/finance/FY14Budget/Documents/FY2014BudgetBook.pdf.

68. Foucault (1995).

69. Tyler (2006), 3.

70. Ibid.; Tyler and Huo (2002).

71. Tyler (2006), 3.

72. Sampson and Wilson (1995).

73. See Hagan et al. (2005) for a more in-depth discussion of this interpretation of the "experience of the expected." On the distribution of arrests among a similar population (1995–2002 data) within and across Chicago's neighborhoods, see Kirk and Sampson (2011), 402–3. For a great example of how maps like maps 4.1 and 4.2 can convey the same information on perceptions of injustice (shading) and police contact (dots) in grayscale, see Kirk and Sampson (2011), 402.

74. "Regulars" refers to Lincoln Park's general education track, which is one step above remedial classes and one step below honors courses.

75. His teacher would have written up Louie's actions on a CPS misconduct report.

76. Chicago Board of Education, "Adopt Uniform Discipline Code." The 2014

Student Code of Conduct explicitly grants students this right; see Chicago Public Schools, "2014 Student Code of Conduct," 2.

77. Chicago Public Schools, "2014 Student Code of Conduct," 15.

78. This information is drawn from Chicago Public Schools, *Proposed Budget 2013–2014,* because it gives more detailed information than is available on the CPS website, which notes that the "School Safety and Security" main page and the link displaying "Current Initiatives" are both "out of date and may no longer be relevant." They are "preserved for legal reasons" at: http://www.cps.edu /About_CPS/Departments/Pages/OfficeOfSchoolSafetyAndSecurity.aspx.

79. According to Chicago Public Schools, *Proposed Budget 2013–2014,* 115–18, the OSS has the following functions: administration (overall management of all safety and security efforts for CPS); student safety center and monitoring as a 24/7 communications hub between CPS administration, CPS schools, the Chicago Police Department (CPD), and the Chicago Fire Department (CFD), monitoring surveillance cameras and sharing real-time intelligence with CPD; student safety supplemental support, which involves supporting schools in developing and managing their Safe Passage and Parent Patrol Services; school-based security; and central administrative office security services.

80. Ibid., 115.

81. See Black and Reiss (1970), Piliavin and Briar (1965), Piquero (2008), Singer (2014), and Vito and Wilson (1985). For historical data on the vast number of diversions in Chicago, see Wolcott (2001). For more qualitative data, see Brunson and Miller (2006a).

82. A classic work by the sociologist Gerald Suttles (1968) describes Italian police officers in Chicago dropping "delinquent" Italian youth off to their fathers or families for informal punishment, while formally processing Black youth by taking them to the police station for similar offenses. Madeline Wordes and Timothy Bynum (1995) also find that White juvenile officers are more likely to follow formal procedures while policing urban areas, which may contribute to racially disproportionate outcomes in the juvenile justice system.

83. The origin of the phrase "the soft bigotry of low expectations" is unclear. It was used by President George W. Bush and his former secretary of education, Ron Paige, to decry the low expectations held by teachers (and the rest of America) for "disadvantaged" children about their educability. According to the No Child Left Behind Act, the "disadvantaged" subgroup of students includes "[those who are] low-income, ethnic and racial groups, and children with disabilities and limited English proficiency" (Langan and Aspey 2003), 1. On "unilateral suspicion," see Brunson and Miller (2006b), 625.

84. Half of those funds come from school-based budgets, with the other funds directed from the general CPS fund, federal No Child Left Behind funds, and other school-generated grants; see Chicago Public Schools, *2015 Fiscal Year Budget: Department Narratives Overview,* available at: http://www.cps.edu/fy15 budget/documents/departments.pdf (accessed August 5, 2014).

Chapter 5: To Serve and Protect?

1. Hagan and Foster (2001), Haynie et al. (2009), Macmillan (2001), and Macmillan and Hagan (2004).

2. The mission statement of the Chicago Police Department: "The Chicago Police Department, as part of, and empowered by, the community, is committed to protect the lives, property, and rights of all people, to maintain order, and to enforce the law impartially." See City of Chicago, "Police: Mission," available at: http://www.cityofchicago.org/city/en/depts/cpd/auto_generated/cpd_mission.html (accessed September 6, 2014).

3. Skolnick and Fyfe (1993).

4. Bourdieu (1989), 21.

5. Ibid.

6. This topic received a great deal of attention in popular media during the mid-2000s. "Stop snitching" DVD and T-shirt campaigns were launched in urban areas to discourage individuals from cooperating with the police in their efforts to solve crimes or identify criminal offenders. Many of these admonishments were threatening in tone, such as the slogan on one T-shirt: Snitches get stitches. For an academic analysis of snitching, see Woldhoff and Weiss (2010).

7. See Bolton and Feagin (2004).

8. Hagan and Foster (2001).

9. Ibid.

10. Mortimer and Larson (2002).

11. Hagan (1997).

12. For a description and evaluation of the station adjustment process in Chicago around the time of this research, see Butts et al. (2009), 34. Station adjustments range in formality from "the old stationhouse process of writing the names of juveniles, talking with them about making better choices, and then sending them home and hoping for the best . . . to youth and their families having access to case management services designed to follow their progress more closely and to help youth stay out of trouble."

13. For an extended discussion of the "experience of the expected," an idea promulgated by Orlando Patterson (1997), see Hagan et al. (2005).

Chapter 6: Conclusion: Paradoxes of Progress

1. Kozol (2005).

2. Sharkey (2013).

3. Sampson (2012).

4. Cheryl Corley, "Months After Killing, Chicago School Looks Ahead," NPR, June 1, 2010, available at: http://www.npr.org/templates/story/story.php?storyId=127251139.

5. For instance, the White population at Payton Prep increased from 29 percent in

2009, which was the last year race was used in selective high school admissions, to 45 percent in 2013; see "Elite CPS High Schools Need to Reconsider Race as Factor" (editorial), *Chicago Sun-Times,* July 20, 2014.

Appendix A: Methods

1. Christopher B. Swanson, "Cities in Crisis 2009: Closing the Graduation Gap," Editorial Projects in Education (April 2009), 14, available at: http://www .edweek.org/media/cities_in_crisis_2009.pdf.
2. Since Harper High School is basically all African American, this group makes up a large portion of my sample (twenty-seven out of forty). Also, white students from Lincoln Park and Payton High School are underrepresented. I have only two in my sample (one from each school), but the larger sample of quantitative data revealed that race was not significantly correlated with perceptions for white students, only personal police contact. There is also a bit of a selection bias because I would have interviewed only students who fastidiously returned the survey after having their parent or guardian sign the consent form. There was also a small payment ($10), which served as further incentive for students to get their forms signed. Finally, one school granted me access only to a ninth-grade homeroom from which to draw my sample, skewing the grade distribution of the sample.
3. I organized the qualitative data using Atlas.ti qualitative analysis software and analyzed them using a "person-oriented strategy" similar to the one employed by John Laub and Robert Sampson (2004, 85), which allowed me to assess the students' overall perceptions of injustice from their particular racial, spatial, and experiential perspectives.
4. For a methodological model, I used Laub and Sampson (2004).

REFERENCES

Advancement Project. 2005. *Education on Lockdown: The Schoolhouse to Jailhouse Track*. Washington, D.C.: Advancement Project (March). Available at: http://b.3cdn.net/advancement/5351180e24cb166d02_mlbrqgxlh.pdf (accessed August 5, 2014).

Alderden, Megan. 2005. "Juvenile Arrests 1999–2004." *Juvenile Justice* 2(2). Chicago Police Department, Research and Development Division.

American Psychological Association. 2008. "Are Zero Tolerance Policies Effective in Schools? An Evidentiary Review and Recommendations." *American Psychologist* 63(9): 852–62.

Anderson, Elijah. 1999. *Code of the Streets: Decency, Violence, and the Moral Life of the Inner City*. New York: W. W. Norton and Co.

Bell, Derrick. 1987. *And We Are Not Saved: The Elusive Quest for Racial Justice*. New York: Basic Books.

Black, Donald J., and Albert J. Reiss Jr. 1970. "Police Control of Juveniles." *American Sociological Review* 35(1): 63–77.

Bobo, Lawrence D., and Devon Johnson. 2004. "A Taste for Punishment: Black and White Americans' Views on the Death Penalty and the War on Drugs." *Du Bois Review* 1(1): 151–80.

Bolton, Kenneth, Jr., and Joe R. Feagin. 2004. *Black in Blue: African-American Police Officers and Racism*. New York: Routledge.

Bonilla-Silva, Eduardo. 2006. *Racism Without Racists: Color-Blind Racism and the Persistence of Racial Inequality in the United States*. Lanham, Md.: Rowman & Littlefield Publishers.

Booher-Jennings, Jennifer. 2008. "Learning to Label: Gender, Socialization, and High-Stakes Testing in Elementary School." *British Journal of Sociology of Education* 29: 149–60.

Bourdieu, Pierre. 1989. "Social Space and Symbolic Power Source." *Sociological Theory* 7(1, Spring): 21.

Bowles, Samuel, and Herbert Gintis. 1976. *Schooling in Capitalist America*. Princeton, N.J.: Princeton University Press.

———. 2002. "Schooling in Capitalist America Revisited." *Sociology of Education* 71(1): 1–18.

Briggs, Xavier de Souza, ed. 2005. *The Geography of Opportunity: Race and Housing Choice in Metropolitan America*. Washington, D.C.: Brookings Institution Press.

Brooks, Richard R. W. 2000. "Fear and Fairness in the City: Criminal Enforcement and Perceptions of Fairness in Minority Communities." *Southern California Law Review* 73(6): 1219.

Brooks, Richard R. W., and Haekyung Jeon-Slaughter. 2001. "Race, Income, and Perceptions of the U.S. Court System." *Behavioral Sciences and the Law* 19: 249–64.

Browning, Sandra Lee, Frances T. Cullin, Liqun Cao, Renee Kopache, and T. Stevenson. 1994. "Race and Getting Hassled by the Police: A Research Note." *Police Studies* 17: 1–11.

Brunson, Rod K. 2003. "Police Don't Like Black People: African-American Young Men's Accumulated Police Experiences." Criminology and Public Policy 6: 71–102.

———. 2007. "Police Don't Like Black People: African American Young Men's Accumulated Police Experience." *Criminology and Public Policy* 6: 71–102.

Brunson, Rod K., and Jody Miller. 2006a. "Young Black Men and Urban Policing in the United States." *British Journal of Criminology* 46: 613–40.

———. 2006b. "Gender, Race, and Urban Policing: The Experience of African American Youths." *Gender & Society* 20: 531–52.

Buckler, Kevin, James D. Unnever, and Francis T. Cullen. 2008. "Perceptions of Injustice Revisited: A Test of Hagan et al.'s Comparative Conflict Theory." *Journal of Crime and Justice* 31(1): 35–57.

Burdick-Will, Julia. 2013. "School Violent Crime and Academic Achievement in Chicago." *Sociology of Education* 86(4): 343–61.

Butts, Jeffrey A., Elissa Gitlow, Jan DeCoursey, Brianna English, and Ada Skyles. 2009. "Process Evaluation of the City of Chicago's Juvenile Intervention Support Center." Chicago: University of Chicago, Chapin Hall. Available at: http://www.chapinhall.org/sites/default/files/JISC_Report_04_21_09.pdf (accessed August 17, 2014).

Carter, Prudence L. 2005. *Keepin' It Real: School Success Beyond Black and White*. New York: Oxford University Press.

———. 2006. "Straddling Boundaries: Identity, Culture, and School." *Sociology of Education* 79(4): 304–28.

Cassidy, Lauren, Daniel C. Humphrey, Marjorie E. Wechsler, and Viki M. Young. 2009. "High School Reform in Chicago Public Schools: Renaissance 2010." Part 3 of a five-part series. Chicago: Consortium on Chicago School Research (CCSR) and SRI International (August). Available at: https://ccsr.uchicago.edu/sites/default/files/publications/Part%203%20-%20Ren%202010.pdf (accessed August 17, 2014).

Charles, Camille Zubrinsky. 2000. "Residential Segregation in Los Angeles." In *Pris-*

matic Metropolis: Inequality in Los Angeles, edited by Lawrence D. Bobo, Melvin L. Oliver, James H. Johnson Jr., and Abel Valenzuela Jr. New York: Russell Sage Foundation.

Chicago Consortium on School Research (CCSR). 2004. "Public Use Data Set: 2001 Survey of Students and Teachers—User's Manual." Chicago: CCSR (April). Available at: http://ccsr.uchicago.edu/downloads/28762001_survey_manual.pdf (accessed December 21, 2014).

Chicago Police Department. 2008. "Juvenile Arrest Trends: 2003–2008." *Juvenile Justice* 4(1). Available at: https://portal.chicagopolice.org/portal/page/portal /ClearPath/News/Statistical%20Reports/Juvenile%20Reports/JuvArr2008.pdf (accessed August 5, 2014).

———. 2009. *2009 Annual Report.* Available at: http://home.chicagopolice.org/wp -content/uploads/2014/12/2009-Annual-Report.pdf (accessed August 5, 2014).

Coates, Ta-Nehesi. 2014. "The Case for Reparations." *The Atlantic,* May 21, 2014.

Collins, Patricia Hill. 2009. *Another Kind of Public Education: Race, Schools, the Media, and Democratic Possibilities.* Boston: Beacon Press.

Cullen, Francis T., and John Paul Wright. 2002. "Criminal Justice in the Lives of American Adolescents: Choosing the Future." In *The Changing Adolescent Experience: Societal Trends and the Transition to Adulthood,* edited by Jeylan T. Mortimer and Reed W. Larson. Cambridge: Cambridge University Press.

Davis, James. 1959. "A Formal Interpretation of the Theory of Relative Deprivation." *Sociometry* 22: 280–96.

Dawson, Michael. 1994. *Behind the Mule: Race and Class in African American Politics.* Princeton, N.J.: Princeton University Press.

Devine, John. 1995. "Can Metal Detectors Replace the Panopticon?" *Cultural Anthropology* 10(2): 171–95.

———. 1996. *Maximum Security: The Culture of Violence in Inner-City Schools.* Chicago: University of Chicago Press.

Feagin, Joe R., and Melvin P. Sikes. 1994. *Living with Racism: The Black Middle-Class Experience.* Boston: Beacon Press.

Foucault, Michel. 1995. *Discipline and Punish: The Birth of the Prison.* New York: Random House.

Frazier, John W., Florence M. Margai, and Eugene Tettey-Fio. 2003. *Race and Place: Equity Issues in Urban America.* Boulder, Colo.: Westview Press.

Friedman, Warren, and Marsha Hott. 1995. "Young People and the Police: Respect, Fear, and the Future of Community Policing in Chicago." Chicago: Chicago Alliance for Neighborhood Safety.

Fryer, Roland G., Jr., and Steven D. Levitt. 2004. "The Causes and Consequences of Distinctively Black Names." *Quarterly Journal of Economics* 119(3): 767–805.

Gieryn, Thomas F. 2000. "A Space for Place in Sociology." *Annual Review of Sociology* 26: 463–96.

Graham, Philip. 2004. *The End of Adolescence.* Oxford: Oxford University Press.

Hagan, John. 1997. "Defiance and Despair: Subcultural and Structural Linkages Between Delinquency and Despair in the Life Course." *Social Forces* 76(1): 119–34.

Hagan, John, and Celesta Albonetti. 1982. "Race, Class, and the Perception of Injustice in America." *American Journal of Sociology* 88(2): 329–55.

Hagan, John, and Holly Foster. 2001. "Youth Violence and the End of Adolescence." *American Sociological Review* 66: 874–99.

Hagan, John, Paul Hirschfield, and Carla Shedd. 2003a. "First and Last Words: Apprehending the Social and Legal Facts of an Urban High School Shooting." *Sociological Methods and Research* 31(2): 218–54.

———. 2003b. "Shooting at Tilden High: Causes and Consequences." In *Deadly Lessons: Understanding Lethal School Violence: Case Studies of School Violence Committee,* edited by Mark H. Moore, Carol V. Petrie, Anthony A. Braga, and Brenda L. McLaughlin. Washington, D.C.: National Academies Press.

Hagan, John, and Bill McCarthy. 1998. *Mean Streets: Youth Crime and Homelessness.* Cambridge: Cambridge University Press.

Hagan, John, Carla Shedd, and Monique R. Payne. 2005. "Race, Ethnicity, and Youth Perceptions of Criminal Injustice." *American Sociological Review* 70: 381–407.

Hagedorn, John M. N.d. "Institutionalized Gangs and Violence in Chicago." Available at: http://www.uic.edu/orgs/kbc/International/reports/chicago.pdf (accessed April 22, 2014).

Hailey, Chantal, and Megan Gallagher. 2013. "Chronic Violence: Beyond the Developments." Washington, D.C.: Urban Institute (March 11). Available at: http://www.urban.org/publications/412764.html (accessed April 22, 2014).

Harris, Angel L. 2011. *Kids Don't Want to Fail.* Cambridge, Mass.: Harvard University Press.

Haynie, Dana L., Richard J. Petts, David Maimon, and Alex R. Piquero. 2009. "Exposure to Violence in Adolescence and Precocious Role Exits." *Journal of Youth Adolescence* 38(3, March): 269–86.

Henderson, Martha L., Francis T. Cullen, Liqun Cao, Sandra Lee Browning, and Renee Kopache. 1997. "The Impact of Race on Perceptions of Criminal Injustice." *Journal of Criminal Justice* 25(6): 447–62.

Hirsch, Arnold R. 1998. *Making the Second Ghetto: Race and Housing in Chicago: 1940–1960.* Chicago: University of Chicago Press. (Originally published in 1983.)

Hirschfield, Paul J. 2003. "Preparing for Prison?" PhD diss., Northwestern University.

———. 2008. "The Declining Significance of Delinquent Labels in Disadvantaged Urban Communities." *Sociological Forum* 23(3): 575–601.

———. 2009. "Another Way Out: The Impact of Juvenile Arrests on High School Dropout." *Sociology of Education* 82(4): 368–93.

Hochschild, Jennifer L. 1995. *Facing Up to the American Dream: Race, Class, and the Soul of the Nation.* Princeton, N.J.: Princeton University Press.

Holmes, Oliver Wendell, Jr. 1881. The Common Law, e-book. Available at: http://www.gutenberg.org/files/2449/2449-h/2449-h.htm (accessed September 14, 2014).

Humphrey, Daniel C., and Patrick M. Shields. 2009. "High School Reform in Chicago Public Schools: An Overview." Part 1 of a five-part series. Chicago: Consortium on Chicago School Research (CCSR) and SRI International (June). Available at: https://ccsr.uchicago.edu/sites/default/files/publications/Overview.pdf (accessed August 5, 2014).

Illinois Criminal Justice Information Authority. N.d. "Implementing Restorative Justice: A Guide for Schools." Available at: http://www.icjia.state.il.us/public /pdf/BARJ/SCHOOL%20BARJ%20GUIDEBOOOK.pdf (accessed August 5, 2014).

Jacob, Herbert 1971. "Black and White Perceptions of Justice in the City." *Law and Society Review* 6: 69–90.

Jaynes, Gerald D., and Robin M. Williams. 1989. *A Common Destiny: Blacks and American Society.* Washington, D.C.: National Academies Press.

Jones, Nikki. 2009. *Between Good and Ghetto: African American Girls and Inner-City Violence.* New Brunswick, N.J.: Rutgers University Press.

Kaba, Mariame. 2014. "Juvenile Justice in Illinois: A Data Snapshot." Project NIA (April). Available at: https://chiyouthjustice.files.wordpress.com/2014/04 /juvenile_justice_in_illinois.pdf (accessed September 26, 2014).

Khan, Shamus Rahman. 2011. *Privilege: The Making of an Adolescent Elite at St. Paul's School.* Princeton, N.J.: Princeton University Press.

Kirk, David S., and Andrew V. Papachristos. 2011. "Cultural Mechanisms and the Persistence of Neighborhood Violence." *American Journal of Sociology* 116(4): 1190–1233.

Kirk, David S., and Robert J. Sampson. 2011. "Crime and the Production of Safe Schools." In *Whither Opportunity? Rising Inequality, Schools, and Children's Life Chances,* edited by Greg J. Duncan and Richard J. Murnane. New York: Russell Sage Foundation.

———. 2013. "Juvenile Arrest and Collateral Educational Damage in the Transition to Adulthood." Sociology of Education 83: 36–62.

Kirschenman, Joleen, and Kathryn Neckerman. 1991. "'We'd Love to Hire Them, but . . .': The Meaning of Race for Employers." In *The Urban Underclass,* edited by Christopher Jencks and Paul E. Peterson. Washington, D.C.: Brookings Institution.

Klinger, David A. 1997. "Negotiating Order in Patrol Work: An Ecological Theory of Police Response to Deviance." *Criminology* 35: 277–306.

Kluegel, James R. 1995. Review of "Psychological Perspectives on Justice: Theory and Applications," by Barbara A. Mellers and Jonathan Baron, eds. *Social Justice Research* 8(4): 421–26.

Kluegel, James R., and Lawrence Bobo. 2001. "Perceived Group Discrimination and Policy Attitudes: The Sources and Consequences of the Race and Gender Gaps." In *Urban Inequality: Evidence from Four Cities,* edited by Alice O'Connor, Charles Tilly, and Lawrence D. Bobo. New York: Russell Sage Foundation.

Kluegel, James R., and Eliot R. Smith. 1986. *Beliefs About Inequality: Americans' Views of What Is and What Ought to Be*. New Brunswick, N.J.: Transaction Publishers.

Kozol, Jonathan. 2005. *The Shame of the Nation: The Restoration of Apartheid Schooling in America*. New York: Crown Publishers.

Kupchik, Aaron. 2010. *Homeroom Security: School Discipline in an Age of Fear*. New York: New York University Press.

Lacy, Karyn R. 2007. *Blue Chip Black: Race, Class, and Status in the New Black Middle Class*. Berkeley: University of California Press.

Lamont, Michele. 1992. *Money, Morals, and Manners: The Culture of the French and the American Upper-Middle Class*. Chicago: University of Chicago Press.

Lamont, Michele, and Virág Molnár. 2002. "The Study of Boundaries in the Social Sciences." *Annual Review of Sociology* 28: 167–95.

Langan, Daniel, and Susan Aspey. 2003. "Paige Blasts 'Soft Bigotry of Low Expectations.'" National Right to Read Foundation, March 12, 2003. Available at: http://www.nrrf.org/old/paige3-12-03.html (accessed August 5, 2014).

Laub, John, and Robert Sampson. 2004. "Strategies for Bridging the Quantitative and Qualitative Divide: Studying Crime over the Life Course." *Research in Human Development* 1–2: 81–99.

La Vigne, Nancy G., Pamela Lachman, Shebani Rao, and Andrea Matthews. 2014. Stop and Frisk: Balancing Crime Control with Community Relations. Washington, D.C.: Office of Community Oriented Policing Services.

Lee, Jennifer, and Frank D. Bean. 2010. *The Diversity Paradox: Immigration and the Color Line in Twenty-First-Century America*. New York: Russell Sage Foundation.

Lewis-McCoy, R. L'Heureux. 2014. *Inequality in the Promised Land: Race, Resources, and Suburban Schooling*. Stanford, Calif.: Stanford University Press.

Lurigio, Arthur J., Richard G. Greenleaf, and Jamie L. Flexon. 2009. "The Effects of Race on Relationships with the Police: A Survey of African American and Latino Youths in Chicago." *Western Criminology Review* 10(1): 29–41.

Macmillan, Ross. 2001. "Violence and the Life Course: The Consequences of Victimization for Personal and Social Development." *Annual Review of Sociology* 27: 1–22.

Macmillan, Ross, and John Hagan. 2004. "Violence in the Transition to Adulthood: Adolescent Victimization, Education, and Socioeconomic Attainment in Later Life." *Journal of Research on Adolescence* 14: 127–58.

Massey, Douglas, and Nancy Denton. 1993. *American Apartheid: Segregation and the Making of the Underclass*. Cambridge. Mass.: Harvard University Press.

Matza, David. 1964. *Delinquency and Drift*. New York: Wiley.

May, Reuben A. Buford. 2014. *Urban Nightlife: Entertaining Race, Class, and Culture in Public Space*. New Brunswick, N.J.: Rutgers University Press.

Meares, Tracey, Andrew V. Papachristos, and Jeffrey Fagan. 2009. "Homicide and Gun Violence in Chicago: Evaluation and Summary of the Project Safe Neighborhoods Program." Review of Research. Available at: www.psnchicago.org/PDFs /2009-PSN-Research-Brief_v2.pdf (accessed April 22, 2014).

Mortimer, Jeylan T., and Reed W. Larson. 2002. "Macrostructural Trends and the Reshaping of Adolescence." In *The Changing Adolescent Experience: Societal Trends and the Transition to Adulthood,* edited by Jeylan T. Mortimer and Reed W. Larson. Cambridge: Cambridge University Press.

National Research Council (NRC) and Institute of Medicine (IOM). 2003. *Deadly Lessons: Understanding Lethal School Violence,* edited by Mark H. Moore, Carol V. Petrie, Anthony A. Braga, and Brenda L. McLaughlin. Washington, D.C.: National Academies Press, Division of Behavioral Social Sciences and Education, and IOM, Committee on Case Studies in School Violence.

Neckerman, Kathryn. 2007. *Schools Betrayed: Roots of Failure in Inner-City Education.* Chicago: University of Chicago Press.

Newman, Katherine. 1999. *No Shame in My Game: The Working Poor in the Inner City.* New York: Russell Sage Foundation.

Nolan, Kathleen. 2011. *Police in the Hallways: Discipline in an Urban High School.* Minneapolis: University of Minnesota Press.

O'Connor, Carla. 1999. "Race, Class, and Gender in America: Narratives of Opportunity Among Low-Income African American Youths." *Sociology of Education* 72(3): 137–57.

Oliver, Melvin L., and Thomas M. Shapiro. 1995. *Black Wealth/White Wealth: A New Perspective on Racial Inequality.* New York: Routledge.

Pager, Devah. 2003. "The Mark of a Criminal Record." *American Journal of Sociology* 108(5): 937–75.

———. 2007. *Marked: Race, Crime, and Finding Work in an Era of Mass Incarceration.* Chicago: University of Chicago Press.

Pager, Devah, and Lincoln Quillian. 2005. "Walking the Talk? What Employers Say Versus What They Do." *American Sociological Review* 70(3): 355–80.

Papachristos, Andrew V. 2011. "Cultural Mechanisms and the Persistence of Neighborhood Violence." *American Journal of Sociology* 116(4): 1190–1233.

———. 2013. "48 Years of Crime in Chicago: A Descriptive Analysis of Serious Crime Trends from 1965 to 2013," *ISPS Working Paper* No. 12-023, Yale Institution for Social and Policy Studies.

Patterson, Caitlin, and Mariame Kaba. 2011. "Arresting Justice: A Report About Juvenile Arrests in Chicago, 2009 and 2010." Chicago: First Defense Legal Aid and Project NIA (June). Available at: http://arrestjustice.files.wordpress.com/2011/06/arrestingjusticefinal21.pdf (accessed September 26, 2014).

Patterson, Elizabeth A. 2013. "Edward Tilden Career Community Academy High School." Chicago: Chicago Historic Schools (August 26). Available at: https://chicagohistoricschools.wordpress.com/2013/08/26/tilden-career-community-academy-high-school/ (accessed September 22, 2014).

Patterson, Orlando. 1997. *The Ordeal of Integration: Progress and Resentment in America's "Racial" Crisis.* New York: Basic Books.

Pattillo, Mary. 2005. "Black Middle-Class Neighborhoods." *Annual Review of Sociology* 31: 305–29.

————. 2013. *Black Picket Fences: Privilege and Peril Among the Black Middle Class.* Chicago: University of Chicago Press. (Originally published in 1999.)

Peterson, Ruth D., and Lauren J. Krivo. 2010. *Divergent Social Worlds: Neighborhood Crime and the Racial-Spatial Divide.* New York: Russell Sage Foundation Press.

Piliavin, Irving, and Scott Briar. 1965. "Police Encounters with Juveniles." *American Journal of Sociology* 70: 206–14.

Piquero, Alex R. 2008. "Disproportionate Minority Contact." *The Future of Children* 18(2): 59–79.

Popkin, Susan J. 2013. "How Chicago's Public Housing Transformation Can Inform Federal Policy." Brief 1. Washington, D.C.: Urban Institute (January). Available at: http://www.urban.org/UploadedPDF/412760-How-Chicagos-Public -Housing-Transformation-Can-Improve-Federal-Policy.pdf (accessed April 22, 2014).

"A Push for Charter Schools, But Little Difference in Test Scores," *Chicago Sun-Times*, April 15, 2014.

Puzzanchera, Charles. 2009. "Juvenile Arrests 2009." *Juvenile Justice Bulletin* (April). Washington: U.S. Department of Justice, Office of Justice Programs, Office of Juvenile Justice and Delinquency Prevention. Available at: http://www.ncjrs.gov /pdffiles1/ojjdp/225344.pdf (accessed April 22, 2014).

————. 2013. "Juvenile Arrests: 2011." *Juvenile Offenders and Victims: National Report Series* (December). Washington: U.S. Department of Justice, Office of Justice Programs, Office of Juvenile Justice and Delinquency Prevention. Available at: http://www.ojjdp.gov/pubs/244476.pdf (accessed September 26, 2014).

Rice, Stephen K., and Alex R. Piquero. 2005. "Perceptions of Discrimination and Justice in New York City." *Policing: An International Journal of Police Strategies and Management* 28(1): 98–117.

Rios, Victor M. 2011. *Punished: Policing the Lives of Black and Latino Boys.* New York: New York University Press.

Runciman, William G. 1966. *Relative Deprivation and Social Justice: A Study of Attitudes to Social Inequality in Twentieth-Century England.* London: Routledge and Kegan Paul.

Sampson, Robert J. 2012. *Great American City: Chicago and the Enduring Neighborhood Effect.* Chicago: University of Chicago Press.

Sampson, Robert J., and Dawn Jeglum Bartusch. 1998. "Legal Cynicism and (Subcultural?) Tolerance of Deviance: The Neighborhood Context of Racial Differences." *Law and Society Review* 32: 777–804.

Sampson, Robert, and John Laub. 1993. *Crime in the Making: Pathways and Turning Points Through Life.* Cambridge, Mass.: Harvard University Press.

Sampson, Robert J., and William Julius Wilson. 1995. "Toward a Theory of Race, Crime, and Urban Inequality." In *Crime and Inequality*, edited by John Hagan and Ruth D. Peterson. Stanford, Calif.: Stanford University Press.

Schuman, Howard, Charlotte Steeh, Lawrence Bobo, and Maria Krysan. 1997. *Racial Attitudes in America: Trends and Interpretations,* rev. ed. Cambridge, Mass.: Harvard University Press.

Sharkey, Patrick. 2013. *Stuck in Place: Urban Neighborhoods and the End of Progress Toward Racial Equality.* Chicago: University of Chicago Press.

Sibley, David. 1995. *Geographies of Exclusion: Society and Difference in the West.* London and New York: Routledge.

Simon, Jonathan. 2007. *Governing Through Crime: How the War on Crime Transformed American Democracy and Created a Culture of Fear.* New York: Oxford University Press.

Singer, S. T. 2014. *Trouble in Suburbia: Delinquency and Modernity in America's Safest City.* New York: New York University Press.

Skiba, Russell J., and M. K. Rausch. 2006. "School Disciplinary Systems: Alternatives to Suspension and Expulsion." In *Children's Needs III: Development, Prevention, and Intervention,* edited by George G. Bear and Kathleen M. Minke. Bethesda, Md.: National Association of School Psychologists.

Skiba, Russell, Cecil R. Reynolds, Sandra Graham, Peter Sheras, Jane Close Conoley, and Enedina Garcia-Vazquez. 2006. "Are Zero Tolerance Policies Effective in Schools? An Evidentiary Review and Recommendations." Washington, D.C.: American Psychological Association, Zero Tolerance Task Force (August 9). Available at: http://www.apa.org/pubs/info/reports/zero-tolerance-report.pdf (accessed September 26, 2014).

Skogan, Wesley G. 2005. "Citizen Satisfaction with Police Encounters." Police Quarterly 8: 298–320.

Skolnick, Jerome H., and James J. Fyfe. 1993. *Above the Law: Police and the Excessive Use of Force.* New York: Free Press.

Southern Poverty Law Center. 2004. "Brown v. Board: An American Legacy." *Teaching Tolerance* 25(Spring). Available at: http://www.tolerance.org/magazine/number-25-spring-2004/department/brown-v-board-american-legacy (accessed May 2, 2013).

Star, Susan Leigh, and James R. Griesemer. 1989. "Institutional Ecology, 'Translations,' and Boundary Objects: Amateurs and Professionals in Berkeley's Museum of Vertebrate Zoology, 1907–39." *Social Studies of Science* 19(3): 387–420.

Steinberg, Matthew P., Elaine Allensworth, and David W. Johnson. 2011. "Student and Teacher Safety in Chicago Public Schools: The Roles of Community Context and School Social Organization." Chicago: University of Chicago Consortium on Chicago School Research (May). Available at: https://ccsr.uchicago.edu/sites/default/files/publications/SAFETY%20IN%20CPS.pdf (accessed April 22, 2014).

Stinchcombe, Arthur L. 1964. *Rebellion in a High School.* Chicago: Quadrangle Books.

Sugrue, Thomas J. 2010. *Not Even Past: Barack Obama and the Burden of Race.* Princeton, N.J.: Princeton University Press.

Sunshine, Jason, and Tom R. Tyler. 2003. "The Role of Procedural Justice and Legitimacy in Shaping Public Support for Policing." Law & Society Review 37(3): 513–48.

Suttles, D. Gerald. 1968. *The Social Order of the Slum: Ethnicity and Territory in the Inner City.* Chicago: University of Chicago Press.

Suttles, Gerald. 1972. *The Social Construction of Communities.* Chicago: University of Chicago Press.

Swann v. Charlotte-Mecklenburg Board of Education, 402 U.S. 1 (1971).

Tatum, Beverly Daniel. 2003. *"Why Are All the Black Kids Sitting Together in the Cafeteria?": A Psychologist Explains the Development of Racial Identity.* New York: Basic Books. (Originally published in 1997.)

Teske, Steven C. 2011. "A Study of Zero Tolerance Policies in Schools: A Multi-Integrated Systems Approach to Improve Outcomes for Adolescents." *Journal of Child and Adolescent Psychiatric Nursing* 24: 88–97.

Tilly, Charles. 1998. *Durable Inequality.* Berkeley: University of California Press.

Tyler, Tom R. 1990. *Why People Obey the Law.* New Haven, Conn.: Yale University Press.

———. 2006. *Why People Obey the Law,* with a new afterword. Princeton, N.J.: Princeton University Press.

Tyler, Tom R., and Cheryl J. Wakslak. 2004. "Profiling and Police Legitimacy: Procedural Justice, Attributions of Motive, and Acceptance of Police Authority," Criminology 42(2): 253–81.

Tyler, Tom R., and Jeffrey Fagan. 2008. "Legitimacy and Cooperation: Why Do People Help the Police Fight Crime in Their Communities?" Ohio State Journal of Criminal Law 6: 231–75.

Tyler, Tom R., and Yuen J. Huo. 2002. *Trust in the Law: Encouraging Public Cooperation with the Police and Courts.* New York: Russell Sage Foundation Press.

Tyson, Karolyn. 2011. *Integration Interrupted: Tracking, Black Students, and Acting White After Brown.* New York: Oxford University Press.

U.S. Department of Education. Office for Civil Rights. 2014. "Data Snapshot: School Discipline, Restraint, and Seclusion Highlights." Issue Brief 1 (March). Available at: http://www2.ed.gov/about/offices/list/ocr/docs/crdc-discipline-snapshot.pdf (accessed September 26, 2014).

Venkatesh, Sudhir A. 2000. *American Project: The Rise and Fall of a Modern Ghetto.* Cambridge, Mass.: Harvard University Press.

Vito, Gennaro F., and Deborah G. Wilson. 1985. *The American Juvenile Justice System.* Beverly Hills, Calif.: Sage Publications.

Voices of Youth in Chicago Education (VOYCE). 2011. "Failed Policies, Broken Futures: The True Cost of Zero Tolerance in Chicago." Chicago: VOYCE (July). Available at: https://s3.amazonaws.com/s3.documentcloud.org/documents/216318/voyce.pdf (accessed August 3, 2014).

Waters, Mary C. 1990. *Ethnic Options: Choosing Identities in America.* Berkeley: University of California Press.

"Whites Getting More Spots at Top Chicago Public High Schools," *Chicago Sun-Times,* April 28, 2014, available at: http://chicago.suntimes.com/?p=166698 (accessed May 2, 2014).

Willis, Paul. 1977. *Learnng to Labor: How Working Class Kids Get Working Class Jobs.* New York: Columbia University Press.

Wilson, William Julius. 1987. *The Truly Disadvantaged.* Chicago: University of Chicago Press.

———. 1996. *When Work Disappears: The World of the New Urban Poor.* New York: Knopf.

Wolcott, David. 2001. "'The Cop Will Get You': The Police and Discretionary Juvenile Justice, 1890–1940." *Journal of Social History* 35(2): 349–71.

Woldhoff, Rachael A., and Karen G. Weiss. 2010. "Stop Snitchin': Exploring Definitions of the Snitch and Implications for Urban Black Communities." *Journal of Criminal Justice and Popular Culture* 17(1): 184–223.

Wordes, Madeline, and Timothy S. Bynum. 1995. "Policing Juveniles: Is There Bias Against Youths of Color?" In *Minorities in Juvenile Justice,* edited by Kimberley Kempf Leonard, Carl E. Pope, and William Feyerherm. Thousand Oaks, Calif.: Sage Publications.

Young, Alford A. 2004. *The Minds of Marginalized Black Men: Making Sense of Mobility, Opportunity, and Future Life Chances.* Princeton, N.J.: Princeton University Press.

Zubrinsky, Camille L., and Lawrence D. Bobo. 1996. "Prismatic Metropolis: Race and Residential Segregation in the City of Angels." *Social Science Research* 25: 335–74.

INDEX